D0898981

WHY WE WIN

WHY WE WIN

Great American Coaches Offer Their Strategies for Success in Sports and Life

Billy Packer with Roland Lazenby

MASTERS PRESS

NTC/Contemporary Publishing Group

Library of Congress Cataloging-in-Publication Data

Packer, Billy.
    Why we win: great American coaches offer their strategies for success in sports and life / by Billy Packer with Roland Lazenby.
        p.   cm.
    ISBN 1-57028-184-X
    1. Coaches (Athletics)—United States—Interviews.   2. Sports—United States—History.   I. Lazenby, Roland.   II. Title.

GV697.A1P282   1998
796'.07'7—dc21   98-47086
                                                   CIP

Published by Masters Press
A Division of The McGraw-Hill Companies

Copyright © 1999 by Billy Packer and Roland Lazenby. All rights reserved. Printed in the United States of America. Except as permitted under the United States Copyright Act of 1976, no part of this publication may be reproduced or distributed in any form or by any means, or stored in a database or retrieval system, without the prior written permission of the publisher.

2 3 4 5 6 7 8 9 0 1   QWF/QWF   1 0 9 8 7 6 5 4 3 2

ISBN 1-57028-184-X

This book was set in Palatino
Printed and bound by Quebecor World Fairfield

Interior design by Heather Lowhorn

Interior photographs:
Page xviii: AP/Wide World Photos, 1962; page 26: copyright © Brian Spurlock/Spurlock Photography, Inc.; page 51: AP/Wide World Photos, 1964; page 72: courtesy University of North Carolina Media Relations/Olympic Sports Office; page 96: copyright © Brian Spurlock/Spurlock Photography, Inc.; page 116: copyright © Brian Spurlock/Spurlock Photography, Inc.; page 142: copyright © Jay Crihfield/Spurlock Photography, Inc.; page 165: copyright © Rick Stewart/Allsport USA; page 182: copyright © 1996 Otto Greule/Allsport USA; page 200: copyright © Brian Spurlock/Spurlock Photography, Inc.; page 218: copyright ©1993 Patrick Whitmore/Allsport USA; page 234: courtesy University of Iowa Sports Information Office; page 250: copyright © Brian Spurlock/Spurlock Photography, Inc.; page 272: copyright © Brian Spurlock/Spurlock Photography, Inc.; page 286: copyright © Brian Spurlock/Spurlock Photography, Inc.; page 304: copyright © Brian Spurlock/Spurlock Photography, Inc.

McGraw-Hill books are available at special quantity discounts to use as premiums and sales promotions, or for use in corporate training programs. For more information, please write to the Director of Special Sales, Professional Publishing, McGraw-Hill, Two Penn Plaza, New York, NY 10121-2298. Or contact your local bookstore.

This book is printed on acid-free paper.

*This book is dedicated to coaches' spouses,
who bear the real burden of competition.*

Contents

Preface

Why do they win? How do they win? As a young assistant coach at Wake Forest in the early 1960s, I marveled that certain coaches managed to have winning teams year after year. Was it the talent on their teams? Their knowledge? Their ability to motivate? What grand formulas separated the legends from the rest of the crowd? What were the game's best coaches thinking as they led their teams to championships? A decade later, when I became a television sportscaster, I was afforded the opportunity to get to know many of the coaching legends of our time and to observe them from close range. My first assumption was that athletic success was similar to that old three-part formula for finding valuable real estate—location, location, location. In sports, it seemed to me that the trick to building championships was talent, talent, talent. And then more talent.

In those days, I often ran into fans who asked me to name the best coaches in college basketball. My answer usually ran along the lines of no. 1) John Wooden, no. 2) Bob Knight, no. 3) Dean Smith. At face value, it seemed like an easy answer. After all, those were the guys winning the most games. The longer I stayed in the business, though, the more I came to look for a more detailed explanation. Why were certain coaches far better than others? Was the best coach really the guy with the best won-lost record? The one with the most championships? Was the best coach simply the best recruiter? The best mastermind on the bench? The best teacher of fundamentals? None of the above?

Over the years I began to look at the subject differently, and as I did, I got away from the lists and measurements. In some seasons it seemed to me that the best coach was some man or woman who never got national attention, someone who maybe didn't even make the playoffs. I began looking around the competitive landscape to see which coaches were maximizing the efforts of the available talent. It occurred to me that some of the best coaches might even be losers. Not very often, of course. But sometimes.

I had once figured that given time, the best coaches would automatically rise to the top. But the longer I observed the proceedings, I began to note what a factor good fortune played in the course of events. It became clear that in this age of instant gratification some deserving coaches might never get the opportunity to rise to the top of the game. And for those who did find a way up, their fortunes often hinged on something as simple as a single decision. For example, I remember that Bobby Knight had put together a powerful Olympic basketball team in 1984 comprised of some of the best collegians in the country, including Michael Jordan, Patrick Ewing, and Sam Perkins.

This Olympic team played a series of exhibition games against a collection of National Basketball Association stars. It was fascinating to see the Olympic youngsters routinely whip the NBA teams. One of the final games in the series was played in Phoenix, and I broadcast the game for CBS. The coach for the NBA exhibition team in that game was Pat Riley. True to the pattern, the Olympians again defeated the NBA stars. That night after the game, Gary Bender, my broadcast partner, and I visited with Pat Riley in our hotel lobby.

I remember being struck by Riley's mood. He had been a Los Angeles Lakers broadcaster in 1981 when the team abruptly fired Paul Westhead and named Riley the head coach. In storybook fashion, his Lakers won the NBA title that spring of 1982. But the next two seasons had brought disappointing losses for the Lakers in the NBA championship series, first to the Philadelphia 'Sixers in 1983 and the Boston Celtics in '84. The dissension in Los Angeles had been substantial after these losses, and now Riley was left hanging, waiting over the summer of 1984 to learn whether team owner Jerry Buss would decide to replace him. In fact, Pat was scheduled to meet with Buss in the coming days to learn his fate. Riley had a great deal he wanted to accomplish with the team, but he didn't know if he would get that chance.

As fortune would have it, Dr. Jerry Buss did elect to keep Riley in the job, and Pat went on to lead the Lakers to NBA championships in 1985, 1987, and 1988, thus establishing his reputation as a great coach and great motivator. I point this out only to make it clear to young coaches that in another set of circumstances, Pat Riley might have missed that opportunity to demonstrate his competence in such a high-profile arena. Even for the great ones, the factor of good fortune weighs large. There is, of course, no guarantee that good fortune will follow those who are deserving. But, as Riley's example has demonstrated, the odds of that happening are enhanced when preparation and determination intersect with opportunity. You have to work hard to get into position to be fortunate, in coaching or any other business.

However they arrive at their greatness, coaches have always fascinated me, probably because my father was one for many seasons. That, in large, explains my motivation to write this book with Roland Lazenby. I had a desire to speak with many of America's greatest coaches in hopes that they would offer their insights into winning, leading, and succeeding in a highly competitive environment. For the purposes of this book, I have limited the selections to coaches who have won two or more national or international championships over the course of their careers. Although I had my opinions about a number of their personalities, I wanted most of the information to come across in the interview format. I also wanted to limit the questioning to a set of specific topics so that the reader might be able to informally compare various coaches' beliefs about methods and philosophy. Mainly I wanted to know why they won. After all, the mystery was substantial. The personalities of a John Wooden, a Pat Summitt, a Tommy Lasorda, and a Bill Walsh were all dramatically different. They all took different paths to championship status. I wanted to see where they were alike, and where they were different. Sometimes their answers reflected a consistency, but each interview produced a host of surprises.

One of the most fascinating was Anson Dorrance, the highly successful women's soccer coach at the University of North Carolina. Subsequent to the interview, two of Dorrance's former players filed a lawsuit against him, which in turn brought a large number of his former players stepping forward to avow that they had never witnessed or heard of any improper behavior on coach Dorrance's part. The legal process will have to work its course in settling the dispute, but the reader will still find Dorrance's observations here invigorating. Each contributor was asked the same basic questions with some slight variations and encouraged to provide specific examples from his or her experiences. In reviewing their responses, it becomes clear that a pattern or formula emerges for some of the leaders interviewed. Still, there's little question that much of coaching remains a matter of personal style, a mixing of organization and strategy and philosophy and personality and preparation and a zillion other things. That's exactly how it should be, and in the final analysis, it makes this project a collection of their wisdom and insight, a companion for other coaches young and old, big timers and Little Leaguers, all looking for that extra edge. What they have to say also makes sense many ways in matters of business and even of family relationships, or in any venue where respect and communication and understanding are prized.

It's in that spirit that Roland Lazenby and I bring you this collection of visits with great coaches who have been willing to offer thoughts on why they've won. We hope that you find a number of items here to help you along, whether it aids the growth and development of your team, improves interaction with your family and friends, helps you rethink your plans for the upcoming season, or better yet, even brings you an extra win or two when your fortunes don't look so good.

Billy Packer

Acknowledgments

The authors wish to thank Tom Bast for his belief in this project, and to express their appreciation for the editorial help of Heather Lowhorn, Mike Ashley, and Susan Storey. We wish to acknowledge the fine help of the excellent sports information staffs at the University of North Carolina and the University of Tennessee, plus the help of Arthur Triche and his public relations staff with the Atlanta Hawks, and Jeff Twiss and the staff of the Boston Celtics. The help and support of Talbot and Kim Masten, Mike Shank, Lindy Davis, Mike Meyers, Mike Morris, and numerous others is appreciated. We also wish to thank our families who make the most special contributions of all. And a special appreciation goes out to the coaches interviewed, who graciously gave of their time to make this project a success.

WHY WE WIN

Red Auerbach

In the 1940s, Arnold "Red" Auerbach was the boy wonder coach of the NBA, and in the 1980s he was the league's general manager emeritus. In the four decades in between, he saw just about every scenario. He engineered the team's transition from Bob Cousy to Bill Russell to Tommy Heinsohn to John Havlicek to Dave Cowens to Larry Bird, the guy who wheeled and dealed other NBA managers into dizziness. He had the vision to acquire Russell and Sam Jones and Larry Bird and countless others. He understood the challenge of building a championship team, evidenced by the fact that he played a major role in the winning of 16 NBA titles.

His coaching days, however, ended following the 1965–66 season, after his Boston Celtics had won their eighth straight (and ninth overall) NBA World Championship. The Celtics went on to win two more championships over the next three seasons with Bill Russell as player-coach. Regardless, Auerbach said he had no regrets about stepping down when he did.

"I had to make a choice," he explained. "Everything is a matter of timing."

The timing in this case concerned the club's general managership. Long-time team owner Walter Brown had died in 1964, leaving Auerbach to fill the dual role of coach and general manager for two seasons. That task left him exhausted. He once explained to good friend Lefty Driesell that the mere act of putting on his sneakers to go to practice had become drudgery. At the end of the 1965 season, he decided to do the general manager chores exclusively.

Without tremendous fanfare, Auerbach closed the chapter on the most successful coaching career in the history of professional sports. In his 20 seasons of coaching, he won 938 regular-season games, a record that would stand for three decades until Lenny Wilkens eclipsed it in 1995–96.

An immensely proud man, Auerbach says he takes the most pride in the consistency of winning that the numbers represent. He also takes pride in the fact that the Celtics accomplished their championships with meager team resources. Brown, after all, had funded the team out of his own pocket for years, which meant that the entire Celtics organization consisted of four people. Auerbach had no assistant coaches. He did his own scouting and managed the team's business affairs, right down to booking plane flights and hotel rooms.

Obviously, much of Auerbach's philosophy is born of surviving, then thriving, in difficult circumstances, for both him and his Celtics. Raised in Brooklyn, he was the son of a Russian immigrant who labored long hours operating a small laundry. Life was not easy. But neither was running an NBA team in the league's formative years, particularly in Boston.

After distinguishing himself in New York high school basketball, Auerbach attended junior college, then went on to play for George Washington University, beginning a long-term love affair with the District of Columbia. When the Basketball Association of America, the forerunner of the NBA, formed in 1946, Auerbach was hired as the 29-year-old coach of the Washington Capitols and immediately directed the team to a regular season divisional crown. The Caps lost in the playoffs, but Auerbach's reputation had been established. Across the league, opponents quickly learned that his wavy red hair was true to the stereotype.

"He was flamboyant, gutsy, on top of everything. And fiery. I mean really fiery," Celtics radio announcer Johnny Most said of the young Auerbach in his early years in Boston. "But the important thing about him was that he knew the rules better than the officials. And he pulled the rule book on the officials all the time because he knew them. And he had the bite of intimidation. Like when his team was not playing well or playing lethargically, he'd go out there and start to scream at the fans or the referee and get them on him.

"Sometimes he used to get himself thrown out of a game, and the guys would respond by ripping off 20 points in a row or something like that. They'd explode. And there was no assistant coach in those days."

In 1985, the Celtics honored Auerbach with a celebration of his 35 years building the team. Dozens of old Celtics returned, stars and role players alike, long-termers and short-timers, all to honor Red. The occasion prompted Bill Russell to reflect on exactly what set Auerbach apart. "He never made any pretensions about treating players the same," Russell recalled. "In fact, he treated everybody very differently. Basically, Red treats people as they perceive themselves. What he did best was to create a forum, but one where individuals wouldn't be confined by the system. And he understood the chemistry of a team. People tend to think teamwork is some mysterious force.

It can really be manufactured, and he knew how to do that, to serve each player's needs."

In short, Auerbach constructed a system from which he could orchestrate greatness. In this pursuit, the "pride" became a primary motivational tool. "Motivation is a very hard subject to address because there are so many reasons, so many factors involved," Auerbach says. "Basically you play percentages and you do the little things. You try not to get beat by the little things because they all add up. For example, I remember when I was coaching and we had a dress code. Everybody had to wear a shirt, tie, and a jacket to every game, except on the road they could travel with a sports shirt. No beards or none of that. And you say what good does that do? Does that score any points? No. But it does do good because it gave the players a feeling of superiority. They were better dressed and acted differently than these other teams that were coming in sweat shirts and dirty socks and no socks and so on. It was not original on my part. I copied that from the old Yankee manager, Joe McCarthy. If you want to be a champion, you've got to feel like one, you've got to act like one, you've got to look like one. . . . That's all part of your motivation. Whether it's that or whether it's the way you conduct your practices or the way you may teach your players to speak in public."

Billy Packer: Red, what would be the most important ingredient of a championship team?

Red Auerbach: I would say the chemistry of the ball club. The ability to get along with each other and the type of discipline that would be prevalent throughout the team. In other words, you can't have too many chiefs and no Indians, so to speak. You've got your ball club. They've got to respect the person in charge. They've got to feel they can respect his decisions. In addition to that, they've got to realize, in my opinion anyway, that the statistics mean very little as far as their careers are concerned. To win championships, I used to tell my players that your salary is dependent solely on your contribution to winning, not how many points you score. Because there are no stats to measure defense. There are no stats to measure hustle. There are no stats to measure obvious mistakes. The only stats you had back in the 1950s and '60s was point-scoring and rebounding and later on, of course, blocked shots. So therefore, in those days you could do that—make your ball club as individuals aware that their salary is totally dependent on their overall contribution. And we stuck to it.

Q: I'm surprised you didn't say talent when asked to list the most important ingredient. Is that not necessarily the most important ingredient of a championship team? Have you seen championship teams that didn't have the talent?

RA: Yes, I certainly have. I think talent, naturally, is important; you can't make chicken salad out of chicken feathers. You've got to have a good semblance of talent. But I remember there were certain teams that had an abundance of talent and couldn't win because of the selfishness of the various players relative to their stats. They felt that their salary depended on how many points they scored, period. Or how many rebounds they recorded as opposed to what they did to contribute to winning.

Q: Putting together the team, what's the first thing you're looking for?

RA: The ball. You can't win without the ball. Therefore your first ingredient is to get somebody who can get you the ball.

Q: Meaning rebounding?
RA: Meaning rebounding.

Q: Now that would jump off to me to mean that if you were starting a team right now, would a Dennis Rodman be a guy that you would want? You don't think of him as a team man, but he's a guy who can get you the ball. Explain that to us.
RA: No. No, Dennis Rodman, on paper, does all the great things relative to getting you the ball where you could start your fast break. Basically though, he is concerned with his individual accomplishments relative to rebounding. He's not concerned with getting that ball and getting it downcourt, with starting a fast break. Secondly, with his off-court antics and other facets of his game, I wouldn't want him on my team. I just wouldn't want him. It's not worth it. Take a guy like a Bill Russell, who can rebound, in my opinion, better than Rodman; who could block shots better than anybody who ever played the game, and was as quick as a cat and could run the court, everything like that, and was totally unselfish. Totally unselfish . . . as far as winning the game. All he wanted to do was win. Nothing else mattered. And Rodman, you can say he wanted to win. Sure, he wanted to win because it's self-serving to him. I mean everything he did was calculated. When he got thrown out of a game and did something to the crowd and threw his shirt in the crowd and all that stuff, that's all translated into money. The fact that it hurt the team in that game, that didn't bother him. He knew that if he was suspended and it cost him $50,000 or $60,000, he would more than make it up in commercials because of his identity, the way people market identity today. They don't market character or anything like that. They market exposure, identity. You see him in a hotel commercial or something like that. If he was a normal type athlete that played the ball game as it should

be played, he'd be another guy. He wouldn't get the high profile he has. For example what if Karl Malone did those things? Then, he'd make millions of dollars. As it is, Karl Malone can't get a commercial because he's a nice guy. Same with David Robinson. They're nice people. They can't get a commercial.

Q: **We all hear about people who are champions because they're supermotivated. Can a coach be the motivator, or is motivation something that is within a person that a coach can bring out?**

RA: Well, both. First of all, the most important thing in coaching in my book, is communication. It's not what you say as much as what they absorb. For example, a lot of people know the X's and O's. A great coach will take that, explain it to them and look at them, and he knows that they absorb it. Another coach would say it the same way, the same words, but nobody would absorb it. It just goes through. It's just like a coach that rants and raves. After a while his players turn him off. They say, "Hey, we're 10 points down at halftime. He's going to come in. He's going to hit the locker. He's going to scream. He's going to yell. I might as well be ready for it." So they get in the corner. They sit there with their heads down. Some people think that approach works because the players will put out enough effort so they won't have to listen to the coach's crap, see.

Q: **But you were known as a guy who occasionally got hot with your players?**

RA: Never.

Q: **Never got hot with them?**

RA: Well, I shouldn't say that. I would cuss once in a while in general. Never cussed a player as an individual. I never cussed a player. And my players, you could talk to any one of them, the dressing rooms at halftime, after the game, were disciplined. I mean sometimes you start off sarcastic, and you get funny. Sometimes you start off funny and you get mad. Sometimes you start off a little mad and you get funny. But you've got to remember the worst thing that coaches do in the game of basketball is talk too much. They overcoach. For example, I had guys with me for 10 years. Cousy. Russell. Sharman. Those guys. How much could I say every practice, every pre-game, every halftime, every postgame? They get tired of listening to the same crap all the time. So I used to pride myself in avoiding repetition. Avoiding having them know what's going to happen.

Q: Keeping them on edge a little bit?

RA: Right. For example, many a time I'd walk into the dress-ing room about 15 minutes before we'd go out, before I'd kick the visitors out of the dressing room. I mean every-body. No owners. No nothing. That was not a place for people to gather. This was the place for the players and myself. And I would pace up and back for a few minutes and I'd say, "You know, I've got nothing to say." I'd say, "You've played these guys before. Let's go out and get the job done." That's a pregame talk. And that's more ef-fective than going through all the old routine. How many times could you tell Satch Sanders, "When you play Baylor, Satch, you're not going to block his shot. Don't try to block the shot, just stick your hand up and as he takes the shot, see that he doesn't get the second one. In case he misses, you make sure you keep him off."? How many times could I tell him that? We play them six times a year, you see. So I avoided all this repetition. And after a while, the ballplayers would not know what's going to happen.

One day we were in the playoffs, and I didn't know what the hell to say. I walked in and I said, "Hey Ramsey, give them the pregame motivating speech." And he's a comical guy from Kentucky, but very bright. And he walked up to the blackboard and wrote down, "You win—$10,000. You lose—$5,000." And he sat down. Everybody laughed, and the tension was broken.

Every once in a while I'd say, "Hey, you think you guys are nervous in a playoff game, a seventh game? Figure out how nervous they are, knowing they're going to play you guys." I'd say, "Their hands are sweating. Their hands are wet. What the hell are you worried about? What got you here? Do it. Get out. Out!"

Q: You were blessed through your career, as you mentioned, not just with Bill Russell but with guys like Tommy Heinsohn and John Havlicek and Bob Cousy. Guys who had tremendous internal motivation themselves. Did you ever have a player that you felt didn't have this self-motivation, that the other guys helped him develop? Did you have a guy who wasn't so motivated who actually went on to become a real competitor? Or is competitiveness an innate thing?

RA: That's a good question. I think that competitiveness only has to be evident, prevalent, in a few. It's catching. Certain players will instigate the feeling and affect the others that they go along right with it. If you've got a Larry Bird, he'll affect everybody in that dressing room. He won't take any crap. If a guy is not ready to play or a guy doesn't want to do it, then he'll get on them. He won't even wait for the coach. That's the same with the teams that I had. A lot of them were quiet. Russell never said anything in the dressing room. Cousy was very quiet. Most of them were quiet. They were getting ready for the game. Today, you go into a dressing room, there's a million people in the goddamn place. They've got the music blowing and they're talking and this and that. And then, before the game, they throw some people out, but a lot of them still stay there. You know, the ball boys and the trainer and the equipment man and the alumni in college. They're all around the goddamn place. And I think that is total distraction.

Q: For so many years, you'd hear about some kid that has great potential. Is potential a negative word or a positive word?

RA: Well, I don't know. Potential to me is that you have the possible ability for greatness. Now, how to achieve that may depend on the person, may depend on the coaching, may depend on outside activities. It may depend on money. It might depend on a lot of things. But you're born with the possibility.

I once gave a lecture on potential limits. For example, you take two people. And one guy, you train for five years on how to jump the running broad jump. Five years. You take another one, a similar athlete, similar height and weight and everything like that. Never trained a day in his life. He comes out there and beats the guy by five feet. And you say, well, how can that be? Well, his potential limit may be 30 feet. He may never achieve his potential limit of 30 feet, but with proper training, and proper coaching, and proper diet, and everything in place, he may get up to 28 feet. See? The other guy's potential limit, no matter what he does, is 20 feet. So the most he'll go, probably, is 17 feet, maybe 18 feet. With the same coaching, the same thing. That's what you mean by potential limit. The potential limit is up there. How close you come to achieving it depends on all these different factors. Outside activities. The money. The coaching. Your attitude. How hard you want to work. Do you want to pay the price? And that's what I mean by potential.

Q: Over your fabulous career did you ever discover any shortcuts to success? Because that's what people today always seem to want to look for—the shortcut.

RA: No. You see, when we won a championship, I used to go and meditate myself. I'd say, "You know, you're a lucky guy. You have coached the greatest basketball team in the world. Now, that's some great accomplishment. Now, everyone's after you. Now, what are you going to do? Isn't this a wonderful feeling? Everybody looking up to you as the coach of this great organization or whatever it is."

My players would come back in the fall, and I'd say to them, "Did you have a good summer? Wasn't it a great feeling all summer knowing you were a member of the greatest basketball team in the world? Now everybody is after you. Everybody wants to take that away from you. Now, isn't that worthwhile, tightening your belt and getting it again? And going through this again—that great feeling? Instead of saying, 'Well, we lost because . . . ' or 'We didn't feel real good'?"

One thing that used to bother me was the people who look for reasons why they're going to lose, rather than look for reasons why they should win. But they've got their alibi all set before it even starts, you see. And that was my theory. And every year I used to do that when we would win these championships in a row.

Q: You were known for building an organization where loyalty mattered. How about loyalty? Is it a two-way street? Is it something, that if you're going to have a championship team, it's got to be there?

RA: Well, loyalty takes time. And it takes cooperation from owners and so forth. It takes time to build up. But to expect loyalty from a player, you've got to be prepared to give it. Unfortunately in most situations, in most teams, they want it, but they won't give it. We had an organization and still have an organization where we try to help our own, those who have been true to us and given everything they can. For example, we've had so many players make their home in the Boston area, and so many players we've helped get jobs. And all of our guys right now, practically everyone in the organization is a former Celtic guy. Cousy and Heinsohn do our TV. Cedric Maxwell does the color on the radio. I can go on and on and on. Now, you reward them not only that way, but you reward them for their loyalty by being loyal to them in that if they ever get a problem away from basketball, you try to help them. Which we've done in their personal and private lives.

Q: What is your position on goals? So often young coaches come along and especially business organizations, they'll have meetings before the year starts, and they lay out all the goals and anticipations and rewards for goals. In accomplishing so many championships, were you goal-oriented? Did you set out with a goal in mind, or how did you plan that? Are you a guy who sets goals?

RA: Oh, yes. The goal was to win. When we started building a team, I figured out I don't want to get a better team. I want to pick the best team out there. Then I want to get a team that can beat that best team. And I go with that in mind. And if it took role players, fine. For example, the first few years here, we had a hell of a team, interesting to watch, everything like that. But come March, April, we'd run out of gas because we had no center. Ed Macauley, a Hall of Famer, was a great player, but he only weighed 180 pounds and these guys would wear him down by that time, see? So in the playoffs we'd have problems. So we made up our mind we had to get somebody to get the ball on rebounds and carry us through March and April instead of falling through fatigue.

Q: If you had to pick a characteristic of a top player, would you say his mental approach to the game or his physical approach to the game would make him more of a champion?

RA: I don't think you could measure that at all. I think so much depends on the individual. Some guys, they have the physical attributes to be a great player, and they become a great player or sometimes, they louse it up. If the guy's got a mental attitude and if he doesn't have the talent to go along with it, he's not going to get there. I've seen a lot of guys, unfortunately, with great, great mental attitudes, but they just can't get there.

Q: So let's suppose I had to make a choice. I have a guy with great ability, but no mental approach to the game, or I have a guy who has a great mental approach, but limited ability and I only have one spot. Which guy would you probably take?

RA: First of all, it depends on the position. Secondly, it depends on the rest of your personnel. Because sometimes the guy with the poorer mental ability with the great physical attributes can be hidden by the other guys, and they could help him out and do that.

Q: That's part of putting together your team?

RA: Exactly.

Q: As an example, you may have a guy who has a lot of ability, physically, who doesn't have either the mental or the competitive drive, but knowing that you've got

other guys that can bring that to the plate, they may pick him up in the area of his weakness?

RA: Like I said before, it's the chemistry. A lot of teams are happy only when they win, but the true measure of a team is how do you keep them going and keep them in good control when you're losing and hoping to turn it around. And that is the tough part, and that's where the chemistry is so important. Because if you've got a team that wins and is happy, and all of the sudden they go into a tailspin and they start sniping at each other and start fighting each other, you've only got one place to go from there, and that's down deeper.

Q: **Red, if you had something that really disturbed you about a player or about a team, what would be the thing that would be most disturbing to you?**

RA: What would bother me more than anything else was when they didn't play to the best of their potential. In other words, you always felt that this team was a better team than they played. Why did they lose this many games? Was it just because they were unlucky? Or the ball didn't go in? No matter what happens, that's the way you've got to approach it. You think, it's all right, if it was because the ball just didn't go in, but they hustled and they played hard. You accept that. But, it's disturbing if they had a reasonable amount of shots and you see they're not rebounding well, and they're not thinking and they lose their attention to what's happening out there. And then they get careless and they lose games. And that's how you lose a lot of close games.

With my teams when we'd be down to the end of a game and we'd have a time-out, I wouldn't make my players nervous. I wouldn't pull out a clipboard and give them a new play like these guys you see on TV. They get a clipboard. They draw X's and O's and throw in a new variation of a play. To me, that makes them nervous. I mean, you practice twice a day for so many months. You play so many games. Why can't you come down with 20 seconds to go, and say, "Hey, run the four play. Damn it, execute it right. Run the four play, get it done." Boom, it's over. Ten, 15, 20 seconds of your time-out. The rest of the time, let them relax. You don't have to keep yacking at them.

Then again—I think this is very important—most coaches treat their players very poorly. They have no confidence in players as intelligent people. And I always felt that if I had a Bob Cousy or a Russell, or Heinsohn or Havlicek or any of those kind of guys, I had to have confidence in them. Many of them were 30 years old, 33 years old when I coached them. They'd been with me so long. They're college graduates. Are they stupid? They're not stupid! Why can't they contribute something to me? So many times, I would say in a time-out, "Anybody see anything out there that they want to try?" And most times they'd say no, but sometimes they'd say, "This guy is turning his head on me a little bit. I think we can backdoor him or pull the string or whatever." But I always used the intelligence of my players. I didn't treat them like they were beneath me. They're not. I take Cousy, what am I, 10 years older than Cousy? So what? Or Russell? Whatever. Or eight years older than Sharman? Does that make me smarter? But coaches today, they think that their form of discipline is that they should be in total control, every practice, every game. And they're like the dictator. They know it all. And it's not so. That's how you get the respect of your players is you treat them like people. You see, I always used to hate the expression, "How did you handle Russell and Cousy?" You don't handle them. You handle animals. You deal with people. They've got a problem, we go one on one. We talk about it. That's what I find is the biggest problem in coaching today. Coaches, most of them, have total disregard for players' intelligence.

Q: Red, was there ever a time when you were disappointed after a victory, but in some way were pleased in some aspects when you lost?

RA: Well, I did something unusual one time we lost a game. First of all, I always used to refer to the team as "us." I never say "my Celtics." They weren't my Celtics. They were our Celtics. I never treated them that way; no one ever heard me say "my Celtics." I never used that term. But I remember, we lost a game. It's very quiet, and I came in the locker room. I said, "You know, you guys are down, we lost the ball game. I tell you something. I've got a confession. I stunk." I said, "I did a horseshit job on the bench. I don't think I was up for it. I wasn't thinking right. I don't think my moves were good." I said, "I stunk this game. Now forget it and get the next one."

Another thing that was rare, I always would predicate a lot of what I did when the game was going on based on my plans for the next game. You see where a team is 20 points ahead with five minutes to go, the coach is out there doing all that bullshit. Sit down. Think about the next one. How you're going to prepare for it. A good example is this story, which I've told many times. It's been written but it's true. We had a blizzard. And I wasn't coaching then. Bill Russell was the player-coach. He didn't make the game. So, you know, being a guy with a lot of ego, I was sitting in the stands and I came out and I took over the team because he had no assistant. And with about 20 seconds to go, in walks Russell. It was bad weather, and he was wearing his hat, the whole bit. He looks up there, we're 15 points ahead with 15 seconds to go, 20 seconds to go. He gets that grin. We win. We go in the dressing room. I lay into him like you wouldn't believe. I said, "You big son of a gun, where the hell have you been?" He said, "Well, I got stuck in the blizzard." I said, "Look, you and your Lamborghini with the six carburetors," I said, "shove them all." I said, "Goddamn it! Havlicek walked four miles." I said, "You and your stories, I can't believe . . . ," Then Don Nelson grabs me, touches me on the arm. He knew I was hot, and he says, "He's the coach now, and these young kids don't understand." I say, "He's no goddamn coach to me. He's a player." And I get up, and I say, "Furthermore, Russell, goddamn it, when you're not here there are two people that are not here. That's Bill Russell the coach and Bill Russell the player." I said, "I think that's a horseshit thing." And I storm out. Why did I do that after we win? Why did I do that? I wanted to win the next game, and I made Russell so mad that I got it. You see. But people don't understand that. They don't project, you see. Those are many of the things about the psychology of coaching and management, that being a step ahead.

Q: What about the delegation of authority? When you started out, you were the head coach, cook, and bottle-washer. Today, we see in companies, and we see even in coaching now where you've got the head coach, the assistant coaches, the TV guy, the scouting deal, and an organization that involves 150 people, including a specialized sales force. How important is it for a man to be able to delegate authority where those who are working for him feel that they're really part of the team, too?

RA: I think the game of basketball doesn't need all that is happening today. We didn't have videotapes. We didn't have assistants. We had 10 or 11 men, however many, you've got a game going on, and my mind was in tune. I knew how many fouls on any one of my players. I knew how many time-outs were left through memory, through experience. Through running the thing. Today, they've got one coach that takes care of the time-outs. One coach that takes care of the personal fouls, and they've got all that kind of stuff, and they get in each other's way. I can't stand it when a guy does something out there on the floor, and this coach gets him and says, "What the hell did you do this for?" And then the other coach gets him and he says, "Do it this way." And they get in each other's way. To me, when the game starts, one guy should run it. The only thing good about assistants is that they take away the nitty-gritty, everyday grind the coach doesn't have to do. I remember Bill Reinhart, the great coach at George Washington telling me years ago, that the duty of an assistant coach is to see that the freshmen become sophomores.

Q: **Do you actually play as you practice? Bill Russell told me that he hated to practice. He said that once after the Celtics lost, he walked into practice and saw that you had like five cigars laid out on the sidelines. He said, "Holy cripe, we're going to be in here the full day, 24 hours." He went out in the scrimmage and played like it was the seventh game of a world championship, and you stopped the scrimmage after a very short time, kicked them all out of practice and asked Russell to come in. And you said something along these lines: "Bill, every time I've ever asked you to do something for me you were there for me in the game. I really made a mistake expecting you to do it every day in practice." Could you amplify on that story a little bit? And what is the bottom line, do teams play as they practice?**

RA: Well, not exactly. However, individuals do. Not all of them. There are exceptions, but that's after you become good. You don't make a team by loafing in practice. You make a team by what you show in practice to earn the playing time. But relative to that story, we had a practice one day, and I couldn't get Russell to do a thing. He was loafing, and a couple of other guys picked it up, and they were loafing. And no matter what I did, I said, "Look, all I'm asking you for is a 20-minute scrimmage." I said, "Is that so much? I want a 20-minute scrimmage. I want to keep your timing." I couldn't get it. I blow the whistle. I said, "That's all, get out! No shooting around. I don't want to see you. Just get out!" (laughing) So they go out, the next day, they're wondering what happened, what I'm going to do, see. So I said, "I've got these five cigars. I've got no place to go. I'm not even going to go out there. I'm going to sit here at the desk. My feet are up and I'm going to watch this practice. If I don't get a 20-minute practice of game situation, playoff situation, we're going to do it over again until I get it. And I've got five cigars to prove it."

So Russell—he must have had some place to go—he played like it was a playoff game. He blocked a thousand shots and all. Finally, I went over to him, I stopped him and I said, "Look, I've done a lot of crazy things in my life. But Russell, I didn't mean for you to play that hard." Then I started to laugh. That's the dumbest thing I ever said. I started to laugh (laughing). "I didn't mean for you to play that hard!" And that's what happened. But that was the story and that was true.

But actually, as far as playing as you practice, there's a tendency to pace yourself at practice, especially once you have a team made. And when you pace yourself in practice, unconsciously, when the game starts, you pace yourself during that game a lot. Instead of playing all out, you pace yourself and you try to pick your spots, which is terrible, because there's no substitute for hustle. So that's what I meant in saying you play as you practice, because it's so. There are exceptions like Russell. He always felt he only had just so much in his legs, you know. I said, "That's bull."

One day he came over to me, he says, "Can I miss practice?" I said, "Why?" He said, "I'm tired." I said, "Good reason, don't come." Haaa! Like one time after a game, he was tired. I said, "What the hell are you so goddamn tired about. You played 45 goddamn minutes. I'm paying you to play 48."

That's the kind of humor we used to have, all those things going with all our players. And that's what kept them fresh. I felt, anyway, that I had compassion. If a guy had a problem, I listened. Cousy came over to me one time, he says, "Can I miss practice tomorrow? I got a chance to do a commercial in New York." I say, "What are they going to pay you?" He says "Five thousand dollars." His salary was only 15 or 16. That's one-third your salary for one day. I say, "Hey, take me with you!" I said, "Forget practice." I let him go. But there are coaches today that wouldn't do that. They think that's the end of the world for a guy to miss practice.

Q: To be successful, how important is it to manage your time?

RA: I don't know whether I was a workaholic or not, but I was in the office every day. Every day unless I was on the road or had some place to go. For example, if we had a game on Wednesday, and there was a college doubleheader in New York on Thursday and we had a game on Friday, I'd play my game on Wednesday, I'd call practice in the morning on Thursday, and I'd go down and take the plane to New York. I'd get there like 1 o'clock or something. I'd go over to the Garden, and watch the teams practice. Then I'd wait for the games, and scout the games. And I'd come back the next day. I felt I could get more information sometimes watching them practice and talking to the coaches, who I knew practically every one of them, than I could just by going to the game. Sometimes you go to a college game and all you see is a zone defense and they're playing catch, catch, catch. And you can't scout a kid, see. So I would do that and come back Friday for the game. Now, today, coaches don't do that. Very few pro coaches go to college games. The guy who I admired a lot was Nellie (Don Nelson). Nelson, you used to see him all over. While he was coaching, he'd get a day off and go scouting someplace. Most of these other guys, they don't do that. They figure they've got scouts and so forth, see. Maybe they're right, I don't know, but I never bought that. To me, the day was a day. You can't just sit around.

Q: Looking back over all the championship teams you put together, did you have a formula, and if so, was it a secret formula? Or did things fall in place as you moved along?

RA: No. There was absolutely no formula. The team, we didn't have any money. In other words, the Knicks would buy a player or things of that sort. We couldn't do that. We had to do it picking last in the draft and that was it. And try to make it a good pick. And so we would try and fill in a piece as much as we could every time. For example, when Cousy and Sharman retired, we had the Jones boys, Sam and K.C., ready. When Frank Ramsey retired, John Havlicek moved in. That was the way we used to do that, but we had no money. We couldn't be like the Yankees before the playoffs. They'd buy a player, you know.

Q: What was the best or most important piece of advice that had to do with your final successes?

RA: I don't think there was anything I could recall in particular. I used to admire my college coach Bill Reinhart at George Washington, the way he would do things. I liked [Celtics owner] Walter Brown, his demeanor. But I always felt the main thing was that my word was my bond. If I told a kid something, and the owner would say I can't go along with that, I would pay it out of my own pocket rather than see my word go down the tube. Because to me, that was important. And I think that the players knew that. You know, that you've got integrity, and you learn that from those kind of guys.

Q: What was the best advice you felt that you handed down to either one of your teams or one of your players?

RA: The main thing I used to tell them, do some listening. Don't be so domineering that you want to show and prove that you're the boss every day. You're a head coach, fine. Organize your staff. Do your job. But listen to people. Listen to people. Don't get to the point—and there are a lot of coaches that do this—where you absolutely have to prove that you're in complete command at all times. I know coaches—I'm not going to mention any names—you miss a practice, that's the end. If you get hurt and you come back ready to play, they're mad at you. It takes a long, long while before you get back in the lineup. One thing I used to tell all my guys who are coaches, try not to hold grudges. If you get down on a player for anything specific that he's done, I said call him in and talk to him. Lay it on the line. There's no better way to do it than that. Just talk to him, but don't hold grudges.

It's like the stupidity of college coaches, a lot of them. They give these kids a set of rules. If you're late for curfew, you don't start the next game. If you're late twice, you're suspended for a game. He's punishing himself.

The man is absolutely stupid that would do that, I don't give a damn who it is. What you do is you have sets of rules with no specific penalty laid out. That used to be my stock and trade. They never knew what I was going to do. For example, Kevin McHale missed a plane. I wasn't coaching then. I was the president. The coach says to me, "Well, what should I fine him?" Because, you know, most places have an automatic fine. I said, "Nothing. He's been with you eight years. He ever missed a plane?" He says, "No." I said, "So something was the matter with his kid or he got stuck in the tunnel or he overslept. So what's the big deal? You fine him, he gets pissed off." Not that it's the money, it's the idea. I said just forget it. Take him aside, say, "Hey Kevin, forget it. Don't do it again." That's the way you handle those things.

I swear to you, I coached for 20 years, I only fined a guy once, five dollars. And I never collected it. I don't believe in it, and basically I think that's a very important thing, and these college coaches should be aware of this. Don't set rules. I remember Charlie Scott or somebody was in Phoenix, he was fined $6,000 one year. I said for what? He says for little things. He says, "I turned on the radio in the airplane, I shouldn't do it. Two hundred dollars. I come five minutes late—three hundred dollars. Stuff like that, you know."

There are other ways, than to do that. You've got to get the players to owe you, see. Rather than antagonize them to show who's boss, you have them owe you. You do them a favor without showing two sets of standards or anything like that. You do a favor for one. You do a favor for another. You do a favor and they owe you.

I used to tell my players, "You're intelligent people. It's easier for you to study me than it is for me to study all 12 of you. Therefore it's easy, so you learn my eccentricities, my likes and dislikes, just as I learn yours." That's very important.

Also, you learn there are certain players you don't yell at. Certain players, you don't bawl out. Certain players, you know, you slap on the back—nice going. Some other players, not as much. But you study your players. For example, I never bawled out Cousy. I never bawled out K. C. Jones. But I would bawl out Jim Loscutoff. I would give Frank Ramsey hell once in awhile. Even Havlicek. And Russell, I'd get on him all the time. And another thing, I very seldom really gave a substitute hell. They've got enough troubles. They don't need all that.

Q: Do the things you were talking about, the characteristics of the team, of the coach, the way you deal with people, are those philosophies just as solid today as they were in the '50s, '60s, '70s, and '80s?

RA: No. No, it's entirely different. I think, sure, I could coach today with the X's and O's, and running the team, and do as well as I ever could. At my age, it's physical; it's not mental. But it's different. The money has changed everybody. It's changed them from the time they're 15 years old. They show some talent. The family gets in it. They talk to coaches, AAU coaches, whatever. They talk to agents, so forth, so on. They change the whole thing as it used to be. It used to be fun. It's like the old cliché. Years ago, the ballplayers would come to practice with a gym bag; today, they come to practice with attaché cases, followed by their agents, followed by the Madison Avenue boys or whatever. It's entirely different.

How do you approach it because of the salary cap and other factors that have been involved in the game? I really don't know. Like for example, when a player today who is getting $6 million a year says to the coach or the owner, "Look, I want to be aware of any deal that's made. I want you to go over it with me." And he tells that to the coach, too, and the coach says, "What the hell is going on here?"

The player tells the coach, "Look, I don't have to take any crap from you. I've got a no-cut, guaranteed, five-year contract, and if I don't like you, I'll get rid of you." And there have been a lot of cases where players have gotten rid of coaches. And those are, to me, your big problems today. The players are getting more and more power, and they've taken it over.

John Wooden

More than any other coach, John Wooden set the age of modern college basketball in motion. His UCLA teams popularized the sport and attracted national television. Beyond that, his zone press foreshadowed the age of high-tech defenses.

All the same, Wooden was very much a coach from the old school, given to wearing horn-rimmed glasses and quoting inspirational verse. Because of that, when writers described him, they reached for idyllic images, of one-room Indiana schoolhouses and church deacons (Wooden was a deacon in his Santa Monica, California, church). He was once described as "the only basketball coach from the Old Testament." This image cloaked the fact that Wooden was an intense competitor. With his great eye for detail, he focused those competitive energies into a laserlike precision, which he used to cut the hearts out of opponents. In the dozen seasons between 1964 and 1975, his teams won 10 NCAA championships. This competitiveness as a coach was an extension of his intensity as a player. He had been an all-state high school performer in Indiana, and later a three-time All-American at Purdue under coach Piggy Lambert. His understanding of the game grew from the lessons Lambert taught him about up-tempo basketball. After a stint in the Navy during World War II, Wooden coached two years at Indiana State, then moved on to UCLA in 1947. It was an unheralded urban school in those days with a losing basketball team and a small gym. But Wooden changed that. He did it with his knack for precision, particularly in his practices.

"I am not a strategic coach," he once said. "I am a practice coach." Each session was organized tightly to run his players through a barrage of drills, conditioning, and scrimmaging. He always saved the scrimmaging for the end so that his players would learn to function when they seemed most tired.

Like a computer-aided-design system, his mind seemed to view the game from every angle. Quite often he would watch his practices from the gym's upper seats to view the entire floor. As Marv Harshman, the former Washington State coach, once said, Wooden made adjustments during a game better than anyone. It was his complete view of the game that aided these adjustments.

In his first 13 years at UCLA he admitted to growing frustrated by the program's lack of national success. "I wanted to win a national championship very much," Wooden recalled, "and I think it's quite possible that, prior to winning one in 1964, I might have wanted it so much I hurt my players in one or two instances."

Wooden had come to UCLA in 1949 and immediately turned a loser into a winner. But his teams fought for more than a dozen years to rise above regional competition. For much of that period, UCLA had a tiny gym. And although he won, Wooden's ability as a coach was held in question in the West, where Phil Woolpert at the University of San Francisco and Pete Newell at the University of California were winning with disciplined, patient offenses.

"The Wooden teams were all different but all alike in the regimen," recalled broadcaster Curt Gowdy, himself a former college star. "They ran those high-post offenses. I noticed little things about them, how they'd hold their arms up in the free throw lane ready for the rebound, how they'd always bank their side shots. I asked Wooden about that. He just thought it was an easier way to shoot than aiming straight for the hoop. His teams had beautiful skills fundamentally.

"Wooden was a deceiving man in that he mildly rolled up his program during the games," Gowdy said. "In practice he was tough. When he was a player he was tough. He would drive and crash into the bleachers on layups and played the game hard. His teams played that way."

Today, nearing his 90th birthday, Wooden remains an acute and active observer of the basketball scene, as his comments reveal.

Billy Packer: Is there such a thing as the thrill of victory and the agony of defeat?

John Wooden: It depends on how you would define victory and define defeat. I don't think you necessarily have victory when you outscore someone, and I don't think you are necessarily defeated when you're outscored. I think the real thrill comes from the preparation to get where you're in that area where you have the opportunity to outscore an opponent. But getting there . . . it's like Cervantes said. The journey is better than the end.

Q: Could you define for us what is a championship team? It might not be the guy who won the trophy. What is the key ingredient to a championship team?

JW: When you have a group working together, to me, it's one of the most difficult things you have to do, and most important. To get each individual to accept the role that you, the leader, feels is necessary for the team overall to become near their level of competency. Individuals may be better suited for another role than the one in which you have them, but you may have someone else who's even better suited for that role. Between the two, you get better total results by having someone in a role that might not be his best role. To get them to accept that is one of the difficult things.

Q: We often think that one of the basics for a championship team is to have the best talent. Is that the case? Have you ever had a championship team in which you didn't think you had the best talent?

JW: First of all, no one wins championships without talent. No one. However, not everyone wins with talent. Yes, I've had teams that I think did better than other teams that I felt had more talent. But what I might consider better talent for me might not be better talent for the other person. I think we're all different, the styles that we use to get the most overall effect. Some might give up a little more in quickness to get more size. I would give up a little size to get more quickness.

Q: Have you ever started a season thinking, "I have the physical talents to have a great season," but when that season was over you have a feeling that that talent wasn't best exposed? Has that ever happened to someone as successful as yourself?

JW: Yes, I've misjudged it on occasion. Perhaps, to begin with, I was judging them from the physical point of view alone.

I thought they had the physical abilities. But there's so much more to it than the physical abilities, and I failed to recognize it, not knowing them. This would be true when I had new players that I thought were extremely talented coming in to begin with. I would know their physical talent, but wouldn't know all the other things about them which I needed to know to be able to work them into a unit. It's the unit that's the important thing, not the individual. Yes, I've been wrong in my judgments of different players many times.

Q: **You've said to me many times over the years that winning, in terms of the objective, might not have so much to do with the score as it does with meeting your potential. I've heard your players from the past discuss that in terms of your motivation. Could you explain that?**

JW: Well, my players never heard me mention winning. One creed that my dad gave me when I graduated from grade school was, "Make each day your masterpiece."

That became one of my creeds. I tried to get that across in teaching youngsters. You're not going to make a great jump all in one day. But you're going to increase a little bit every day, and pretty soon each of those little bits amounts to something pretty strong. I feel that winning in one sense is something only individuals can determine for themselves, whether they won or lost. You're the only one who really knows. It's like character and reputation. Reputation is what you're perceived to be; character is what you really are. And you are the only one that really knows your character. You're the only one who really knows if you did everything within your power to prepare yourself to function at your highest level.

Don't try to be someone else, that's another thing I tried to get across. Don't try to be better than someone else. That may be impossible. But it's possible for you to make the effort to do the best that you can do. That's another thing that my Dad tried to get across, that very idea. If you get yourself too engrossed in things over which you have no control, it will adversely affect the things over which you do have control.

That's why I eventually came up with my own definition of success, which is peace of mind obtained only in the self-satisfaction of knowing that you made the effort to become the best of which you're capable.

This may amuse you. I've talked to Bill Walton a little bit. In fact, he calls me every week. He asked me to critique him as a broadcaster one time. I said, "One thing, Bill, quit telling me that the players overachieve. No one ever overachieves. We're all underachievers to one degree or another. Don't tell me he's an overachiever, and don't tell me he's a hustler when he's just running around not getting anything done. I want my players thinking out there. I don't think you would have ever referred to your former teammate Keith (Jamaal) Wilkes as a real hustler out there, but he was always thinking out there. He always got things done and was always at the right place at the right time. So quit saying that. And don't tell me that somebody gives 110 or 120 percent. That's impossible. We're working toward perfection. We know that's impossible to obtain because we're all imperfect."

Q: **Is motivation something that comes naturally within a player, or can a leader of a team actually motivate his players in some ways?**

JW: I think the person in position of leadership, whether it be a team, a business, or some other operation, has to gain the respect of those under his or her supervision and make them subconsciously want to put out a little more effort than they might ordinarily put out, even the subordinates might think they were trying. I think the leader really can do that. I have said one of the greatest motivating things that a coach has is the bench. They all love to play, all of them. You sit them on the bench, and they come around pretty good. They all want to play. I've also said that one of the greatest motivating factors is the pat on the back, although with some individuals, you have to make the pat a little lower or a little harder. To some degree, I think that's true.

But a leader motivates by leadership, just by example, by what he's doing, in my opinion. Now, there are different coaches who motivate by different methods. For me, there was no yelling for me at any time in our dressing room before games. We came out on the floor, we came out quietly. We didn't come running out. I wanted to save that energy for when the ball goes up with the center jump. "I want you to go out and get warmed up," I told them. That was our purpose—to get warmed up completely. I think the best method of motivation is by example.

Q: We are now in an era where coaches talk about having relationships with their players. What about relationships between players and coaches, between leader and player?

JW: I like a statement that the late Amos Alonzo Stagg made one time. He said he never had a player he didn't love. He had many he didn't like and didn't respect. But he loved them just the same. I think players know that you really care for them, even though they might not be getting to play the amount of time that they would like to play. You can do that by other ways. You can use the pat on the back, the nod, the smile, the hello, for players that I think aren't going to get to play very much. They need that, more than the players that are going to be getting it from the media, the alumni, and so on. So I think it's necessary to make sure that they get recognition, because we all want that.

Q: **Moving from that, can you discuss the mentality of the "star player," the athlete who has been told by everyone that he is great, sometimes to the point that he thinks he is far better than he really is. For example, you mentioned Bill Walton, a very eccentric individual during his years in college, certainly not like a Dennis Rodman today, but very much a product of that star mentality. How about the star player? How do you keep him in focus?**

JW: On the floor, a player like Bill Walton was perfect. On the floor. It was off the floor where certain of his eccentricities came into play. He played for me at UCLA during the early '70s, during that antiestablishment era. But on the floor, he was the perfect player. I've had some, however, that felt that they were the stars and maybe felt like they should be treated like stars. Well, my feeling is you get best results by *not* treating everyone the same. The general feeling is, if you don't treat everyone the same you're showing partiality. To me, that's when you show the most partiality, when you treat everyone the same. You must give each individual the treatment that you feel he earns and deserves, recognizing at all times that you're imperfect and you're going to be incorrect oftentimes in your judgment.

When I've said that the bench is the best ally you have in dealing with players, I've had other coaches tell me, "I can't put him on the bench. He's potentially the best player I have."

I tell them, "You explain yourself when you say potentially. You're not saying he *is* the best player. You're saying potentially. They don't pay off on potential. They pay off on results, how you produce. So if he's just potential, he's not your best player. Someone else who doesn't have that potential might be your best player. Although this other player is a lesser talent, it might be better for other players to be on the floor with him at the same time than it would be for this player with potential."

Q: Have you ever been in a situation where, in the short term, you had to put your beliefs on hold because it would help you advance in the long term?

JW: There's always fine lines in almost everything. My feeling is that I've had players where, when we're having trouble getting going, I put those players in to get some scoring. But then you have to get those players out in a hurry before they lose the game. They can get you back in the game, but they can get you out of it just as fast. I've had players like that, yes. I've had players that as a starter would never be as effective as they were when I brought them in off the bench. I've had others who if I didn't start them wouldn't be effective as a substitute. There again, a person in position of leadership has to study all of those under him and analyze their best contribution for the group as a whole.

Q: We saw the University of Kentucky in 1996 with a star-studded cast, almost a throwback to the years when teams did have 10 or 12 top-notch Division I players. It looked like coach Rick Pitino did a fine job of getting those guys to understand their roles within the team. How difficult is it to get players, or people for that matter, to accept that their role is in the best interests of the team?

JW: I feel that's one of the most difficult challenges that a person in position of leadership has, because there's always roles that seem to be more important in the public eye, and people want to be in those roles. It's like a play.

And I used to tell my players that the assembly of our team is like a play. Now, we might have an Alcindor, say, who is going to have the lead role. But if we don't have a good supporting cast, we won't have many encores, and we won't be able to go on the road.

I also equate it to an automobile. An Alcindor can be the powerful engine, and you as an individual are just a nut that holds the wheel on. Now, what good is that engine if we lose that wheel? So the nut on the wheel is just as important, in some regards, as the engine. The tough part is getting them to accept that each role is important. Everyone needs to feel needed and feel to a certain degree that they're important. So you have to pat them on the back and encourage them in those supporting roles. Also, the star must not refer to them as his supporting cast. He doesn't refer to them that way. They're all the cast, trying to get the job done. I want no excessive jubilation when you outscore another person or team in a game, and conversely, I want no excessive dejection if we're outscored. I want you to feel good, of course, when we do the outscoring, but nothing excessive.

Also, getting outscored should not be the reason for your dejection, rather you should be upset knowing that you didn't do what you needed to do to prepare for the situation.

Q: The greatest satisfaction you had as the leader of young athletes, what would it be? The championships?

JW: I would say in my earlier years it would have been championships, but as I matured and became more experienced my satisfaction became, what's going to happen to these youngsters after they're out from under my supervision? What's going to happen to them after basketball? I like very much to refer to Amos Alonzo Stagg again. After a particularly great season, a reporter said, "Well, is this your greatest season, coach?" And Stagg said, "I won't know for 20 years."

I think my greatest satisfaction is that practically all of my players graduated, and practically all of them have done well. Certainly reasonably well in the professions they chose. I get an awful lot of satisfaction out of looking around and seeing so many attorneys, ministers, surgeons, and those in other professions.

Q: This is a different era today in athletics in terms of media and public relations. Would the emphasis on public relations have changed how you ran your life and your program if it had been a factor in the 1960s and '70s?

JW: There is no progress without change. We know that. But all change isn't progress. I think the basic way I ran my team would not change. Those things would still be effective today, and they were effective before I used them. And I think they'll be effective long after you and I are gone. And that is, in sports, the three things—and I have them in the heart of my pyramid—that are, first, you have to get your players in the best possible physical condition—and that must be preceded by mental and moral conditioning. The next thing is that they must be able to properly execute the fundamentals. They must be skilled. I don't care whether it's a basketball player, a surgeon, an attorney, whatever, they must be skilled. And it isn't enough that they know how. They must be able to execute it. And they'd better be able to execute it quickly or they won't be able to do it at all. The third thing is probably the most difficult. Once you have talented players schooled in the fundamentals, the next step is to get them to be a team, to be considerate of others, to accept their roles, and to have the proper team spirit. That's going to be absolutely essential to get them to work together.

Q: Looking back at your incredible record, it's hard to think it, but was there ever a time that you faced failure?

JW: I never believed in teaching through fear. There are those who do, and I could name some and it appears that they've gotten fine results. But I always wanted to keep the positive approach. And sometimes I just had to let my players know that they weren't going to be successful. Sometimes the other person is just better, and there's nothing you can do about that. But there is something you can do about making the effort to become the best of which you're capable. And that's all I asked. Don't worry about the other fellow. Don't think about him, about beating him. Just think about being able to execute to the best of your ability and hope that might be good enough to outscore him. But if it isn't, you still haven't lost if you've made that effort.

Q: In regard to shortcuts to success, we all seem to be looking to follow a master. If I do what he does, then I'm successful. Do you think there really are any shortcuts?

JW: There's a statement, about those who keep so busy learning the tricks of the trade that they never learn the trade itself. There are no shortcuts, no easy way. The cornerstone of success, of coming close to reaching your own level of competence, is hard work. There is no substitute for that. You have to work hard, and you have to enjoy what you're doing. If you don't enjoy it, no matter how hard you seem to work, you're not going to be working as hard as you can because you're not enjoying it.

Q: We hear about "loyalty," or the lack of it, often in athletics. The loyalty between a leader or coach and his athletes. Is it a factor in the mix of championship teams?

JW: I think it is. But I think it's like a lot of other gifts. It begins with the person in position of leadership. If you listen to the people you're in charge of supervising, they're more apt to listen to you. Therefore, they'll be more loyal to you. But loyalty to yourself is far more important than being loyal to someone else, because if you are loyal to yourself, you're going to be loyal to all others. I think it's very important. I don't think people can function near their level of competency unless they have someone, or something, to whom they're showing loyalty.

Q: **In regard to goals, some coaches start each season by establishing their expectations. They say, "This year I think we can be 23–7." Sometimes they're that specific. What goals did you have in mind in terms of your leadership and building a championship?**

JW: Well, if you're setting goals as far as games won and lost, you have no control over those teams you're going to play. There are some circumstances where you have an inferior team facing an inferior schedule. Even though you have a good record in those circumstances sometimes, in my way of thinking, you're not as successful with that kind of team as you might be in another year, when you have a better team but a tougher schedule. Your goal should always be trying to come as close as possible to reaching your own particular potential. There's no way to judge that. I suppose winning percentage is a way to attempt to judge it, but it's not an accurate or valid way at all. When I was teaching, you had to win your conference to get into the NCAA tournament. In December each year, we played nonconference games. I tried to get across to our players that these nonconference games were to get us ready for conference play. If we win the conference, then we're going to get an encore, which is a trip to the NCAA tournament. So, our goal becomes to win the conference. But, to do that, we've to think each day about improving

ourselves a little and get to the point where we can function individually and as a group at a high level.

Q: The word "competitor," is this something that can be
   developed? Or do you think that competitive drive in
   an individual is innate, something God-given?

JW: I think it can be developed to a great extent. In my pyramid of success, I have competitive greatness as the very
   top. You're not going to be a great competitor unless
   you're prepared. You're not going to be prepared if you
   don't work hard and aren't enthusiastic about what
   you're doing. You're not going to be prepared unless you
   can function quickly. You're not going to be prepared
   unless you are considerate of others. You're not going to
   be prepared unless you're in proper condition. You're
   not going to have poise unless you have these other
   things (and poise is just being yourself). So all of these
   things, I think, work up to making you a competitor.

   Yes, you can make yourself a better competitor by preparing yourself to be able to function. Now, a lot of
   players are extremely spirited, but I wouldn't say they're
   the greatest competitors in the world, and I've seen others who don't look nearly as spirited who are great
   competitors.

Q: So this is something misjudged by the fan. Exhuberance
   may just be a show of emotion, but it lacks the focus of
   true competitiveness?

JW: Definitely.

Q: What about the old phrase, "You play as you practice."
   Is that accurate?

JW: To some degree. Not 100 percent. There are players who
   don't practice well but who compete well. I know you
   have talked to Red Auerbach, and I've heard him say

that when he had Bill Russell with the Celtics they had better practices without Bill Russell. He said he had two sets of rules, one for Bill and one for the team. But Bill was always ready to play when game time came. But you couldn't do that with a lot of other players. I'm sure that you couldn't. They wouldn't be ready to compete unless they were there at practice and working hard every day. So it depends somewhat on the individual, but I think as a whole, you must have organized practices where you're getting the group to work together, meshing their individual skills within the framework of the team.

If you're not doing it well in practice, the odds are you're not going to perform in a game. But I have heard stories. For instance, the great double-play combination, Tinker to Evers to Chance, I've heard they fought each other and didn't like each other at all. And the old Oakland team [Athletics] when they won their championship, they had fights and everything else. But the way they played the game you'd never know it.

One of my championship teams—I won't name which one—but off the floor they didn't like each other. There were only a couple of players liked by everybody. There were some liked by a few, and then there were a couple of players that almost nobody liked. But I've heard people say that on the floor, boy, that was one of the best-working teams they'd ever seen. I found out then that you didn't necessarily have to have the greatest chemistry off the floor to have a great chemistry on it.

Q: When I was interviewing Red Auerbach, I mentioned something about "handling Bill Russell." He corrected me immediately. He said something I'd heard you say before. The coach doesn't "handle" players. Do you recall that?

JW: That came from something Wilt Chamberlain said. When Wilt was acquired by the Los Angeles Lakers, I attended the press conference announcing his joining the Lakers. Bill van Breda Kolff was coach of the Lakers at the time, and one of the reporters asked Wilt, "Can van Breda Kolff handle you? We've heard that you're difficult to handle." Wilt said, "No one handles me. I am a person, not a thing. You handle things. You work with people. I think I can work with anyone who will work with me." Now just that very year, my book, *Practical Modern Basketball*, had just been published, and I had a section in there, titled "Handling Your Players." I left that meeting and immediately went home and crossed that out. I called the publisher so that in later editions there would be no section called "Handling Your Players." A little thing, yes, but perhaps an important thing. There was a time when I referred to all my players as "my boys."

But in the early '60s that phrase took on racial connotations, and some of the black players didn't like being referred to as boys. So I tried to quit doing that. Sometimes I reverted back because I had been doing it for so long. It didn't refer to color, or anything else. I've had players reply when I slipped, "That's all right, coach." But for some, it wasn't all right.

For years, I had called Alcindor by his first name, Lewis. But then he changed it to Kareem Abdul-Jabbar. I had called him Lewis so long, that sometimes I would slip. He'd say, "That's all right, coach." But if somebody else called him Lewis, he didn't like it at all.

There are many things you have to be aware of when you're coaching, when you're in a leadership position. You're always learning. To the day you die, you should always be learning.

Q: Coach, one of the things I've noticed in watching your teams practice over the years, was your organization,

particularly the use of time and the importance of it in building a championship team.

JW: It's extremely difficult to manage time. Time is a such an important thing in preparing a team. I had three rules that I always used in preparation. (I started out having a lot of rules and a few suggestions, and I ended up having a few rules and a lot of suggestions.) But my three fundamental rules were: 1) You be on time. 2) You never criticize a teammate. That's my job. 3) You never use profanity. If you violated any of those three things, then you didn't get to practice that day. You were off the floor for the day. Our players knew that we started on time.

When I first started coaching, I used to keep them overtime if things weren't going well. But if you keep them overtime, they're tired physically. And if they're tired physically, they'll be tired mentally. If they're tired, they won't be the most stable in the world emotionally, either. So you're not going to be able to accomplish much. So I learned to budget my time extremely well. We had 5 minutes or 10 minutes, never over 15 minutes for any one particular drill. If things weren't going well, we quit them. Maybe I had to add a few minutes for a drill the next day. But managing that time was something I learned as I coached.

On the other hand, I also learned never to be extreme, never to say never. If a player was going to be late and he came to me ahead of time to explain it, if I bought the explanation, fine. If I didn't, then he didn't get to practice that day. And they knew darn well that if they didn't practice they didn't get to play. A certain amount of playing time would be taken away from them.

Q: You've had some strong people work on your staff at UCLA over the years. What are your philosophies on the delegation of authority?

JW: You must have good people working with you. One time at UCLA I had two assistants, one of them was Denny Crum. I had many players who played for me who I thought would be outstanding coaches. But Denny was a player I had who I thought was born to coach. The only other person I've been around who had those same qualities was Jim Valvano. I was around Jim for three years when I worked Harry Litwack's camp in the Poconos. He was a player at the camp, and I remember thinking at the time, "That kid was born to coach."

But on my staff at UCLA, I had Denny Crum and Gary Cunningham. I wanted Gary Cunningham to concentrate on our set offense. I wanted Denny to concentrate a great deal on our pressing defense. When we got into games, during every time-out, Denny spoke briefly on the press, Gary spoke briefly on our set offense, and I spoke briefly on our set defense and fast break and tried to bring it all together. Prior to the game and at halftime, the three of us did much the same thing.

I would sit with Denny and Gary practically two hours every morning planning practice sessions for that afternoon. The practice sessions themselves would never last over two hours. But for each 10 or 15-minute session, each assistant knew exactly what he was going to do.

My players, I wanted them to have complete respect for my assistants. If I wasn't there, I wanted things to go on just as if I was. That was a great situation. Then there were other things. Denny coordinated all the recruiting. Gary coordinated all of the players' academic progress and helped with planning toward their degrees. He also arranged for tutors and summer jobs and things like that. I had to oversee it all, but they had the specific responsibilities. In practice, if my assistants did something that I thought was incorrect, I would never correct them before the players. I waited until we were alone to get an explanation for what they had done. Maybe what they had done was better than the way I wanted it done, but I wanted to know why.

A person is no better than his assistants in many ways, just as you're often no better than the talent of your players.

Q: Looking back at the championship teams that you had, what was their greatest asset?

JW: I would answer that by saying what a number of coaches have said to me through the years. A couple of things have come out. One was that we were consistent. I've always believed in consistency. It has been said that consistency is the last refuge of those without imagination. I've always wanted to be consistent. Another thing that was said about our UCLA teams is that we kept it simple. Our opponents always said we were easy to scout but difficult to play because we executed well.

I think those would be the things that I did. We weren't complicated. Now, I know some great coaches in the game who were very complicated. But we kept things simple.

Q: The best advice you were ever given that relates to building a champion?

JW: Not in words, perhaps, but more in presence. In seeing Piggy Lambert, under whom I played in college at Purdue. His primary success was that he kept the three things that I had in the heart of my pyramid. I think we were always in better condition. One time we were playing Indiana University, which was then coached by Everett Dean, one of the nicest, kindest people you ever met, and a fine coach, too. Piggy always called his opponents Mister. He said we would beat Mister Dean "because he's too nice a person." He said we would beat them at the end of each half because we'll be in better condition.

Well, another thing, Piggy insisted on quickness. He always had to have quickness. It had to be under control. From him I also learned that you could have activity without achievement, and that doesn't help you much. We want achievement with our activity.

Then we learned that we better play together as a team, if you wanted to play.

Now those three things are the most important of all. Of all time, I'd say. Yesterday, today, and tomorrow. Yet I can't say that I ever heard Mr. Lambert mention those things. Yet he emphasized them, and I came to understand them from being under his supervision.

Q: You hear so much today about the psychological approach to coaching. Do you think it's necessary to keep players happy?

JW: Adolph Rupp was a great coach, and a reporter said to him one time, "You know your players don't seem so happy. They don't seem to like you so much. How come?"

Rupp replied, "I'm here to coach them, not coddle them."

You'd like to see them reasonably happy, but that's not your job. You hope that you have their respect; that's far more important than having them happy. Having their respect and getting them to accept the roles you designate for them, even though they might disagree, that's the most important. You have to teach them while practicing the idea that we can disagree without being disagreeable. You must always listen to them, and you must explain why you do things to them, although they might disagree. They must know why, and they'll be more accepting if you listen to them.

Q: Does the coach hoping to build a championship team have to develop a system and a philosophy that becomes the foundation for the team?

JW: I think that will evolve as time goes by. Eventually you will come to that, and that will vary with the talent or material on your team. I would think it might be important in pro competition where you might have players on your roster for longer periods than in college. I don't believe that the system is nearly as important as your philosophy for getting them in the best possible condition, teaching them to execute and play together as a team, and keeping balance. I think the two most important words in life are love and balance. If we all had love to the extent we should have, I think we wouldn't need many other words. Love and balance. Balance keeps things in perspective.

From the physical standpoint, I think the most important thing in most sports is quickness under control. From the mental standpoint, the key is balance. We have to keep things in perspective. We have to keep balance. Physical balance. Emotional balance. Mental balance. Offensive balance. Defensive balance. There's a need for balance in just about every area you can think of. In sports, you must have quickness under control and balance. In life, you must have love and balance.

Q: **Let's get completely away from basketball for a second. How important is it to have interests away from the job? And is it possible to have other things in life and still be successful in the job?**

JW: Absolutely. Other things are more important than the job. Not that the job is unimportant, but you've often heard the statement, "He's so busy making a living he forgot to make a life." Now what's more important, making a living or making a life? Can you do both? I think you can. With me, I've often said—and I know it isn't right, but it's what I've said—the three most important things to me are first my family, then faith, and then my profession. Now, my faith, the Lord should be first, but I place Him second, and I think He understands.

I think you can balance your life. I tried not to bring my job home. I tried to be concerned with the things that were happening at home when I was with my wife, my family, and my children. I tried to do that. Now, can you do it 100 percent? No, I don't think you can do it 100 percent. But for the most part, you can.

Something I used to do in recruiting—made out a little questionnaire and sent it to the recruit's coach. Also sent it to five coaches whose teams had played against the recruit and asked them to fill it out. I called them first. That left me with six perspectives coming in. From those six, I made one composite. If one person has one thing different from everybody else, then I usually discounted that. I always found out about grades.

After each season had been over for five or six weeks, I'd then take up a topic and explore. For example, I might take up rebounding. I'd contact great rebounders or coaches who coached great rebounders. I'd get the books, and I'd take everything together and just study rebounding. Then I'd take all the information and create a composite, just as I did in recruiting.

I did that with all the great fundamentals. Rebounding. Free throw shooting. Offense against zone defenses. Everything over a period of time.

Ara Parseghian

In 1964, Notre Dame picked Ara Parseghian, the son of an Armenian immigrant, as the next in a line of esteemed coaches, and he quickly won his way into Irish hearts by becoming an overnight sensation. Those who knew Parseghian weren't surprised at his success; he had a football background steeped in excellent coaching. After service in World War II he had enrolled at Miami (Ohio) University, where he earned little All-America honors. Just short of graduation in 1947 the 24-year-old Parseghian took up the offer of Paul Brown and the Cleveland Browns to turn professional. He played just two years before a hip injury ended his career, then returned to Miami as an assistant to another legend, Woody Hayes. When Hayes left for Ohio State in 1951, Parseghian assumed the head coaching duties at Miami, where in five years he won 39 games and lost just 6, a record good enough to earn him the top job at Northwestern. Not only did he revive Northwestern's program, his teams won four straight games over Notre Dame, a factor that led to his hiring in South Bend.

Parseghian made sweeping changes upon his hiring in the spring of 1964, discarding the old split-T offense and picking up variations of the slot-T and I formations used by the pros. Parseghian had his mind set on the passing game.

His first real task was to find a quarterback, and amid the scrap heap of talent on campus he discovered one, a forgotten senior, John Huarte, who had failed to letter in 1963 as a third-string junior. Huarte had attempted only 50 passes in two varsity seasons, but Parseghian found him to be just the athlete he needed to run the offense. He could move and throw, and the only ingredient missing seemed to be confidence.

Over the spring, the Notre Dame staff worked intensively to school Huarte in the offense, to refine his skills, and to assure him that he would be the starter that fall. The reward was a stunning transformation. Huarte led the Irish to a 9–0 record and the very verge of a national title until a late loss to Southern Cal killed that dream. Huarte, though, was voted the Heisman trophy, and Parseghian was named collegiate coach of the year. His career at Notre Dame was off to a glorious start.

In 11 seasons at South Bend, he would guide the Irish to three national titles and big wins in the 1970 Cotton Bowl, the 1973 Sugar Bowl and the 1974 Orange Bowl.

The Sugar Bowl on December 31, 1973, was the site of his ultimate victory, with his undefeated Irish driving for a late field goal to edge undefeated Alabama, 24–23, in one of the greatest college football showdowns ever.

In 24 seasons, Parseghian amassed a coaching record of 170

wins, 58 losses, and 6 ties, a .739 winning percentage. In 1980, he was voted into the National Football Foundation Hall of Fame. For many years he has served as a network television college football analyst.

Billy Packer: Ara, in your experience, was there ever such a thing as the thrill of victory or the agony of defeat?
Ara Parseghian: Absolutely (laughing). I guess there's a lot of things in my life I have experienced that have been agonizing. But in a profession where you are trying to prepare a team as a coach, the feeling that you get from seeing a game plan and a group of kids execute it, is a great thrill. Obviously, when you pour your heart and soul into all this and things don't come out the way you want, it is agonizing. It's tough. You're emotionally upset, but one of the things about the coaching experience is that it's a microcosm of what you're going to face the rest of your life, the ups and downs of life. From that standpoint, I think that I learned an awful lot by being involved in athletics.

Q: Can you profit from that agony of defeat in any way?
AP: Yes, absolutely. I recall during my high school days, college days, and pro days, when I was with the Cleveland Browns for a couple of years, we always had winners. Then I went back to Miami of Ohio, and I was a freshman coach under Woody Hayes for one year, and then head coach for five years, and we won there by sizable amounts. But then I went to Northwestern, a private school where the program had been run down, where they had people recruiting who were not involved in coaching, and coaches who didn't recruit. Of course when it got to game time, one blamed the other. The second year that I was there, we lost all the games, the only losing season that I had in

25 years of coaching. And what an experience that was. I profited from that. I learned more in that losing season than I did in any winning season. The following year, we went to every measure possible to get an edge if we could. I learned a great deal from that losing season, believe me.

Q: What do you think is the key ingredient of a championship team?

AP: Well, I don't know that there is any key ingredient. It's a combination. It's good chemistry. It's loyalty. It's good personnel. It's a combination of a number of things. Not just one. I don't think you can answer that question with just one answer. If it was that easy, you'd have more people being successful, I guess (laughing). It's a combination of all those things. I think also that a team will reflect the intensity of a coach. I had the great benefit of being under coaches like Sid Gilman, when I was in college; Blanton Collier, when I was with the Cleveland Browns; Paul Brown, when I was at Great Lakes [a naval training center], and I played there during the war years, and then with Paul Brown for two more years, and so I had the opportunity to be under some great coaches. Well, that gave me a tremendous opportunity to learn from some of the greatest. And they all had particular characteristics, each of them. But I think a team will reflect a head coach and his intensity, and his knowledge and so forth.

Q: I've talked to so many of you outstanding coaches, and you would think, the simple answer is that, well, the key is talent. But surprisingly, very few mention that first. Did you ever feel that you had an outstanding team that had less than the best talent?

AP: It's a combination of things. A coach can have great talent and do a good or bad job with it. A coach can have poor talent and do a good or bad job with it. I think one of the significant accomplishments that we had, when I look back on it now—I didn't realize it at the time how important it was, but as you get more experience you can look back on it—when I was at Northwestern, we took one of the Northwestern teams that had what you wouldn't call great talent, took them to the polls' number one spot for three or four weeks. We did that back in those days when there were no scholarships limitations as there are today. A team could bring in 80 or 90 players if the coaches wanted. We were restricted by academic restrictions and financial circumstances with tuition being high. So, as I look back on it now, that was a hell of a team, but it did not have outstanding talent. I remember one of the centers, Jay Robertson, made the All–Big Ten team. We sent him to the East-West All-Star Game. Jack Molinkoff was coaching at the time. And when we sent Robertson out there, Jack Molinkoff said, "Are you kidding me, this is your center?" He was about 195 pounds, but quicker than hell and tough. You asked whether we had a good team without great talent. That's a good example. We had talent, but not the kind of talent that we were competing against. That's the way I felt about it.

Q: When the season is over and you've won a championship, do you ever look back and say, "When did we start to develop the championship attitude on a team?" Is there a point that the attitude starts to develop, or was it there from the get-go?

AP: I think there's a certain game that will occur where you see your team, when you're playing against a certain opposition, and you know you are a good football team. You sort of see your football team come together and play with a kind of intensity and talent that you'd like to see them perform with. In the championship seasons that we've had, I've sensed that about midseason. I just felt like all of the sudden the pieces were all there. The inexperience that we were concerned about on our roster was often a factor. By midseason those inexperienced players had developed enough so that we could go through the rest of the season.

In every year that I've ever been involved with a championship team or an outstanding team, there is a game during the season that you get by, that maybe you were a favorite in the game, but you get into the ball game and you get into a real dogfight. And it can go either way, and maybe there's a break there that ultimately makes the difference. A good example of that is the Nebraska-Missouri game [in 1997], where Nebraska was favored by four touchdowns or whatever it was. The Cornhuskers fell behind, but then with a break at the end of the ball game, a kicked ball, fourth down, clock running out, they were able to tie it up and win it in overtime. You're going to have a game like that on your schedule. It's going to be there. There might be two of them, and you've got to get by those games. Championship teams, during the course of the year, will have one or two of those games. And sometimes luck enters into getting over that hump. Penn State was faced with that dilemma [during the 1997 season]. They didn't get over the hump, whereas Michigan did. It's another one of those notches during the course of a season.

Q: Is motivation a factor that stems from coaching, or do you feel that motivation comes from within the players?

AP: Both. I think that the team will reflect the intensity or the passiveness of a coach. That's my view. I think a coach sets the stage. I think a coach builds the mentality, and not just with a motivational talk before the ball game. He starts on Sunday and Monday, building to a point where the team knows why they're going to the field. I know it's very dificult to keep a team up. In football, it's very difficult to keep a team up for 11 or 12 games. There's going to be a game along the way that you can't keep them at the peak. The idea is, in those crucial games, to have them at the highest level of intensity. And they will reflect that. Sometimes you will benefit from two or three guys on the team, or maybe just one guy that is a tremendous leader and infects the other guys with that same intensity. But basically, I think that motivation comes from both, not just one.

Q: Is it important as a coach to be liked by those that you are coaching?

AP: No. It's not a popularity contest. But I think that it is very important for a coach to be fair. In whatever discipline he doles out, he should treat every player equally, whether he's the star on the team or whether he's a prep player on the team. I think it's impossible for a successful coach if you've got a hundred kids, to have every kid like you, because he has hard decisions to make as to who's going to be number one and number two. You can't run a popularity contest and be successful.

You want all the kids to feel they were well-prepared for the game, both offensively and defensively, strategy-wise. And they also say I was always fair. Being fair when you have to make hard decisions regarding positions, hard decisions when you have to decide who you're going to discipline and what the discipline is for, you outline that up front. I don't think that you can get every kid on your team to like you, and if you're running that kind of a show, I think you're in trouble.

Q: Is it important for you to have a personal relationship with players at the time they are playing for you? I don't mean after they graduate. But at the time, is it important to have a personal relationship?

AP: We pursued and followed their academic work and whether or not they missed class. If they did miss class, they would be called into the office. Is that what you want to call a personal relationship? It was for a purpose. When you say personal relationship, expand on that.

Q: A friendship, a buddy-buddy relationship with a player.

AP: Well, the closest you would come to that would be maybe with a quarterback because you probably spend more time with him. But I think there must be a line, and there must be respect. Without that, you can run into problems. You can't be buddy-buddy to everybody on the football team, and you're not there to be buddy-buddy. You're there to coach and be fair, and do the best job you can.

Q: Is "potential" a blessing or a curse, when it comes to putting together a championship team?

AP: When you say potential, I see these two things. I see potential and I see performance. I remember in my early years of coaching, I had a kid, and this, gosh, goes back to 1951, my first year as a head coach. He's 6'4", about 220, could run like a deer, and boy, there was potential. And a kid, 185 pounds, beat him out. You know, we didn't want that to happen. We figured this kid is going to be a superstar, because that was big back in those days. Well, the difference was performance, and not potential. The big kid had great potential, but he didn't perform. The other kid performed, and he didn't have the potential of the other kid, but he wound up winning the job.

Q: I think you make a very good point there. There comes a time where you have to cross the line and say, "Hey, we have the potential to do such and such, but our performance is X." And that decision, is that a tough one to make?

AP: I don't think so. In coaching clinics what I said was, "When you walk on to that field, there is X number of football players out there. They represent a certain potential, and you will be able to determine that as you work and place them in various positions." This is what I call personnel alignment, taking those players, putting them in the best possible positions for them to become the best possible team that they can. Now, you may look at a team, particularly early in the season where you think that this guy is the best player. Well, it turns out he doesn't perform on the field although he appeared to have the best potential and the best preseason. So you have to make adjustments during that period of time. It's a constant evaluation. We had our velcro boards where we continually changed personnel. Every coach had one in front of him, and every name on the team was there, offense and defense, and we looked at it every day to see whether or not one guy could be moved to make us a better football team.

There's the guy with the great potential. Could he play center? We need help at center. Could this guy do this? And that was constantly going on. But I looked on that as crystalizing down to using the best personnel. We had both potential and performance.

Q: The term "role model" is so easily thrown around today. Does it apply for a coach in the eyes of his players?
AP: I think that it definitely does. I think that your behavior, your attitude, your habits are all observed by your players. And this doesn't mean that they will follow you right to the end because certain kids are going to compromise the rules regardless of what happens. I said many times that 5 percent of the squad gave me 95 percent of the problems. The rest of the 95, I didn't have to worry about. They were no problem. But regardless of what the circumstances

are, what the rules are, those are the guys that gave you the most problems.

Q: Does the coach have to be a positive role model in the eyes of his players for a championship team to develop?

AP: I definitely think so. I think that you handle yourself with class and dignity, I think they're going to reflect that. They're going to appreciate that. At least certainly on the collegiate level, that's my experience.

Q: Looking back now at your career, what was your greatest satisfaction as a coach?

AP: Boy, that's a tough question. I think the thing I enjoyed the most, and that I missed the most when I got out, was working with the kids on the field, watching them grow individually, both physically and emotionally and in the expression of their talent. And then implementing a strategy on the field to go to the next challenge, which would be the next game, and then watching them implement the strategy and the performance. That, to me, was the part of coaching that I think I enjoyed probably the most.

Q: Could you, in effect, do all of those things to your satisfaction, and yet when you looked up at the end of the game, you were on the losing end? Can there be satisfaction there?

AP: Well, there's never satisfaction in a loss because your goal is to win, but if your team has given the best effort they possibly can, and I know that there are some limitations and I know that the other team played better than we did on that particular day, then it's more palatable, I guess. It's never acceptable to lose. But there are times also where your team may have gone out there and made all kinds of mistakes, then it's very difficult to digest because you know they're better than that and they had a bad day. We all have bad days. But losing never was much fun (laughing).

Q: With today's press scrutiny, does it make it tougher than in the past to develop as a coach and to develop the team the way you'd like to?

AP: That's a tough question. I think there is more scrutiny today, without any question, in all sports. But, I think if a guy is honest with himself, and he doesn't try to fake out everybody as far as the press is concerned, I think he can go forward, and not be affected by it. I was in the hot seat there at Notre Dame for 11 years, and you know, there's always the critics, even when you win. You didn't win by enough. You didn't look good in winning. You didn't play the right people. And then, of course, the writers can pick up on that. But you have to go forward with the idea of doing the best job that you can, and knowing there's going to be a certain amount of criticism. Do I believe it's tougher today? Yes, I do, because there's more publications out, more people have opinions, and the very fact the media is in competition with themselves, they'll stretch beyond what I think they did during my coaching years.

Q: The fear of facing failure, whether that be immediately before a game or before a season, was that something that was constantly out there for you as a coach?

AP: Yes. The fear of failure, I remember . . . (laughing) . . . the first time I was a freshman coach out at Miami of Ohio. Woody Hayes was the head coach. He hired me, and we had five freshman games. And the first freshman game, my first time out coaching, I was thinking, "Oh my God, will we even make a first down. It's going to be embarrassing." Then you go to the field, and your team plays well and wins. Then you realize you get a feel for it. But the fear of failure, I think for me, was always there, particularly when you're a heavy favorite, then it puts a hell of a lot of pressure on you, I think. You're expected to win. Those circumstance are even more difficult. And we were the favorite so many times during my Notre Dame years. The expectations were always great, and if you didn't achieve those, the disappointment was even greater. I'd rather go in and play a team that we were a "pick 'em" deal or a one- or two- or three-point favorite, than I would go in as a big favorite, because so many things can happen. You were always concerned because you can't control a number of things. As good a coach as you can be, you can't control the officials. You can't control the weather. You can't control the turnovers, which can be very critical, the penalties and so forth. There's certain factors you can't control. And that's why the game is exciting, and that's why there are upsets in this game.

Q: Looking back at all the great experience you've had, have you ever found any shortcuts to create the success for a championship team?

AP: I don't think there are any shortcuts, particularly in the conditioning area. One of the first lectures that I always gave my players, I said, "You know, this is one of those situations where it doesn't make any difference where you come from, how much money your dad has, what kind of resources your entire family has. Nobody can come in here and give me a hundred dollars and say, 'He's in shape.' You have to earn all those things." Football is a particular game where there is a lot of physical, two-a-days in the early going, and there's sacrifices that have to be made. And as a result of that, you have to earn the right to that. I don't see any shortcuts.

Q: Does loyalty have to be a two-way street for a ball club to become a champion?

AP: Yes. I think so. One of the things I did from a loyalty standpoint, when I would hire a new coach, I would tell them, I don't care how much football you know. Our philosophy will be one that you will embrace, I'm sure. But I demand your loyalty because there are going to be people chopping at us, there's going to be people after us. And I would clench a fist and say, "We have to be that tight, all of us together." And it's the same way with a team. You have to give loyalty. I used to tell my players, "You will never ever see your name in print being criticized by this head football coach or any staff member." And that's the way it always was. If there were things to be said, they were always said behind closed doors. Kids know if they made a mistake. You'd never ever see any of the assistant coaches that were under me criticize a player publicly. I told them that, and that was the thing that I lived with all the way through. They knew they weren't going to be criticized.

Bear Bryant was the best at taking the heat for any loss. You don't blame any coaches. You don't blame any players. You give credit to the opposition because they played better than you that day. They won.

That was our philosophy, and I watched Bear Bryant do exactly the same thing. He took the rap right down the line on it.

Then you watch your players and you watch your coaches work the following week. We never lost two games in a row in 11 years at Notre Dame. And somebody pointed that out before the season started this year. I wasn't even aware of it. In that regard, loyalty is a major part of your team strength.

Q: What about goal setting before a season? Did you ever go so far as set a goal for what your team's record should be?
AP: No, we really didn't. We looked at the schedule. We knew what our long-range goals were. We had a situation where

we couldn't go to the bowl game in the early going. When I first started coaching there, Notre Dame didn't go to bowls. We didn't belong to a conference. We couldn't win a conference championship. We couldn't win a bowl game. The only thing that we had to shoot at was the polls. So it was very important for us to not lose any games because it moved you down in the polls. That was a lot of pressure back in those days. You might be able to recover from an early season loss, but you weren't going to a bowl to make it up and you weren't going to win a conference championship. And a late loss, obviously, made it impossible as far as national rankings were concerned. So we aimed at winning every game because we knew the impact of it. If we wanted to win the national championship, we wanted to go undefeated. That was the only way we could get the goal we wanted.

Q: Is a winning coach born with leadership skills, or can they be developed?

AP: I think maybe in some people leadership is innate. And I think that those who have some leadership ability build on their experiences as a coach as they go through their coaching profession. I'd like to think that I was a helluva lot better coach after five years of coaching than I was the first year. Or after 10 years of coaching or 15, or whatever it may be.

I've learned that the idea is not to repeat mistakes. I've seen coaches come into circumstances and they're making the same mistakes five years down the road as they did the first year. My basic feeling on leadership is that I think some of it is innate, and then I think you can develop it and improve on it.

Q: You have two guys on your squad who from a performance level are basically even, and you have to make a

choice. Would you pick a guy who has more intelligence
or more raw physical talent, assuming that they're both
basically the same in regard to performance?

AP: Well, you've already said they were equal. So if they're
equal, there'd be other factors involved. For example, is
one a senior? Is one a junior? Are they both juniors? You
say they're equal?

Q: **Equal in terms of what they seem. What's going to be
the dividing characteristic if you had to pick, and there's
two characteristics you're judging by, intelligence or
physical ability? Which do you think is the one, the guy
you want to have on the field?**

AP: That's a hard one because a guy that has the intelligence
maybe won't make the mistakes, but he may not be physically capable of doing the job. The way we evaluated it,
we took a lot of film, and we matched the kids up to see
who was the best at that position. And we expected them
to be intelligent.

I worked in private schools for the last 19 years I
coached, so we had a pretty high level of intelligence
and we were able to do some things strategically and
through what we called "automatics" that you may not
be able to do at some of the other schools. So we generally had pretty good intelligence. But if it was down to a
point, where one kid had physical ability and the other
kid had intelligence and he wasn't quite as good, I think
I would probably play the kid with intelligence. I can't
tell you why at this stage because even though the kid
may have a lot of talent, going the wrong way doesn't
help you.

Q: **(Laughing.) . . . Can you create a competitor, and I say
this both individually as a player and as a team, or do
they have to have that inborn?**

AP: I think you have to set a stage and a climate for it, yes. I think they, too, have to feel what you feel. I think a coach is a salesperson. I think he has to be able to, from the on-set, from the first meeting and during the course of the season and during the course of every practice session, set a stage. I used to have notes that I would read to them: "What does this game mean?" "Next Saturday's game is not going to be won on last Saturday's performance."

I'd go through a whole list of things, starting to set a stage and tempting them with their competitive instincts, and building the crescendo.

I learned two things from Paul Brown. He was a great organizer. He didn't overwork his teams, and he brought them to the peak at the right time. You never felt like you were overworked. You always felt like you were underworked, and you always felt like you were well pre-pared, and that he would motivate you when you went to the field. I think that you can certainly improve com-petitiveness and refine it, and it's your job as a coach to do so.

Q: What's more important, pregame preparation or in-game adjustments if you're going to have a championship season?

AP: If you gave me my choice and I could only have one of those, I would take the pregame preparation. With the preparation, I would feel that at least I've seen your team, even if you come out with something different, I would feel that I know your personnel. I know your general strat-egy. I'll take the pregame, even though you have to adjust during the game. I'd rather have my team prepared for what I anticipate, then take my chances on adjusting.

Q: Does a championship team play as it practices?

AP: No. They don't (laughing). During the course of a foot-ball season, you have days where these kids are worried about their girlfriends or worried about their tests they have to take or an exam they've got. A number of things that they've got going on. A family problem, maybe. So every day is not a good practice day. That doesn't mean that they're not going to perform on Saturday.

Coaches are the worst in the world trying to predict whether the team is ready or not. God, I've walked into a locker room, and our kids are just jumping up and down, and they go out and lay an egg. We didn't lay many eggs, but there were those days. Other times, we have practice during the week and I'm saying, "Where the hell are these guys? They're preoccupied with something else." And then we go play the game, and they look like gangbusters (laughing). So that's what makes coaching real exciting.

Q: Do you feel it's important to have a mentor or mentors that helped you along the way to develop as a coach?

AP: It's like a master's degree or doctorate degree. And I had the good fortune of being under some top-notch people: Sid Gilman, who was a great technician; Blanton Collier, who was another great technician; Paul Brown, who was a great organizer and a great motivator and a great preparer; Woody Hayes, who had a great rapport with his teams.

Q: That's a group of Hall of Famers there.

AP: Exactly. Just think about that. How many guys had the opportunity I had? Not many. I don't think many have had the kind of exposure to top coaches that I've had.

Another factor was my playing experience. When I was in high school, my mother didn't want me to play. I finally got to play when I was a junior. I started out, I played offensive guard and center. I played defensive line and linebacker, and then I graduated up and became a fullback, a halfback, and a cornerback. So I have played virtually every position in football except defensive end and quarterback. So I look back on it now, that helped me from an experience standpoint. I know what it feels like to get down and play defensive line or offensive line. I know what it's like to play linebacker. I know what it's like to be a running back. I know what it's like to be a cornerback. And so that, too, probably influenced my ability to understand most of the aspects of the game. That was very helpful to me.

Q: The best advice ever given to you in terms of building championship teams?

AP: Well, there's no single one, I guess. You're a sum total of all those experiences. My experiences with Sid Gillman, watching him from a technical standpoint. The hard work. The dedication and all those things.

If there was one thing it was, don't repeat mistakes. That was one of the things. I've forgotten where I got it. But I lived with that. If I made a sideline mistake, and it affected the team, I said to myself, "I'll never make that mistake again." I've gone through that where it's just like somebody stamping it in there in my brain. And you build on that. Experience gives you all that. "I've made that mistake. I'm not going to make it again."

Q: Is there a formula for championship success? Did you develop one?

AP: The basic fundamentals don't change. Strategies change. Tactics change. Personnel changes. But the basic fundamentals don't change. So you would start with that.

If I went back to coaching today after having been out all these years, I know that I would have to bring myself up to speed on what the technology is, on conditioning, on what new equipment is being used for improved blocking and tackling, all those things. But the idea is that the

fundamentals are still the same. You have to put forward
a team that's well-conditioned, that can execute the basic
fundamentals.

You have to keep those while working around whatever
strategies and technology are now in play. You have to go
by not what you believe in, but by what they do best. This
is what I considered, what I called personnel alignment.
What I liked to do offensively or what I liked to do defensively didn't always mesh with what that talent was. I was
not going to take a finesse team and try to run power football. Nor would I try to take a power football team and run
the opposite of that. If you have an ordinary passer, then
you have to build a kicking game, you've got to build a
defense. You've got to play a different game on the sideline. Those are all part of coaching because, as much as I
would like to be able to go in and say this is what I'd like to
do offensively, then it's not what my team does best. So
that's one of the basic fundamentals, the ability to look at
your talent, see what they do best and build a team that
hopefully will become a championship team.

Q: **When we look at the history of sport, probably no job
in the country is more demanding than that of football
coach at Notre Dame. How about the use of time? How
important is that to the degree of success of building a
championship?**

AP: I think it's very important. I think you have to be extremely
well organized. I think you've got to get the most of your
players when they're on the field. I think that was a trait I
learned well from Paul Brown's practices, and being well
organized, and having everything, maximizing of the
practice session to bring them up to where you want to
bring them.

I was a nut on time. We'd have our meetings. I was a
guy that had slip-on loafers and clip-on ties. You were

always on the go. Every minute that you wasted between the time a game ended and the next game started was wasted time because you only have so much time in there. Back in those days we were playing 10-game schedules, went to 11-game schedules, and then you had to wait another year! It's all there. You had to lay it all on the line on a Saturday afternoon, and then if things don't go well, you've got to wait until the following year to make it right. So time is very, very important.

Q: To be successful, do you have to develop a philosophy?

AP: Yes. I think you definitely do. I think you have to have a philosophy. And you have to live by it, or adjust to whatever demands come that might change that philosophy. But I think you have to have a philosophy about your coaching. That applies to your life, as well.

Q: When did you develop your philosophy? Was it your first year as a freshman coach, or did it develop over time?

AP: I think it took a number of years. My experience starting out as a raw coach, as a freshman coach, I was very young. When I got the head coaching job at Miami of Ohio, I was 27 years old. I stayed there until I was 32, I guess it was. When they were making the determination about who would succeed Woody Hayes at Miami, they solicited the approval of Paul Brown, who was a Miami graduate. He said I had played for him, and he thought I had some ability and so forth. He told them, "Ara doesn't know what he doesn't know." Looking back on it now, I was young. I was a player. I had only coached the freshmen one year. But I grew and built on the basic philosophy during those early years. I think probably it took until I got to Northwestern where I saw all sides of it, saw big-time football. I saw the disadvantages of a private school with high costs, high admission standards. I saw the opportunities of a state school like Miami, where I could get kids into school. Then I went to another private school. But I think by the time I was at Northwestern for about three years, I had built a pretty good philosophy over that period of time.

Q: **What was your greatest satisfaction as a coach, your greatest disappointment as a coach, looking back?**

AP: The greatest satisfaction, I suppose over all those years, is to win a national championship. When we played Alabama in the Sugar Bowl, Bear Bryant and I had never competed against one another. Alabama and Notre Dame had never played. It was the North against the South. It was the Baptists and the Catholics. It was Bear Bryant saying this was the best offensive and defensive football team he had ever had. And we were both undefeated and it was on the line. You're going to win the national championship or you're going to lose it in one game. And we were fortunate enough to win the football game, so that was arriving at a national championship and doing it and playing against what was considered the absolute best. Even by Bear's own admission, this was the best offensive and defensive team that he had ever had.

In other games, there may have been some moments of personal disappointments. The losses, you take them all hard, but the one that was really difficult for us was in 1964, my first year at Notre Dame. Notre Dame hadn't had a winning season in five years. They had been 2–7 the year before I arrived. We came in and we turned the program around. This is what I'm talking about, the talent was there and we put it in the right spot. We motivated it, and they got on a roll, and that's what coaching is about. In any event, we ran nine straight games. We went out to Southern California in our last game. We were leading 17 to nothing at halftime. This game is going to be put away. This is going to be a sensational turnaround, a national championship, an undefeated season from a 2–7 season our first season there.

Then Southern Cal scores a touchdown and it's 17–6 or whatever it is, 17–7. We drive in the fourth quarter, score from the two-yard line to put it to bed, and they call it back for holding. Anyway, there's a bizarre set of circumstances that occur the rest of the game where there were three or four major penalties against us in the game. We wound up losing the game 20–17. And that, for the kids and for the team, was an extreme disappointment. I felt bad for everybody that followed Notre Dame, the whole Notre Dame family, the staff and the kids because we had this in our hands. It just goes to show you can't count anything in your hand until the final whistle blows. So those two games, going back to one of your first questions, reflect the ecstasy and the agony of coaching.

Anson Dorrance

With the rise of the football program at the University of North Carolina a few years back, then Tar Heels basketball coach Dean Smith was asked about the crowding of his own program. "This is a women's soccer school," Smith replied. "We're just trying to keep up with them."

The answer was entirely appropriate, considering that the UNC women's soccer program under coach Anson Dorrance has won 15 of the 18 national championships since the sport began deciding a collegiate national champion two decades ago.

Each season, the faces change on Carolina's roster, but Dorrance has established a brilliance for attracting talented players to his program and motivating them to top performances.

"Obviously Anson Dorrance knows what it takes to win, and that is very rare," says Mia Hamm, a former Carolina athlete who was named National Women's Collegiate Player of the Year in 1992 and 1993. "He makes another kind of investment in his players beyond just training. He cares about them as people. He knows what motivates certain types of players and ties it all in to team chemistry and camaraderie."

The numbers that substantiate this praise are staggering. In the sixteen seasons that the NCAA has sponsored a tournament, Dorrance's teams have reached all 16 Final Fours. Since 1986 alone, his clubs are 283–4–9.

His 1997 team finished with a 27–0–1 record and claimed yet another national championship.

"Anson's accomplishments on the field are unparalleled," says Atlantic Coast Conference Commissioner John D. Swofford, a former UNC athletic director. "He may well be the single most successful coach in intercollegiate athletics. I think of Anson as a Renaissance man. He's so talented in so many different ways. And he has analyzed and made a science of coaching female athletes. No one knows the ins and outs of that better than Anson Dorrance. He is a great ambassador, not only for women's soccer, but for the University of North Carolina as well."

Billy Packer: Is there any such thing as the thrill of victory or the agony of defeat?

Anson Dorrance: Based on the kind of event you've won, there's a kind of thrill; and based on what you've lost, there's kind of an agony. The event highlights the thrill or extends the agony.

Q: Do you ever profit from any of the agony or any of the defeats that you've had in the great illustrious career you've had?

AD: Oh, unquestionably. I think what ends up happening whenever you lose, you review everything you could have done to win, and there's a sort of an extended period of self-examination until you win again. And of course, one of the most uncomfortable games to lose is the last game of the season, because then you sort of agonize through the entire off-season until the next season rolls around. So there's an extended period of review after any kind of loss, and the only sort of panacea for it is to win again.

Q: What is the key ingredient of a championship team if it's something other than talent?

AD: I think there are several keys. One is to have a collective will. The best teams we've ever had here had a sort of a collective power that was almost unbeatable. And we had this collective power, irrespective of talent. There were some teams with very average talent, that collectively were just so overwhelming. That was the key. It's tied into team chemistry, really. And it's tied into a philosophy that we've sort of encouraged from the beginning—the concept of playing for each other. I think most people don't understand this. Playing for championships or titles is very overrated. It always stuns me when someone outside our team fabric comes up before a critical game and assumes that the team's going to be motivated because of the event. In my experience, teams aren't motivated for championship games; they're motivated for each other. And the motivational factors go beyond the event they're playing for. They basically relate to connecting with all the people that surround them on the team. So I think team chemistry is a critical element, and perhaps even the most critical element in a championship season.

Q: How do you start to develop that championship attitude among a group of kids?

AD: I think the first thing you do, especially in my environment where we're losing and gaining players every year, you want to reestablish the connection, the chemistry. It's almost like a rite of passage for a new player to come in and be accepted by the group that's won before. And what has to happen is every player that comes in really has to humble herself for the task. It's impossible to be a consistent winner without humility. And a lot of the humility is accepting first of all that you can get better—the player herself, can get better, and also that you're going to sacrifice yourself for the team. And so what happens in our preseason when any player comes in, regardless of their accolades before they get here, there's a wonderful kind of humbling process as they realize the environment that they've entered. And then after that's done, then almost the opposite occurs. Once the players and the group have been humbled individually, then you try to create a collective confidence where everyone plays a certain role to help the team win. And the other critical aspect is that everyone in the organization has to have a role and everyone is valued for their humanity. So it's not a hierarchy of talent within the team fabric, it's a collection of human beings.

Q: **Did that humility aspect start at the top with you and filter down so that now those who are remaining off your championship teams basically establish a trial period for the newcomer?**

AD: I don't know how we got into this. I think maybe the way we ultimately did is again, losing. I started out as a men's coach, and when I was a men's coach at UNC, there always seemed to be a common thread as to why we lost. And the common thread related somehow to an arrogance my team had going into the game, and basically, a lack of humility. And so, I guess, in learning to prepare my early teams to win, one of the first things we tried to achieve was to let everyone know that we should certainly respect everyone we were going to play. And the way you demonstrate your respect for an opponent is by playing your best against them. So we tried to humble ourselves going into any kind of contest, which would elicit our greatest effort, and that translated into creating a humble attitude toward any contest we were playing in, which again extended itself into our preseason as the players came on to the team. And I think what's humbling from a coaching perspective is that you can lose any game, and all of us have. We've lost to teams we should never lose to, and I think that's a wonderful lesson for anyone who coaches, and certainly should be a lesson for anyone who plays.

Q: Does a player's motivation have to come from within, or can it provided solely by the coach?

AD: Some players are intrinsically motivated. You rarely have to motivate them. They come into the game with such a collection of buttons they can push on their own that these are truly the remarkable players. I think the way the coach assists in motivating the team is to find personal elements to draw on before the game begins. And a lot of people, when they ask me about motivation, they expect an answer that's a formula. Like, well, if you do this then your team's going to be motivated. Some people feel that the motivation can take place weeks before the event actually begins, and it can't. I don't start writing and reviewing my motivational material until about an hour or two before a contest. And oftentimes, some of my best motivational ideas occur within 15 to 30 minutes of when I'm addressing the team as a group. What you're basically doing is you're waiting for what you feel about your team, what you're going to share with your team that's particularly personal and unique. And so there's never a formula. And it's usually something incredibly personal, and it's something that galvanizes the entire group that wouldn't galvanize another group. In other words, it's not a speech you can recite into a tape recorder and then hand it over to another organization or team and assume that particular thing is going to motivate them. It's something personal and unique to the experiences and the events of your particular group.

Q: **If you don't mind me prying, could you think of one such incident that came to you at almost the last moment?**

AD: I can give you what happens consistently. I think one thing that I've been very proud of over the years is our motivation for a championship game. And I'm very proud to hear a commentator on television or an associate or colleague talk about how well my team played during a championship game. And I think that's been characteristic of the teams we've had here over the years, and I'm very proud of that. And what invariably ends up happening, and maybe it's even a part of our tradition and fabric now, is the seniors who are graduating provide the motivation with what amounts to a final statement about their career at the university that we read before the championship game. And they're incredibly personal. These statements are something the team, only our team, could appreciate, and it's galvanizing. And what ends up happening in these events is all the underclassmen play with a collective fury for the group that is leaving them. And I think that's been consistent over the years. And every note has been different, but it's all touched on a personal chord.

Q: **Is it important for a coach to be liked by his players?**

AD: No, not at all (laughing). Although invariably, the route to becoming liked is through respect. And I think one of the great mistakes that all the young coaches make as they are entering the profession is the feeling that they have to be liked. And what ends up happening is they end up trying to win a popularity contest, and they end up sacrificing the respect of the team. It's much more critical to be respected. And long term, ultimately, through respect, I think you gain a kind of affection from the people you've trained.

Q: **You've coached both men and women. Is it important to have a personal relationship at the time those players are playing for you?**

AD: I think with the women it is. I think a young woman will die for you if she feels there's some sort of personal connection and that you care about her for reasons beyond the game. With the men, it's not as critical. With the men, oftentimes your relationship with them develops the most after they've graduated, as they've looked back and appreciated all the things you tried to do to get them to another level. And, I think, in men's athletics, some of that effort to get the athlete to a higher level is a very stressful one for both the player and the coach. On the women's side, though, to get them to another level, the relationship is sometimes best served if there is a personal connection because I think women have the superior understanding that their relationships are more critical than the game itself. And that's what they treasure and take from most of their athletic experiences.

Q: **The word "potential," is it a blessing or a curse?**

AD: It can be both. I define potential for my players when I sit down with them. And it's kind of a joke, but it's also not a joke. I say—and I'm sure it's a cliché and I'm sure other coaches have used this—potential means you're not worth a damn right now. And what you're trying to tell the someone who has potential is that unachieved potential is still nothing. So it's a blessing in that you dangle it before someone to show her what she can achieve. And it's a curse in that all these people who have potential feel a pressure to achieve. We've had athletes who are motivated on both sides of that potential divide. And I've had athletes who have had great potential, and yet are bothered by the insistence of a coach who feels they have to fulfill it. And when you can sort out that the athlete doesn't like the pressure of achieving her potential, then you back off, and you appreciate the young athlete for whatever she decides to give you. The irony then is that without the pressure of having to achieve potential, invariably, they will select to go ahead and fulfill their promise. And then there are others that the best thing you can do for them is to let them know how great they can be, and that, in itself, gives them a vote of confidence to know they can achieve their game at a much higher level.

Q: **The term "role model" is thrown around an awful lot now. Does it apply to the coach in the eyes of his players?**

AD: Oh, unquestionably. I think you have to live what you're teaching, and we certainly try to do that here at UNC. We believe in having the athletes maintain a year-round fitness base, so we, as coaches, participate in that. We believe that you should always strive to be the best that you can be, and so we try to do that in all parts of our lives. And we also feel you should take responsibility for any loss, and so we try to do that. Any time our team loses, as a coaching staff, we take full responsibility. And what ends up happening, we feel over time, is that all of us collectively take responsibility for our failures. And I think as soon as anyone does that, they're basically making a statement that they're going to change and improve.

I think too often, in not just athletics, but all walks of life, everyone claims to either be a victim or blames their circumstances on something beyond their control. And as soon as you do that, you relinquish the opportunity to change your circumstances. So, yes, I think the role model has to start with the coach.

Q: What is the greatest satisfaction you've had over the years of coaching?

AD: Well, when I was young coach, I really felt that if we won a lot that would be incredibly satisfying. And I had a personal epiphany in December of 1991. I was the coach of the U.S. national team that won the world championship, the United States. That was the first world championship for any American soccer team in history. And it was funny. Building up to that event, I really felt that winning it would sort of exorcise all those demons and make me feel on top of the world, and I was stunned when it didn't. I was stunned it wasn't a great feeling. In fact, all I felt when we won was incredible relief that I hadn't let the country down. And it just wasn't a very satisfying experience. And then what started to dawn on me is that the things that I appreciate most are the personal connections with all the players that I've trained while I'm training them and after they're done. And that kind of connection, for me, is the most satisfying.

I've already planned on something I'm going to say during this year's championship banquet. I don't personally believe in wearing championship rings. The only ring I wear is my wedding ring. There were a couple of tapes given me by WCHL, our local radio station, and the first tape was given to me after our 400th win. We played Alabama over at Duke in a Duke Tournament, and we won our 400th win, and the radio station went around talking to all the players, basically about their experiences at UNC and their experiences about playing for me and my staff. And the things they said were just absolutely overwhelming. I have never felt as exhilarated following something as when I finished listening to that tape. And these were obviously testaments from a collection of players who were in full support of everything we were doing. And it made me feel great.

And then they did another tape following this year's championship game, and since I enjoyed that first one so much, I think they're going to make a habit now of giving me these tapes. And it was the same sort of thing. After the championship game, they went around and interviewed all the seniors about their experiences of winning, and their experiences being at UNC for four years. And the things they said were just incredibly connective, and just made me feel unbelievable. So for this year's banquet, what I'm going to do when I speak to the team is I'm going to show them these two tapes and let them know that no ring I could ever wear would make me feel as good as what was given to me by all of them, the two tapes I was holding. Those are the things that I cherish. No triumph has ever made me feel as good as just listening to what my players had to say.

Q: How about on the other side, the greatest disappointment?

AD: I guess it's the opposite side of that. Obviously, there's some people you get very close to as a coach, and then, I think, acts of disloyalty are what cut you to the quick. And eventually, you'll recover from any kind of loss, but I think a player that you feel close to, if they do something, or basically imply that your connection is less than what you hoped it was or felt it was going to be, it's devastating. There haven't been many of those, but the few I've experienced have been worse than any loss I've felt as a coach.

Q: You mentioned about winning the world champion-ships, and obviously, an incredible feat, how about the fear of facing failure? It sounds like you connected with that on that world championship.

AD: Oh, there's no question. I think all of us as coaches pre-tend we don't hear any of the critics, but I think all of us do. A profession like ours requires an incredibly thick skin, but after a while, the criticisms weigh on you. And I think what you always end up fearing as a coach is, whenever you've had any kind of success, your critics attribute any kind of success you've had to things, advantages you've had. And basically, the implication is that you don't re-ally have a clue but you've been incredibly lucky, and when that string of luck runs out, you're going to demon-strate that basically, there's nothing there. And I think what ends up happening for all of us, these nagging doubts are there in the back of our minds, and you have this great fear that all of a sudden, whatever advantage you had is going to be eliminated. And then the criticism that's been piled upon you all those years is going to surface and you're going to realize that basically they were all cor rect, that there was nothing there. And I think that's the great terror that all of us have who have had any kind of success or run, is that it's going to be exposed. And so I think certainly all of us that want to continue to compete at a high level are working furiously against this doubt that lingers in the middle of any one of us about any sort of success we've had.

Q: Have you ever found any shortcuts to success?

AD: No. And it's interesting. Whenever we come into a sea-son, and if things aren't going as well as I think they should, invariably, I can point to some things that I haven't done that I used to do. Which causes me immediately to try and make up for whatever I haven't done. As you gain experience as a coach, you want to keep doing so many things which consume more and more time. And I'm convinced the reason all of us end up retiring, and most of us can't sustain it as long as someone like a Dean Smith, it's because we realize all the elements that are critical for our success, and we end up becoming exhausted trying to sustain them all.

Q: How do you create respect for yourself as a coach in the eyes of the players?

AD: I can't really articulate that in particular, but let me share what I think is important. What I think is important is that you do what you think is best and this again causes you to make choices that are beyond popularity. A lot of times, you're going to make decisions that are going to upset different people. And I think you've always got to go with your gut. You have to go with what you think is right. And you have to make decisions that are beyond what the players want you to do for them. But I also think what's critical is everything that you do, you should involve your player leadership. And I felt that was always an important thing to do. Whenever we were about to do something that was unpopular, we'd bring in the critical people on the team and review with them why we thought this was important, and get their feedback.

And invariably, they would share an insight that was important that would bend our decision in one direction or another. You have to react to the leaders on your team, making them feel that they're as critical a part of the leadership as the coach is. I think that causes you to win their affection and respect.

The other thing that is critical, and I've mentioned this before, is to take responsibility when things aren't going well. And to take responsibility in public as often as you can. And then to always praise the people who have gotten you to wherever you are. I think too often people seem to feel like they're the critical reason for success of an organization, and whenever a leader starts to feel that, I think he loses his organization.

As long as you give the praise and support to the athletes who are making a difference, and you're genuine about it, I think the people who follow you will always die for you. So we've always made it a point in the press to praise the ones who have made a difference. We've also made a point to let the ones who don't gain the glory publicly, to let them know we've always appreciated the things they've done. Treating your people with this kind of respect, and letting people know why your teams are successful is important. The reason they're successful is because of the extraordinary effort and achievement of the people who play for you. I think that ends up winning the respect of everyone.

Q: Do you set goals before a season starts?
AD: We used to. But we don't have a choice anymore. Our goals are set for us. A program like ours doesn't select to win the national championship anymore. We don't have a choice. It's a goal that's set for us by our own tradition. The goal setting that we do is usually individual. We sit down with the individual players and review their particular goals. But I've even learned a lot in goal setting. I've learned that some players hate setting goals. And for those players, we don't. I think what we have to accept is that everyone is uniquely different, and everyone is motivated by different things. And I remember this one player hated goal setting. And so, in a way, we kind of set a subtle goal for her. She just said she didn't want to set any goals, she just wanted to come to practice and have a good time. So, I said, well, let's make that your goal. And it was like this huge weight was lifted off the player's shoulders. From

then on in practice, I'd come to practice and watch this player just have the time of her life. What was interesting is to realize that every player doesn't have to be a world-beater in everything. Then sometimes, maybe, the most critical thing for a player is to enjoy life. And maybe, that should be the goal.

Q: Does a winning coach have to be born with leadership qualities, or can they be developed?

AD: I have never felt that you can develop leadership to any great extent. And it's interesting, I've been asked to speak at different leadership conferences, and I always feel a bit hypocritical in getting up there and talking about developing leadership because I genuinely don't believe you can. I think what ends up happening is people with leadership qualities, when they're placed in certain environments that require leadership, can demonstrate that they have it or develop this quality that just might be latent or below the surface. I don't think you can take someone who isn't a leader and make them one. I think you can possibly make them a manager, but you can't make them a leader.

So, I'm just not sure you can develop great leaders. I know what we try to do as a coaching staff. The University of North Carolina permits us to recruit four players a year, and with those four players, we want each of them to have certain qualities. But one of the four in our recruiting efforts has to be a leader. In other words, when we watch this particular kid's team play, we want to see this young woman motivating not just herself, but also the people around her. So it's something that we actively recruit, in addition to the athleticism, and the skill, and the physical dimensions of the players that we choose.

Q: Along those same lines, you've got a decision to make as to who is going to play. When it comes down to two

basically even players, what would be the determining factor, assuming one has superior intelligence for the game and the team, and the other one has superior physical skill?

AD: We would usually go with the intelligence or experience. Basically, what that means is that this player can collectively raise the level of the people around her, if she's particularly intelligent, and that's something that we would choose. And I don't want to confuse people, because people seem to think this intelligence translates into the academic world. And I know that oftentimes when I'm brought into a high school to speak or into certain environments to speak, people want me to tell everyone how athletics somehow translates into academic success. And I'm always reluctant to do that. I don't think the kind of intelligence a person requires in athletics translates directly into the sort of academic intelligence that everyone would love for it to translate into. I think there's some instinctive quality that some people have that translates very effectively into this particular world that all of us are coaching in. And maybe it's a leadership quality, maybe it's a vision of the game. Maybe it's an understanding that results from having played the sports for hours and hours and hours. But it's not intelligence as most of us would define it.

Q: Can you create a competitor, or is competitiveness something that the athlete must have?

AD: I think that is a bit different from leadership. I think obviously there are some people that are naturally, incredibly competitive. But in our experience here at UNC, over the course of their four years, people who haven't been outwardly competitive, by the end of their four years, become so. There's no better example than Carla Werden Overbeck. We do a lot of competitive matrices here at

UNC. Basically, I stole all my practice ideas from Dean Smith. When I was a young coach, he used to invite me into his practices, and I used to watch the way he trained, and I was always stunned at his practice organization. It was interesting seeing what would happen. He would have his assistant managers scattered around a basketball gym, and they'd be recording absolutely everything. Whether a guy hit a shot or missed it. How many times they won a one-on-one contest or lost. And everything was recorded the entire practice. And then at the end of practice, all these assistant managers would sprint to the scorer's table, where the head manager would be sitting. And Dean would be addressing the troops, and then at the end of his address, he'd turn around. The head manager would be standing behind him with a compilation of that practice's statistics. And Dean would read off a list of who would leave practice early based on performance, and who would stay and sprint, again based on performance.

I was thinking what a wonderful way to coach, where every player is assessed immediately, where everything in practice was basically important, and everyone had to basically play on the edge of his or her game. And I resolved to take that into my own sport, and I did.

So what we do at UNC is we record everything. One of the things we record is the players' one-on-one ability. Throughout the season, you end up playing a one-on-one tournament with everyone on the team. And we had a kid who came in as a freshman named Carla Werden. Her freshman year, she played everyone on the team one-on-one, didn't beat anyone. Didn't win a single one-on-one game. Then her senior year, she didn't lose one one-on-one game. Now she's Carla Werden Overbeck, her married name, and was the captain of the U.S. Olympic team that just won the gold medal in the Olympics for the United States. Now when you see her on the field, she's one of the most competitive people you would ever imagine. Her evolution in four years was dramatic. I think this was uniquely female, that she accepted the fact that it was okay to win, it was okay to compete, it was basically okay to beat all your friends in practice. And it was an evolution for her, because when she came in here as a freshman, everything she had been taught all of her life about connecting with people was at risk, because women are taught to acquiesce when they relate to people or when they compete. For example, the way for her to befriend the people she was playing with at UNC when she was a freshman, was to lose to them. And then, by the time she was a senior, she realized there was nothing wrong with being a champion and winning. So her evolution in this competitive arena, I think, was a reaction to the way our young girls and women are socialized. And so, yes, she became a lot more competitive in her four years at UNC.

Q: What's most important for you, pregame preparation or in-game adjustments?

AD: I think preparation is the absolute. All things you do before the game begins are certainly more important than whatever happens in a soccer game. In basketball and football, you can make some adjustments during the game that can make you look like a coaching genius. I think a lot of coaches in those sports are judged on their game-day decisions. But in a sport like mine, where substitution isn't really critical, and there are no time-outs, really, all of what you do as a coach is done before the game begins. And the preparation is certainly the most critical. What's reviewed before the game is next most critical. And then what happens in the game is least critical.

Q: Does a champion play as he or she practices?

AD: Unquestionably. And for people to try to pretend that they're gamers and that they're saving it for the game is absurd. And I think your strength as a coach is to get the people who can play with a tremendous fury in games to do the same thing in practice, and to try and have your practice environment as close to the competitive game environment as you can. Because the longer players train on this competitive edge, in this competitive cauldron, the more they're improving.

Q: Do you believe in having mentors, and have you had mentors over your career?

AD: Unquestionably. And it wasn't something I did consciously as a young coach. I think your instinct is to look up to people who have impressed you, and to try to steal and adapt ideas from their coaching style. And my mentors are actually a collage. Unquestionably, Dean Smith is a mentor, and for a thousand reasons that go beyond athletics. He's one of my mentors as a man. And I think a lot of that does translate into how effective you're going to be as a coach. After Dean Smith, there's a whole collection of people whom I've selected based on a great quality they've had. In our sport, Cliff McCrath is the greatest public speaker on the soccer circuit, so he's my mentor for public speaking. Bobby Gansler, who is one of our former national coaches, trained me in coaching schools. He had this wonderful presence in front of a group, where he just seemed to be this powerful presence. And he would walk into a room or stand in front of a group, and he just dominated the room without even saying a thing because he stood with such power. So I wanted to have his presence.

A guy who recently retired from the University of Connecticut, was an organizational genius, Joe Marrone. So I wanted to have my teams and my offices organized like his were, because he was just so well organized. And there was a guy, the coach that I played for here, named Bill Schellenberger, who was just so graceful in victory and defeat. I wanted to exude his class.

And then finally, the guy I did play for here at the University of North Carolina, a guy named Dr. Marvin Allen, was just such a tremendous gentleman. I remember when I was a youngster and trying to sort out what I was going to do with my life, I never really thought about coaching. In fact, at the time, I didn't feel that was really a noble pursuit. I was pursuing a law degree. And what finally convinced me that, well, this was something you could do and have a shred of dignity and nobility, was the guy I played for, Marvin Allen. He was a wonderful gentleman, the way he conducted his life almost gave me permission to pursue something I really loved because he made it honorable. So my mentors were a collection of people.

Q: What is the best advice ever given to you?

AD: Gosh, I've been given some great advice by so many different people. But maybe the best advice I was ever given was right after I graduated from college. I was in the life insurance business. And my first general agent, the first guy I worked for was a guy named Murray Strawbridge. And the life insurance business is an incredibly difficult business, because you're rejected from dawn until dusk by everyone. I think it really toughens you up. I think that most people who would jump into that profession would quit in short order, because you're constantly rejected. What he used to tell me, which made great sense at the time, and has made great sense ever since, is to not take myself seriously.

I felt that was incredible advice. Basically, I never have. I've never taken any of our success that seriously. I've never put the pressure on my players to sustain their level of success. I've tried not to have a tremendously serious attitude about anything we do except the way we relate to each other and the intensity that we compete with in practice. I think that advice from one of my first bosses was outstanding, because, as you know, in any kind of profession where you've got some kind of high profile, if you were ever to take yourself seriously, I think you'd be just shredded.

Q: Is it important to establish discipline on a team, and must there be rules?

AD: I'm not real big on rules. I remember when I was the coach of the U.S. national team, I only had two rules. One was, don't get drunk. The other one was to be on time. I think if you have 60,000 little rules, then you're creating a prison. Then you're going to be forced to react to anyone who breaks any of the rules that you've set up. And if you don't enforce them all to what extent the players think you should, you're losing credibility. So I feel that a lot of rules are not a good idea. I think a better idea is what you suggested in your question. You create an atmosphere of discipline where basically everyone is self-monitoring. And you trust their common sense, and you trust your own. And you address problems as they come up, but don't create the problem by drawing a line in the sand, and then have to whack someone that stumbles across it by accident. I think if we're in the business of developing human beings and people with character, I think you do it with things that all of us instinctively understand. And then address the problems as they come up. Create people of character, not robots.

Q: To be successful, do you have to develop a philosophy of your own?

AD: Getting back to the question about mentoring, I don't think any philosophy that any one of us comes up with is particularly unique. Maybe we've got our own tweak on it. But for us to sit here and pretend that we have arrogantly come up with some incredibly profound course in life or statement that everyone else should have to follow, I think it gets back to the discussion of taking yourself too seriously. I think you can steal from a thousand different sources. I think you certainly have to have guiding principles in your life, but I don't think the guiding principles necessarily have to be yours. They can be someone else's that you've stolen that you feel should apply in your life, and then adapt it to your particular purpose. I think it can be part of your religious upbringing that teaches you basics on how human beings should behave. Also, coaching involves helping develop people in more ways than just one or two. You have to acknowledge that there is a spiritual dimension. There are dimensions beyond the athletic dimension that you're developing. There are a lot of things involved in life beyond your particular area. But I don't know whether this has to be something you would have to sit down and consciously develop as a personal philosophy. I think what ends up happening as you mature as a human being is, you sort out what you feel is right and then try to communicate it to the people who are entrusted to you.

Q: **Do you think over the course of your career, basically who you are today was established a number of years ago, or is it ever-changing?**

AD: Oh, it evolves constantly. It's funny. I had this discussion with a friend of mine recently. You know, I feel sorry for people who look back on their lives and think that their college years are the best years of their life. I look back on my life, and the further back I go, the more insecure I become. And I wouldn't trade my position right now with any previous year of my life.

One of my favorite cartoons is a Calvin and Hobbes cartoon, and one of these days when I can get all the clutter off my desk, I'm going to frame it and put it on my wall. I'm not going to get this exactly correct, but this is the drift: Calvin and Hobbes are sitting in their go-cart on top of the mountain that they always go down, and Calvin is explaining to Hobbes the philosophy of his life. And he's explaining to Hobbes this philosophy as the go-cart is going down the side of this mountain. He's saying, "I want my life to be a never-ending ascension." And, of course, the irony in what you're watching is, here he wants his life to be a never-ending ascension and he's going off the edge of a cliff, plunging into this abyss.

I think it's a wonderful statement about what life can do to you, but what you can do to life. Because I think, life, if we do take it too seriously, can absolutely destroy us all. But it can't touch any one of us if our ambition is to make our life something extraordinary. And I think this never-ending ascension is a wonderful statement about the way all of us should lead our lives. I think what we should all strive to do is to try to make sure every year we live is superior to the year that we've just had. And it doesn't have to be superior in ways that are evident to the people around us. There can be, I think, more profound and deeply affecting ways that involve your character, and I think that's what that cartoon from Calvin and Hobbes says to me.

And so, yes, I think you're ever-evolving. I think all of us should spend a lot of our day connecting with the people who are important to us, certainly the family and friends, but also anyone who is a part of our lives. But also, I think all of us should constantly read. I just made a deal with my 15-year-old daughter. She's dying for a car.

And the first deal I made with her was I would buy her a car if she got straight A's for an entire year. And she's doing okay, but she keeps getting that B+, and so this car seems farther and farther out of her reach, and she was getting frustrated. So I made another deal with her, I told her that, and I made this deal with her. I would buy her a brand new car if she would read for an hour a day, 365 days in a row between now and next Christmas. Because I genuinely feel that reading, educating yourself, is a never-ending process. And I make it a point in my life to try and do that for an hour before I go to bed every night because I think this evolution is a part of our growth as human beings.

Bobby Knight

Indiana University coach Bobby Knight has coached his Hoosiers to three NCAA championships. His 1987 title team, led by Steve Alford, Dean Garrett, and Keith Smart, defeated Syracuse in one of the most thrilling championship battles in Final Four history.

Knight's 1981 championship team showcased the talents of sophomore point guard Isiah Thomas and handily defeated the University of North Carolina for the national title.

But Knight's pride and joy remains his 1976 team. It was one of those rare occasions when everything fit perfectly. The coach was perfect for the players, and the players perfect for the coach. And on their way to a perfect 32–0 record, the 1975–76

Indiana Hoosiers set the standard for modern team play. They were perhaps the most balanced, efficient squad of all time.

There is the vivid image of coach Knight, then just 35 years old but wise beyond his years. And driven. And then there is the not-so-vivid image of his players, a collection of determined athletes with lots of substance and very little flash. They played physically. The defense always seemed excellent, the offense structured and precise. They scored inside and out, depending on what opposing defenses gave them. And when something wasn't given, they took it.

Knight knew he had a great team. He was confident that just about anything a basketball team had to do, his could do. The final factor was his unwavering will. "Coach wasn't going to leave it up to us to be as great a team as we could be," recalled Quinn Bucker. "He was going to push, be it psychological, physical, whatever it took, to be the best team we could be."

This hard-driving approach was already established as a Knight trademark. As a player, he had been a reserve on Ohio State's 1960 national championship team. His real talent appeared when he took his first college head coaching job at Army in 1965. He was perceived as something of a martinet in pushing the Cadets to a 102–50 record over the next six seasons. His Army teams were hampered by the Academy's 6'6" height restrictions, but Knight instilled a fierce man-to-man defense. His Cadets three times led the nation in scoring defense, the kind of tenacity that would make him an icon in Indiana basketball.

"The will to win is grossly overrated," Knight often said. "The will to prepare is far more important."

Prepare was Knight's mindset for the 1975–76 campaign. He drilled it into his players' minds that they had to work doubly hard to realize their vast potential. There were extra windsprints after practice each day that served as a reminder. Beyond that, he wanted his players to focus not on playing against opponents, but against themselves.

They humbled the Soviet national team to open the 1975–76 schedule and then faced second-ranked UCLA. John Wooden's last UCLA team had won the '75 championship, and the defending champions were now coached by Gene Bartow. The Hoosiers whipped them by 20 points, then polished off Florida. In the next game, they blew a 14-point lead against Notre Dame and Adrian Dantley before winning, 63–60. A week later, Benson rebounded a miss by Abernethy and scored with seconds left to send a game against Kentucky into overtime, where Indiana prevailed again, 77–68. From there they moved to the Big Ten schedule. Ohio State fell by two, and Michigan State forced an overtime. But the Hoosiers had an arrogance that seemed to rattle other teams. Even the bench players carried it. In one game, reserve Wayne Radford made six of seven from the field on his way to 16 points and five rebounds. Against Minnesota, guard Jim Wisman had 12 points and seven assists. They all carried a confidence that emanated from Knight.

Continuing their string, the Hoosiers entered the Mideast Regional as the nation's raging power. May scored 33 and center Kent Benson 20 as they blew by St. John's, 90–70. They struggled a bit with Alabama, but May's 25 points and 16 rebounds helped them over the hump. In the regional finals, second-ranked Marquette was the challenge. The Warriors led by one at intermission, but Knight's players turned on the afterburners in the second half to win, 65–56.

To help celebrate the United States' 200th birthday, NCAA officials held the 1976 national championship in Philadelphia's Spectrum.

Indiana's opponent in the final was Big Ten rival Michigan, featuring Rickey Green, Steve Grote, Phil Hubbard and John Robinson. The Wolverines had reached Philadelphia via the Midwest Region and were eager for another shot at beating Indiana.

Michigan took a 10-point lead in the first half, and held a 35–29 margin at halftime. Benson thought Knight might come into the locker room screaming. Instead, the coach quietly told his players that they had 20 minutes to prove they deserved to be national champions.

Indiana answered with a burst of power in the second half. Scott May and Benson scored 25 each, and the Hoosiers rolled to win number 32, 86–68. Benson was named the tournament's Most Outstanding Player and was joined on the all-tournament team by May and Abernethy.

Knight, of course, went on to coach Indiana teams to his other NCAA championships and led the United States to the 1984 Olympic gold medal, a bittersweet accomplishment in that the powerful Soviet Union team missed the games because of a political boycott.

In 1986, John Feinstein published a very fine, phenomenally successful book on Knight and his program, *A Season on the Brink*. It captured a somewhat manic Knight in full midlife crisis, caught at his worst, during great upheavals in his professional and personal lives.

Like other great coaches, such as John Wooden and Henry Iba, Knight has been a consummate student of the game who developed into an exceptional teacher. The difference between Knight and the others is that he has a private persona that created success and a public one that often took away from it.

Knight often came across as an egocentric genius who threw chairs and bullied the basketball world. But that image wasn't wholly accurate.

Certainly he had a unique intensity. Knight is demanding, of himself, his players, and the officials. As trite as it sounds, what Knight demanded was not winning but the absolutely best effort possible. When he got that, he could be quite peaceful after an Indiana loss. Conversely, there were wins that left him disgusted.

After the '76 championship, there wasn't much need for re-evaluation. "One of the major emotional feelings in '76 was relief at winning the championship," Knight said. "I was just so pleased that that team won because it was one of the truly great college basketball teams. You know your team will always identify with that accomplishment. That stays with you, and you like to see kids have a part of it. I tell our players that some day they will be watching the tournament with their kids or grandchildren and they'll say, "Hey, I played in that." And it's a helluva lot better to say you won it."

Billy Packer: Bob, is there such a thing as the thrill of victory and the agony of defeat?

Bobby Knight: You can look back upon a season with satisfaction, that's where winning is pleasurable. "Thrill" would not be a word that I would pick. It would be that you can be satisfied, that you can take pleasure in what happened. I really have never felt that way when we've won individual games. We've tried to put the game in a position where we can win, and that's it with the winning part of it. Agony of defeat, I think there are some games that are really excruciatingly painful to lose, based on how you've played, the opportunities that you've had that you didn't take advantage of, and how you got beat. And I think there are other games, when you've lost, that you just go on to the next game.

Q: Bob, is there ever an agonizing feeling when you look up at the scoreboard even though you've won the game?

RA: Yes, I think it's a feeling of disappointment that you haven't played better. The greatest sense of satisfaction during the course of a game is to see a possession played well by your team, whether it's on offense or defense. If it's defensively, you've pressured the ball; you've helped; you've blocked out; you've gotten the ball back. Offensively, it's that you've executed things well; you've made good passes; you've cut well; you've screened well, and then I think if that continues throughout the course of a game, in all probability, you're going to win. And so, then you feel good about what you've done. But there have been games along the way that we've won that had I been a fan, I would have far and away rather have seen the other team win.

Q: You've had so many championship clubs in your career. What do you think is the key ingredient when you look back on a championship team?

RA: In basketball it's really simple. I think it's an understanding of how you win. The majority of players never understand about how to win, and I think there are a lot of coaches that don't understand how to win. And when players understand what has to be done to win, then you've got a chance to be pretty good. And the very first thing that has to be done to win, in any team sport, is play well defensively. I mean, there's never been a team that has won championships, in whatever the sport, that has not been very good defensively.

Q: The answer wasn't obvious, "well, talent is the thing." Did you ever feel that you had a team that won championships that was not the most talented club?

RA: Yes, but talent was always circumvented by understanding how to play, and by doing the things that won. You know, talent alone doesn't win anything. And talent that's not well-used doesn't win. And talent that is wasted doesn't win. The game really is exactly what it looks like. It's a team game, and I go back to the point about understanding how to win. And that, to me, is more important than anything that a kid can bring to the game.

Q: How do you start to develop the championship attitude? Whenever you see teams win championships, there's

something about them, there's just an attitude. They know how to win. How do you start to develop that, or can it be developed?

RA: I think that winning really has to be important to the players. I've talked to kids after games when we've played, that I know immediately that they may have played well, but winning really isn't important because the game is over and they've kind of forgotten about it. It's been a game where we might have happened to have won. With the best teams that I've had, there have been kids who have had a determination to win that was contagious. And now everybody wanted to win. They just wouldn't let other guys feel that, "We're just going to play; we're going to play and do our best." Well, that's not going to be good enough for those kids who really want to win. "We're going to play and we're going to win," is their attitude. Not all kids are going to react that way. And if you don't have two or three players that really do want to win, then I think you're not going to be a championship team. But two or three who do want it can really develop that same attitude among the rest.

Q: Is motivation a factor on behalf of the leader, the coach? Or does motivation have to come from within?

RA: I think that you're constantly trying to do things. I remember hearing Lefty Driesell once at a clinic years ago, when I was still an assistant coach at West Point. Lefty said, "I may not always be right, but the one thing I'm going to do is show my players that I'm always working and that I'm always trying to figure out how we can win. And that they can look at me and say, well, he is really committed to winning."

I don't think Lefty is Socrates, but that was a pretty good point. And I think that you work and you come prepared every day, and you come wanting people to play well, and you come not accepting anything other than the best effort, and not accepting poor play. I think that eventually carries over to how players feel about how they're going to play individually in a game.

I think peer pressure is important. Calbert Cheaney was always the first kid at practice and the last kid to leave. Having a leader like that means that you can say to other players, "How the hell can you do what you're doing when Calbert does what he's doing, and he's better than you to begin with?"

Trying to get kids to play well is, I think, a very, very difficult thing to do.

Q: Is it important for a coach to be liked by those guys that he is coaching?

BK: When I first became the head coach, within the first week of being the head coach when I was down at West Point, I went down to see Joe Lapchick. And I still remember his address. It was 3 Wendover Road in Yonkers. I said, "Coach, I came down to talk to you about coaching and some things." So, the first thing he asked me was, "Is it important to you that you're liked?" He didn't say by the players, just liked in general. And I thought for a second, and I said, "Well, no, it really isn't. I think it's important that I'm honest, and that people know that I'm honest. And consequently, they respect me for being honest. As a coach, I would like to be respected for what I know and how I teach, but I don't think it would really be important to me that I be liked."

And so from that first meeting that I had with him, that's been my approach all the way through.

Q: Did he have a response to that?

BK: He said that when you make decisions on what's going to please the most people, you are not going to be a good coach. And when you worry about how people are going to feel about what you do, you're not going to be a good coach. You, the coach, have got more facts than anybody. You're the guy that watches kids practice every day.

A great example of this is a circumstance that seems to happen everywhere. I've got two kids, Smith and Jones, and I bench Jones and start Smith. Almost without exception, is the story going to be benching Jones or starting Smith?

Q: Benching Jones.
BK: Without exception. And that just boggles my mind. And when I quit coaching, it'll still boggle my mind because if I moved you into the starting lineup, my feeling is that that is great for you and what a great chance that is for you. But you're not the story. It's the guy who got benched, and that's such a shame, I think, today with kids.

Q: Is it important, while they're playing for you, to have a personal relationship with the players?
BK: What's a personal relationship?

Q: I'm going to say a buddy-buddy, an understanding of everything they're doing in their personal lives.
BK: I think what a kid has to feel with me is that he can come to me with any problem that he has and I'll do whatever I can—whatever I'm allowed to do—to help him. And if I can't help him, I'll find somebody who can, and do whatever they're allowed to do to help him. I think a kid has to feel that he can trust me, and I think a kid has to feel that I have his best interests at heart.

And I don't think that that has to be, as you phrase it, a "buddy-buddy relationship." I think a buddy-buddy relationship is that which you have with the guy you go fishing with, or go hunting with.

Q: The word "potential"—is it a blessing or a curse for a ballplayer or a ball team?

BK: Well, it depends on who's using the word. I mean, how many teams have you seen that are just bad? I mean, you've seen them play, and you just say, "Gosh, that team is not that good. They're not as good as people say they are." Or people can say that about a player with a big reputation. Sometimes you'll see a guy who just isn't as good as he's built up to be. You know, at Indiana we've had certain players for four years of potential, and it hasn't taken us anywhere. And I think that in the initial stages of a player's development, that potential is important. His potential to be a player is a factor in how you're going to work with him to get him to realize that potential. But then, as things go, potential has to be changed into reality. And I think that if as a player works toward development, if we're continually talking about potential, then we're talking about a kid that, for whatever the reason, is not going to become as good as we once thought he would be. So when we first decided how good we thought this kid was going to be, there was something wrong in our analysis. And it might have been something that we knew absolutely nothing about.

Q: Does the scrutiny of the coach today by the press and the fans make it more difficult to do the job than in the past?

BK: I think that depends. I think it goes back to what coach Lapchick had to say. What is it that is important to you? What do you want? Do you want to be everybody's friend? Did you ever read the book *The Best and the Brightest* by David Halberstam? If you'll recall, it was a book about the 60's, but mostly it was a book about the Kennedy administration. A major thread that he wove through the book was planning for the reelection. And so many decisions about our policies in the Vietnam War were discussed and based on what's going to fly best so far as the reelection is concerned. The decisions the Kennedy administration made were often horrible decisions. On a much smaller scale, it's like that in coaching. If you're always running for reelection, then you're going to make a lot of bad decisions.

Q: Your greatest satisfaction as a coach, looking back?

BK: I think it's what the players who have played for us have gone on to do. Here, right now, we have two kids that were four-year players who don't have a degree. And one of them will get it. We have nobody that isn't in a really good situation today. All these kids that have played for us for four years, they've all gone on and done really well.

Q: How about disappointments? If you had to look back at the biggest disappointment?

BK: Obviously, there are games you could pick out, but I don't think you pick out a single game as the biggest disappointment. I think, probably, the biggest disappointment for us here was in 1975 when (Scott) May broke his arm. And I say that because I think it deprived us of a chance to win a national title.

You tell me if you'd agree with this: Indiana, Kentucky, and North Carolina are the three schools with the greatest level of fan support for basketball. Now maybe Kansas is really close, but Duke doesn't have enough support. Would you agree with that?

Q: Duke's alumni base is different, more spread out geographically, not as intense. The other three schools reside at the heart of great regional basketball cultures.

BK: Exactly. And Duke has kind of a little holier-than-thou sort of thing. Maybe a little bit like Michigan's. At Indiana, we've got farmers and people who haven't even been on a college campus, for Pete's sake. So does Kentucky, and so does North Carolina. The atmosphere is just rabid. College basketball is one of the things people care about most.

Which means the disappointments can loom pretty large. That's how it felt in 1975 when May's injury deprived this whole atmosphere surrounding Indiana of a national championship that would have been a real hallmark championship by a great team.

Q: How about the feeling of facing failure? Does that ever come up to you?

BK: I think it's more important that you know how to win, and you understand what it takes to win. And if I expound on that a little bit, one of the first things I would say is this: to win and to understand how to win, you've got to know how to prevent losing. And what's going to cause us to lose are these things: poor ball-handling, bad blockout, shot selection, quickness of execution, or effectiveness of execution. So, we take those things that are going to cause us to lose and we try and eliminate those things. There's a difference in preventing losing and playing not to lose. Do you follow me? And so I think I try to eliminate those reasons why you lose, and I don't care what the hell it is you're in. When I go talk somewhere, I always talk about losing. I think there should be more books written about losing than winning because if you eliminate the reasons why you lose, then you've only got one thing left to do. And that's win.

Q: How do you create respect for yourself as a coach, in the eyes of your players?

BK: I think that if you're an honest person who works hard and deals fairly with players, then the coach will gain the respect of those players. A kids knows that he's going to get a chance when he earns it. And a kid knows also, that if another guy doesn't earn his way, then he's now going to get a chance.

That's the kind of thing that I think is important. And I've always thought that. I was a player that was always looking for a chance to play, almost game-by-game. I'm not sure that back then I could even figure it out. I'm not sure that I ever started as a college player four games in a row. I can think of three I started, but I'm not sure of the fourth. I may have done that once. And so I know how important it is to a kid to get a chance to play. And that's why I want the kid to have a chance to play when he earns it and deserves it. Like the other night when we played Kentucky, (Rich) Mandeville played good minutes for us. When we played Evansville, it was just a [bad] game for big guys because they spread the court and played a bunch of 6'5" guys, and Mandeville did not get to play the number of minutes that he had earned in the Kentucky game. He didn't play but six or eight minutes but made a couple of good plays. I told him, "I owe you time to play because you earned it, but this just wasn't the game to use big guys." And he was really good. And now, he was the first guy I looked to play the next night in a game with Green Bay, simply based on the fact that he didn't get to play as much as he should have earlier.

Q: **Do you set goals before the season starts? And if you set goals, are they along the lines of how many games you think your team can win?**

BK: Yes. I always do that. I try to make them realistic, and try to tell my players I'll be frank with them. If I think we can win the national championship, I tell them that. But then I think if our goal is to get into the NCAA Tournament, I say what we've got to do is play well enough to get there, and then let's see what the hell we can do when we get there.

The last few years we have not played as well in the NCAA Tournament. I know the number of wins, but I'm not exactly sure of the number of losses. We, at one time, had won like 40 games in the NCAA and I think had lost like 16, which was pretty high. But now we've lost the last 3 games that we've played so we've lost maybe 19 now. And so, we have not played as well there in recent years. Once we've gotten there, I don't think we've played as well as we used to.

Q: Bob, is a coach born with leadership qualities or can they be developed?

BK: Boy, I don't know. I think the really good coaches that I have known always felt that they knew a little bit more about it than the guys around them. I think they feel that, "Damn it, this is the way we ought to do it!" And probably, a lot of pretty good coaches were the guys who picked the sides in a sandlot baseball game, or they were the guys who drew up the plays on the ground in the huddle of a touch football game. Or they were guys in a basketball game who were, at least at some point, the leading scorer or the guy who said the most about how the game was going to be played. They were the playground bosses when they were kids.

Q: There are two players on your squad. They're basically even in terms of which one is going to get to play. One has maybe superior intelligence; the other guy, superior physical skills. What guy gets to play?

BK: The smarter kid.

Q: (Laughing.) That's what I figured. Can you create a competitor or does he have to have it inside?

BK: Well, I'll tell you, Mike Krzyzewski was kind of a wussy when he came to West Point. He's the best example that I have. He'd been the leading scorer in the Chicago Catholic League in high school. And I'm not sure, I think his high school team won a lot of games, but as I recall, they pressed a lot and he drove a lot and had a lot of crazy shots going to the bucket and got fouled. The Catholic League was pretty good, and he was the leading scorer for two years in the Catholic League.

Now, he was not a very good shooter, and he wasn't real tough. He played on the freshman team at West Point back when freshmen weren't allowed to play on the varsity. And we worked out against the freshman team a lot when he played. When he started playing on the varsity, he had to make a big adjustment, from being a big scorer to being a smart, tough player who didn't score so much. He came to understand that if he played hard and smart, and played that way defensively and offensively, he didn't have to score a lot of points. I mean, I don't think he ever averaged over six or seven points a game. But he developed toughness and competitiveness and wound up being pretty much a three-year starter for us.

I don't think that it was any thing that I did. I just think that he was able to say. "Well, I really want to play and this is how I'm going to play." And then he really did a great job of that.

Sometimes you try to guide a kid toward toughening up, and he discovers he really doesn't want to play. Sometimes you can make a kid more competitive, but that's not always the case.

Q: What's the most important thing—pregame preparation or in-game adjustments?

BK: I think preparation. I think in-game adjustments are the most overrated thing in coaching. The team that's willing to prepare to win is going to be the team that wins. Most everybody plays to win, but it's preparing to win that I think is the most important thing in successful play.

Q: Does a championship team play as it practices?

BK: You know, there's an old saying that, boy, he scores 30 when you win by 3, and 3 when you win by 30, meaning players do what they have to to get by. I think that's bullshit. I think if the guy scores 30 when you win by 3, he ought to get 50 when you win by 30. I think you've got to play at the level at which you can play just as much as is humanly possible to be really good.

Q: So those champions that you've had, they practiced as they played?

BK: I think some of the best basketball that I've ever seen our teams play, with our best teams, has been played in practice. I talked to Ralph Beard, the former Kentucky great, the other day. And he went with us to Hawaii, and he said without any reservation, the best basketball that Kentucky played with those great teams was in practice.

Q: Did you have to have a mentor or mentors as you're coming along as a coach? Are they important?

BK: They were to me. I don't know how other guys feel, but probably the most enjoyable part about my time in coaching was people I could talk to and call and visit with and ask questions. I talked to Red Auerbach this morning. I think it's important to have people that you know you can talk to. I've had about five of them. Clair Bee and Joe Lapchick were first. And Red Auerbach then became somebody I could talk to because he coached John Havlicek, my college teammate at Ohio State. I got to know Red when I was a JV coach in high school. And he was always really good to me. And then, after that, early, the guy that I talked to far and away the most was Clair Bee. And then there's the relationship I've had with Pete Newell, whom I respect very much. It's has been the same thing with Fred Taylor, my coach at Ohio State. So I've had people I can really call and talk to and ask about things during the time that I've been in coaching that I've really enjoyed. And Henry Iba was the other one.

Q: What's the best advice ever given you by any of those fellows, or for that matter, anybody?

BK: Their gift to me was just talking about what was important in the game as far as coaching. Things like understanding how to play defensively. We'd talk about the best ways of playing defensively. And we'd talk about how your defense has to be part of your offense. If your defense is going to be part of your offense, then you've got to develop a game in getting the ball to the offensive end. So you've got three stages to develop. You're going to have a fast break, a secondary break, and you're going to have an offense. We'd talk basics, just the guts of how to play basketball, that's really the thing I've taken from these people. I've gotten so much from them, and I continue to learn from their ideas and creativity.

Q: In the establishment of discipline on a ball club, must there be rules?

BK: Well, from a coaching standpoint, I think there have to be rules. I think defense is all rules. I don't think you can play defense without rules being established to determine positioning, and to determine movement relative to where the ball goes.

I don't know whether I'd use the word "rules" for offensive play, but there have to be principles of offensive play, which is probably almost synonymous. I think that on offense, the principles are spacing, shot selection, handling the ball. I think you have to have principles there. What is discipline? To a lot of people, discipline is a very negative word. In knowing that some people felt discipline was negative, I've always felt it was a positive word, and I defined it in that vein a long time ago in this way: I said discipline is doing what has to be done when it has to be done. You do it as well as you can do it, and you do it that way all the time. That's what a disciplined person does, and that's how a disciplined person plays. And I think a disciplined team, that means to me that that team plays the way it's got to play, and it plays that way all the time, not just once in a while. It plays well all the time. That's what I think a disciplined team is.

Q: To be successful, do you have to have a philosophy, and how do you develop one?

BK: Well, I'm not sure that we're all capable of developing a philosophy of life or a philosophy of leadership or coaching or anything else. I think that whatever our game is, I think we have to understand how the game can best be played. And to me, that goes one step further. How it can best be played by whatever the rules of the game are? What would be a classic example of an athlete who understood how to play a game?

Jack Nicklaus is a prime example. Every golfer will tell you that Nicklaus just managed the game better, longer than anybody ever did. Bill Russell, absolutely, is also a great choice. And I've always said that the most valuable player ever to play the game of basketball was Bill Russell. And now, I really believe he's been challenged by Jordan in that regard.

Q: Bob, as a follow-up in regard to the philosophy, looking back when you started out in high school, then at

West Point, and then looking at Bob Knight today, how much different is your approach to the game today than when you were a young coach?

BK: You know, Pete Carril made a great statement. He said the older he got, the less tolerant he was. And that made a lot of sense to me. And I've tried to really, really be careful of that because I sense and feel myself being that way sometimes. I don't think that the basic ingredients of what has to be done in the game that I coached have to be changed that much. I think the game has changed. I think the three-point shot has had an incredible effect on the game of basketball. I really think it's taken a lot out of the science of coaching.

Joe Gibbs

Like basketball's John Wooden, Joe Gibbs was a coach who drew great strength from his spiritual beliefs. Unlike Wooden, however, Gibbs didn't assume a head coaching job early in his career. In fact, there was a time that Gibbs feared he would be a career assistant. "I had dreamed of being a head coach," Gibbs once explained. "But you've got to remember, I was 40 years old and couldn't get a college head coaching job. I had two interviews—Missouri and Arizona—and they wouldn't hire me. But both were token things. I was 40 years old, and that's up there in coaching. I didn't know if it was going to happen."

Indeed, Gibbs had lived the typical nomadic life of an assistant coach. The son of a sheriff in the North Carolina mountains, he lived in the South until he was 14, when his family moved to California after his father changed careers. He played high school football well enough to earn a scholarship to San Diego State to play for Don Coryell. It would be the beginning of the fundamental relationship in Gibbs's coaching career.

He worked three years as a graduate assistant to Coryell, then moved on to serve as an assistant coach at Florida State, Southern Cal, and Arkansas.

In 1973, Coryell lured Gibbs to his staff with the St. Louis Cardinals with the promise that he could be running backs coach. His tenure in St. Louis ended with Coryell's firing, which sent Gibbs to a short stint as Tampa Bay's offensive coordinator, where he began work with a bright young quarterback named Doug Williams.

The Bucs, however, went 5–11. "It blew up in my face," Gibbs admitted. He left and took something of a demotion, again working as a running backs coach, this time on Coryell's staff with the San Diego Chargers. But Ray Perkins, the Chargers' offensive coordinator, was hired away by New York, and suddenly Gibbs found himself back at the control of an offense. San Diego's Air Coryell put up an 11–5 record in 1980 and battled all the way to the AFC title game, setting up Gibbs as the head coaching choice of Washington Redskins owner Jack Kent Cooke and General Manager Bobby Beathard.

Two seasons later, Gibbs drove the Redskins to their first Super Bowl victory, a defeat of the Miami Dolphins. The next year, the Redskins again reached the Super Bowl, only to be demolished by the Los Angeles Raiders, 38–9.

Over the next three seasons, Gibbs's Redskins stacked up a 33–15 record but stumbled each year in the playoffs. Finally his relief came with the 1987 club, led by Doug Williams, that ran up an 11–4 regular-season record and demolished Denver 42–10 in Super Bowl XXII.

Gibbs's third Super Bowl championship followed the 1991 season, when his Redskins rolled to a 14–2 finish and pushed aside the Buffalo Bills, 37–24, in Super Bowl XXVI. "I've never felt more humble in my life," Gibbs said afterwards. "The Good Lord has blessed me to have this owner and to be around these players."

After one more season, Gibbs admitted that his high-energy, high-commitment style had worn him down. He abruptly resigned, stunning both Cooke and the throng of Redskins fans.

"We were all devastated at the news," quarterback Mark Rypien told reporters. "You know nothing will ever be the same. You start thinking that the Redskins won't play again. That's what Coach Gibbs meant to us."

Billy Packer: Joe, is there any such thing as the thrill of victory? And does it last?

Joe Gibbs: Yes, I think there's a definite thrill of victory. Does it last? No. I'd say that there's a definite thrill of victory. I think that's the reason why I was in it. The thrill of putting something that's very, very hard to do, together, and then climbing that ladder and then winning. That, to me, is a thrill in life. And it has been, really, from the time I was very small. A lot of people are that way, I think. They're very competitive. God made us that way. And what's the best way to get your kid to do something? All you've got to say is, "Let's see how fast you can do this," and boom, they're off. At least mine have been.

The thrill of trying to do something very hard, that's what I loved about the NFL, and that's what I love about auto racing. It's very, very hard. A lot of people would love to do it, but it's one of the hardest things in the world to do. And I get a kick out of that because it is that hard. There's a definite thrill to it. But I walked out on the football field after our last Super Bowl in '91. And I happened to be standing out there with Charles Mann (Washington's veteran defensive lineman) in that Minnesota dome there, and I kind of looked over at him. He looked over at me. It was over. We had already won it, and I looked at him and I said, "Gosh, the fun of this was getting here. It's not now. Not afterwards."

There is something to saying, "Hey, we won the championship." But it was actually the thrill, it was the practices, the blood, sweat, the tears, the losses, the wins, the climbing that ladder and getting to the Super Bowl and then winning it. That's the fun part, and that's what you remember. That's the competitive part, and it doesn't last, because you turn around and you want to do it all over again. The thrills are not going to last in those kind of sports. The thrill was actually getting it done and doing it.

Q: How about the agony of defeat? Because with any guy that's had the victories you've had, there have been moments of defeat.

JG: Definitely for me. I mean I probably remember the defeats, the real bitter ones . . . they're as vivid as the great victories. And that's what I remember. People say, "What victory do you remember most?" I can't tell you that because there were a bunch of them. Our second season we beat Philadelphia up there in the opening game, and I thought it was one of the biggest victories we ever had, 37–34, in overtime. Nobody remembers that. They remember the Super Bowl, or beating Dallas for the championship in '82, or something.

But there are the bitter losses, and I can just reel them off. Philadelphia, running the clock out against Buddy Ryan. Gerald Riggs fumbles the ball, and it comes all the way over to the sideline. They pick it up and run it all the way back to the 14. Score on us, beat us by a point. We had killed them all day long. Losing to Dallas when they

120

were 0–13, coming to our place. There's no way we should lose that. And so, the bitter Super Bowl loss we had, our one Super Bowl loss, was one of the toughest losses I ever experienced. I didn't realize you could go that far and have a loss like that in the Super Bowl and feel that way. So there is a definite agony that goes with those defeats.

Q: What is the key ingredient to putting together a championship team, if there is one?

JG: I'd say people. For me, I always related everything to people. If it's auto racing or if it's football, you don't win with the X's and O's. They're needed. You've got to be good at it, but you don't win with X's and O's. What you win with is people. You've got to have a great front office, you've got to have a great coaching staff, and certainly you've got to pick the great players. You've got to pick the right players to fit your system. And when I say great, we had some players I thought were great that people wouldn't even recognize, if I reeled off the names. People ask me, "Who are the great players that you coached? Give me the greatest player you coached." And I start off with people like Otis Wonsley, Pete Cronan, Greg Williams, and they say, "Who?" Those are some of our special teams' players. They were great players, and they fit perfectly in our system. They were sold on the Redskins. They believed in it.

Q: If the answer is not raw talent, can you win a championship if you don't have the best talent in your given profession?

JG: Yes. You can win a championship. Now, you're going to have to have talent. You're not going to go in there and luck out against somebody. But many times it's role players. On all our Super Bowl teams, we had more than half our team as free agents. You know, I could tell you story after story about us going out and drafting these players and thinking they were the greatest thing since sliced bread. The first year I went to the Redskins we drafted Mark May and Russ Grimm, and all these offensive linemen. We signed guys like Joe Jacoby for $5,000, Jeff Bostic for nothing, and they go to the Pro Bowl. And some of the rest of the guys, not that group, but in some of the rest of the years we draft all these guys that are the latest and the greatest stuff, and they're busts. I think what you've got to have is people that fit in your system. Now, in there, there's going to have to be talented players. But, I definitely feel that the whole becomes a lot better when it's put together than that part, and having a star. It's very important the way everything fits together, and many times, I think it's the role player that for us was a real key. He couldn't even play for somebody else, but for us he was a particular role player that was great at doing one thing, and we found a way to use him, and let him do his one thing for us.

Q: Can a championship team be motivated, and is there an importance to motivation on behalf of the coach?

JG: Yes. You can be motivated. I worked for four different head coaches, and I talk about those guys all the time because I learned a lot from them. But what I found was all four of them were totally different. I mean, in some cases absolute opposites. John McKay was a pure motivator. Really sharp, smart guy, that was a pure motivator. Everybody coached and played because they were scared to death of him (laughing). Don Coryell was the most down-to-earth guy but an intense guy, who studied things for hours. In his way, he was very smart about just organizing a practice. He was a great common sense coach. Bill Peterson was all hard work. That's the way he got it done. He worked your tail off from the time you got there. And Frank Broyles was one of the most polished salespersons. He could sell anything. If he believed in it, he could sell it. But what you see there are four guys totally different. And there's different ways of getting it done. So I learned a lot from those guys.

Q: Can a player who does not have natural motivation skills be motivated by a coach? Does he have to want to be?

JG: No. I think you've got to have motivated guys. For me, the key is picking those kind of guys who do want to achieve, who do want to be a part of it. As far as you motivating them, you can definitely motivate a team. Don Breaux was a coach with me for years, was an assistant coach in the NFL for a long time, one of the most gifted coaches I've been around. And Don would come to me—and he's worked with different guys—and he would tell me, "Hey, this guy can talk to a team." I think it's very important for a coach to be able to talk to a team. Don Coryell was not a good public speaker. You know, a little bit of a lisp, and everything. Didn't like to talk out in public. But this guy could talk to a team, you know. He got ready to coach like he was going to play the game himself. When I played for him, you had eyeballs as big as his by the time he finished talking about the other team. You hated them. He called them every name in the book. And somehow, by the time it was game time, he hated their guts, and he put that across to you. And so, I think you've got to be able to talk to a team.

That's motivation. I think you've got to be able to lift them up at the right time; you have to be able to knock them down at the right time. Chew their rear at the right time. And I think there's got to be a feel to that, and that's the one thing lots of times where we miss on coaches. I tell people, it doesn't matter how good they look, what kind of a coordinator they are, how well they are with X's and O's, what their background is. Because when they get shifted into that role of being a head coach, what they now have to be able to do, one of the most important things is talk to the team, communicate to that team, and you've got to have a feel. It's just a natural feel of when to get on them and when to back off; when they need to be lifted up. A team is a lot like a person. Sometimes they're suffering from self-confidence. They just don't think they can do it. You've got to be able to pick them up. Sometimes, they're overconfident. You've got to be able to knock them down. Sometimes, they need their butt chewed. You've got to chew it. And you can't teach that in coaches. That's not written someplace, and you're not going to get that. You either have that with people, or you don't. You can talk to a team and you can motivate a team. I don't think you can give that to a coach. I think he may reach a certain plateau, but I don't think he's going to be an exceptional coach unless he has that ability.

Q: The relationship. Is it important to establish a personal relationship with those people playing for you?

JG: I've heard that there have been some very, very successful coaches who didn't have a relationship with their players. A player once told me about another great coach, "He didn't talk to me more than 10 words the whole time I was there. He didn't want to talk to me He didn't care. He just wanted me to do the job."

Evidently there's a way of doing that and still being a winner and winning Super Bowls and all that. But I do not believe, myself personally, that's the best way. I think it's important having a relationship, being able to talk to guys, having a real concern for them and their future. To me, that's the best approach. Players seem to feel that hey, your job as a coach is to help them to be the best they can be. So I think having a personal interest in them is crucial, and the way you show that is crucial. Sometimes you take them off to one side and say, "What are you doing? Why are you doing this? Why are you missing these workouts? It's ridiculous. This should be the third most important thing in your life, and you're off. You're going to weddings and doing all this stuff."

I had a kid tell me one time just that. He said, "Hey, you know, I've got to help my dad. My dad's got a farm. My dad counts on me." I said, "Let me ask you something, how much money do you make?" He made $250,000, or something. I said, "Let me tell you something, take $30,000 and pay someone to go do that, and you take care of your $250,000. You're an idiot because you're throwing away your career by running back there and helping your dad on a farm. And he'd be better off. You could hire two guys for him. He'd have a whole lot more work going on there, and you'd protect your job, because you're going to be out if you continue with this."

You have to have a relationship to say those things, make those points, with your players.

Q: The word "potential," we hear it so much in business and life, and family relationships and in sports, obviously. Is it a positive or a negative word? Is there such thing as potential, and is it a blessing or a curse?

JG: Well, potential is a plus. You want to have potential. Does it mean a lot? No. Because I've had a lot of guys with a lot of potential and they stink. They're just not good. And you've got to be careful to distinguish between potential and accomplishment. That's one of the toughest things as a coach. What you have a tendency to do when that person's drafted, I don't care if it's basketball or anything else, is to be swayed by potential. I know in football what happens is, if a player's got a lot of potential, you draft him high because he's got all this potential. Well, the biggest mistake made in pro sports is just magnifying the error. What you do is get in there and all of the sudden, you say, "Oh, wait a minute, this guy, he's not a worker. He doesn't care about the team. He's selfish." And the greatest error in sports is not just saying, "Okay, we're cutting our losses. He's out of here, we're not fooling with him. He's 22 years old. I'm not going to change him in six months or a year." And when you spot that, it takes guts in an organization to say, "We made a mistake. He's out. We're going to keep somebody else here that's got less potential but is a great team guy and can do things for us."

I think magnifying the errors and keeping those guys is the biggest mistake in pro sports. It takes a lot of guts, takes a lot of guts. The paper is going to rip your rear if you cut a first-round draft choice. But, with the Redskins, that's one thing I think we did. We cut a lot of guys that were second, third, first, and we kept a lot of guys who were down the line. But the players know it more than anybody else. They know, and they're watching. They'll spot them as quick as you do. This guy's a dud. He's a first-round draft choice. You paid him two million bucks. He stinks. Now, they're looking and thinking, "Are they going to keep this guy or are they going to go for this guy that's really a hard worker? This other guy makes very little money but is a better team guy for us."

Soon as you keep that other guy, that potential guy who won't work, they know it. And from that point on, they know that, hey, money's making decisions here. And as soon as you cut that underachieving potential guy, it makes a statement. They say, "Hey, they cut this sucker. He means what he says. I'd better be a team guy, and I'd better be making those workouts because it doesn't matter where I was drafted. I can be cut."

Q: What would you say is the biggest satisfaction you've had in your sport career, in either football or racing?

JG: The biggest satisfaction? I'm not sure I can even answer that. I always dreamed about playing pro sports. I wanted to be a great athlete or drive race cars or something. I couldn't do that. I wasn't good enough. And I switched to being a coach. I still would have rather been a great player, but that wasn't what God meant for me to be. I was obviously supposed to be a coach. So I guess, the greatest thrills are you get picked by somebody like a Jack Kent Cooke and Bobby Beathard to go to the Washington Redskins, one of the greatest traditions in sports. And you pick your coaching staff and you work with the front office, you pick your players. It's one of the toughest fields. I guess that's why I like it so much. There's only 30 jobs like that. Then you climb that mountain. And I've said that it meant more to me, for the people in my sport, the other coaches, for them to look at us and say, "Those guys are doing it the right way. I've got great respect for them." That meant more to me than the fans because your peers and opponents, they're the ones that really know, the people in the profession, your peer group. And so I guess it's that whole process of climbing that mountain, of getting it done, and having other people in your profession that spent their life doing what you do, to say, "Hey, those guys are the ones we respect and are doing it the right way and we've got tremendous respect for them." Just like I had tremendous respect for a bunch of those coaching staffs and coaches.

Q: You win a Super Bowl, and suddenly, hey, there's another year. As you said, the thrill of the victory ends very quickly. Is there a fear of failure, and if there is, how do you overcome that?

JG: There was for me. And I don't think you are going to overcome that. I think if that's in you—a fear of failure—I think that motivates you. Even after we won our third Super Bowl, the next year I was right back in the same mind-set. Man, I don't want to lose. Losing stinks. I knew everything that came with losing, because I had experienced it. We started out 0–5 in Washington. It was horrible. My wife kept a diary and recorded just how bad it was. It was the worst thing that ever happened to anybody. Your kids are called names. You're called names. I hated it. And so, for me, it didn't matter how many times I won that Super Bowl. That's one of the things that helped make my decision when I was offered the chance to coach another NFL team. It really got down to where I said, "Hey, every single thing about this job is great. I ought to take this if I ever become a coach again." But the reality was there, that if I ever do coach again, I'm going to do it the same way. I'm not changing because when I lost, my way of correcting that was to go harder and harder. I hated losing. Even when I won, I never had a real sense of accomplishment because all the time I was thinking that what's waiting out there is all those bad things that come with losing. I hated it.

Q: So actually the fear of failure was a positive motivation?
JG: It was in me. I used to laugh because I'd look at Don Shula, and I'd say, "Gosh, you go down there in Miami and they lose the football game and the press never even brought his name up in a negative way." It was accepted. He did his part. It was somebody else's fault. I said I wished I could achieve that level of respect. In Washington, when we lost, it was, "Gibbs is running a one-back offense. He's an idiot. Why is he running Riggins?" And, hey, I didn't like it, I didn't like those things. Definitely. It ruined my whole year, my whole off-season, everything.

Q: How about shortcuts to success? Many people who will read about you and listen to what you and the

**outstanding leaders in the profession have to say are
looking for that shortcut to success. You talked about
the fact that you worked for a lot of people. Is there any
shortcut to success? Are there any shortcuts to the Super Bowl?**

JG: I learned in pro sports—and in the business world, it's
the same thing—that you don't luck out. You may luck
out in one game or a play or something, you're not in
general going to go in there and luck out. You've got to be
real, real good, and then you've got to have some fortune
go your way. But you're not going to luck out and just
throw something on the table and have it work. My way
of coaching is probably different now that I've learned
that there's been a lot of different ways of coaching. I wish
I could have been one of those guys who could go home
at 7 o'clock, you know, and it all seemed to go right for
them. I couldn't do that. We've always kept our whole
staff in there. We went through every single process of an
offensive game plan all together. We didn't break up and
go someplace, and go home. I felt it was always best to
have six minds looking at our plan. By the time we
thrashed our way through all that and decided what we
were going to go with in short yardage, or whatever, and
the collective minds had said this was good and we all
signed off on it, I had a great confidence in it. But let me
say this, we usually had spent a lot of time doing it. There's
a tremendous price to pay in that because most of the time
we finished, it was 2-3-4 o'clock in the morning. Every
year it would start off, I'd try to do it a different way. I'd
say, "Well, I'm going to have somebody else put the short
yardage game plan in front of the team." And then every
time, the coaches would come to me and say, "Let's not
do this.We've got something that works. Don't do this."
And so I found that there wasn't a shortcut. Every year it
went back to the same thing. We'd say, "Okay, if it's 12

o'clock, we are going home" (laughing). And that would last about a week, and we're back . . . because it wasn't done. And there's only really one great way to get it done, in my opinion. That was when every single part of that thing had been checked, double-checked, checked, double-checked. I don't think there's a shortcut, really, to being successful. Maybe if your dad died and left you a couple of billion dollars or something.

Q: You talk about the staff, everybody working together, how about the word loyalty? You hear it so much. Putting together a championship team, is loyalty a two-way street between players and coaches? And does it have to be there?

JG: I think it has to be there. I think the players that really play for you, they've got to think that your way is the best way, and that the Redskins are the best. I had 12 guys that went through three Super Bowls with me, and I could get those guys in a room every time we were having a bad time, and I'd say, "Hey, this is your team. We're stinking the joint up here. Now, what are we going to do about it? And have you guys got any ideas? Give me some ideas. Do we need to change something here? Now, what's going on?" And I think the loyalty factor was big. Those guys knew there were other good places. We always have a tendency as human beings to look and say the grass is greener somewhere else. But in general, when it came right down to the fact, they had a choice of leaving for another team or staying. They stayed most of the time. When they actually got down to it, they said, "Wait a minute here, I'm comparing this with everybody else and when I talk to these other players, this is a pretty good deal here." I think the loyalty factor is important. I think it's important for coaches, assistant coaches to have it. I think they've got to believe in it. If they don't believe in it and believe you're the best and what you're trying to do is the best, then it wouldn't be much fun working at a place where you thought, "Hey, other people are doing it better than we're doing it."

Q: Let's suppose we get down to the last man that you're going to keep on your ball club. And you have to make the choice between two guys who seem to be equal. What would be more important—the mental approach of the player or his physical abilities?

JG: I'd say that they're never equal, first of all. You're not going to find two guys who are dead equal. And for me, it was always the character. And I started telling our scouts that after I was in the NFL for a while. I learned it was a hard process because you learn by mistakes. It became obvious we had things turned around the way we were picking players. We went back to character. And you go to any scouting room, chances are when the scouting draft is on the board, there will be a color code for character. An orange, for us, meant he had a problem. And so that orange would be on these guys, and the first thing I learned was to take all the orange and put them over here. We aren't taking them. You know, one of the favorite statements I used to hear was, "It was only marijuana."

I'd say, "Yes, and then it's going to be something else right after that. I'm not fooling with that." So we'd take everything and put in all the character things over here. So it was character and smarts. Was he a smart football player? Now, I'm not talking about book-smart. As a matter of fact, we changed our whole testing at the Washington Redskins. We went away from all written tests. We had a learning specialist, that still works with the Washington Redskins, develop a test based off the five smartest football players we had on our team at that time. I said these five guys have what we want. Now you go away, test them, come back and develop a test that tells us what they have. Art Monk, Joe Jacoby, Donnie Warren, players like that. And this specialist came back and did that. And the test had nothing to do with reading. And if we had a question, we'd bring him in and let him take the test for two hours. Our testing specialist would walk back out of that meeting, after giving players a verbal test, and he'd tell us, "Hey, this guy is a con man; and this other guy is going to die for you."

I think it's character, smarts—football smarts, basketball smarts—because I've found that a guy may run 4.8 but he thinks faster. Kellen Winslow ran 4.8, but he played 4.5. I had a lot of guys ran 4.4, and they played 5.4. And they made a bunch of dumb mistakes and get you beat. And so I think it's character, smarts, and then ability. Now, you've got to have some ability. You've got to have an ability to do things in pro sports, or business, or anything else. We started making some progress when we got it right about character and smarts. Actually, what would happen is, we would draft all these other guys and we were keeping the smart character guys.

Q: Not realizing at first that it's something by design?

JG: It was not as much of a design at first. Eventually the scouts started sitting with the coaches and saying, "Oh, this is what we want. We'd better get this kind of a player at this position." Almost every time that worked. You can't have a receiver in the NFL if he's a dumb receiver, I'm telling you. You've got no chance. People say, "Hey, he's out there just running routes." No, what he's out there doing is getting bumped and jammed, and things change. And he's got to make decisions on the run. Now if he makes a wrong decision, he's never where the quarterback expects him to be. You can't have a dumb guy doing that. The guys we had were football smart. Art Monk.

Gary Clark. Ricky Sanders. Those suckers were smart, and I didn't have a dumb tight end. Those guys are moving all over the place. Donnie Warren is a smart football player. Our offensive linemen, you could have talked to any of them. Joe Jacoby, Bostic, Grimm, I defy you to find a guy over there that's not sharper than all get-out. Quick. Make good decisions. Make line calls and all that. You cannot play in those leagues without smarts. I don't know about basketball, but I bet you it's the same way.

Q: In regard to the word "competitor," did you find that guys were natural competitors, or can you make a guy a competitor?

JG: I did a study on that. Mostly what I surmise is that stereotypes mean little. We had a high school guy I played with. His name was Dave Stinson, a redhead. His mother and father had never played a thing in their entire lives. They were looking for ways to keep him out of sports. And I remember one time, his mother had his toes operated on. She did not want him out there playing football. I mean whatever they could do to kill off his wanting to play football or anything else, they were going to do it. This whole family, his brother, too, had never played a thing, so this guy came from a background that was noncompetitive. He should have been a wussy. That sucker would tear your eyeballs out. He wrestled. He was one of the most intense competitors I've ever been around in my entire life.

And you know that wive's tale about great athletes coming from the wrong side of the tracks? I've met some of the wimpiest guys that I've ever known that came from the wrong side of the tracks (laughing). Yet I've had some guys who were raised in a cellophane envelope. They had everything, and they are tougher than all get-out. So I will tell you that I think that you are born with a certain amount of it. It's also a function of who you're around. But I do think you are born with quite a bit of it.

Q: As a coach, can you bring that out if a guy is not a basic competitor? Can you, as a coach, make him one?

JG: No. You can say things to great competitors and you can motivate them. I've gone in the locker room very few times in my career and done that, but one of the times was in Philadelphia. We had made the playoffs, but we were stinking the joint up. And I called them everything in the book and said, "Hey, we're a bunch of frauds. This is a stinking, lousiest bunch of guys I've ever seen. You guys are an embarrassment to yourself and everything . . . "

When you say things like that, chances are you're going to get something back.

Q: Everybody hears about practicing: you play the way you practice. In all your experience, did you find that to be the case? Or were there situations where a team gave you a great week of practice and then just came out the wrong way? Or over the long haul, is that a true adage—that you will play as you practice?

JG: I would say that over the long haul it's true. But I have never been able to tell from week to week how a team is going to play from the way they practiced. Now, over the long haul, though, a hard-working team that gets after it, that knocks the heck out of people and is very competitive, that team's going to be successful.

I have had Super Bowl practices, two of them in particular, where I've said, "Hey, we've got to call this off. We're going to kill ourselves. Guys are killing each other." And sure enough, we played great. We killed them in the Super Bowls. But it's kind of rare. I've also been misled. The old deal in the locker room, "Hey, are they ready?" I've had locker rooms quieter than a church mouse. You say, "These guys are not going to hit a soul." But then they go out there and kill them. You have guys yacking away in there, and you're thinking, "These guys are going to stink the joint up. Their minds are not in it!" And they go right out there and kill them.

I never felt like I could put a handle on it.

Q: The use of time is a function of planning. What is the value of the use of time and how important is that in building a championship team?

JG: Coaching-wise? I think very important. Again, you're talking about shortcuts. I don't think there is one. You've got to put in a lot of time and thought, and one of the things that bugged me about coaching was there was almost never a time to really relax. I'd be sitting at home maybe watching TV and in the back of my mind, there was something in there that said, "Gosh you ought to be doing something else to help the team instead of sitting here relaxing." I mean there was never that thing where I could just totally relax except in the off-season. We had a little lake place, and I used to like that because I'd go down there and totally get away from it all. The whole time during that season, if I took two hours to do something, I always worried. Not that it was something I could really put my finger on, but it was in the back of my mind. On the other hand, I never took a film home the entire time I coached. And so that definitely helped me because when I shut that door, lots of time at night, I could somewhat relax. But there was always that thing there bugging me. I didn't enjoy that.

Q: To build a championship, how important is it to delegate some authority?

JG: I'd say that's one of the weak things for me. When something jumped up, I had a tendency that I was going to go solve it. That's always been my nature and my makeup. The same thing happens around here. We had a group come in and study our front office, the way we operated here and everything, and they said, "We want to show you what's really happening. This is the way the line of command is supposed to work." And they had it all drawn up. And they flipped the thing over and every line, every person in the building, went to me. When I hear something, I think, "Hey, I can fix that." And that's a weakness I think I have, although probably some part of it helped.

I'd say you have to delegate things. I used to, in football. I delegated the defense. I'd go over there and spend a day, three or four hours, with them, grading film, telling them what I thought, but in general, they had to work it out. Special teams had to do their thing. The front office, Bobby Beathard on picking players with Charley Casserly, had to do their thing.

You need to be able to delegate. But I have found, though, the best form of leadership is, "I'm going to be the first there; I'm going to be the last to leave." I've found leading by example is the easiest form of leadership. In other words, it's easy if you're there busting your butt and you're there early, to turn around to somebody and say, "Hey do this, do that." And they're going to do it. They say, "Hey, Joe's doing it. I'm going to do it." And I don't worry about saying something to somebody. "Hey, you need to do this or do that," because you're in the trenches in there and you're doing it yourself. I think it would be hard myself, to just sit back and delegate. I've heard people say that, "Hey, I coach the coaches. I don't do this and I don't that. And I go home and take a nap or something." For me, I think it would be awful hard to lead that way.

Q: You won Super Bowls with three different quarterbacks. Did you change your formula for success based on the personnel, or was the basic ingredient the same even though the guys behind the center were different?

JG: I think really good coaches adjust to people and their abilities. Coaches may have a system and all that, but when I watch most of the really good coaches of any kind, or the management of people, they adjusted to the talent they had. If you go all the way back to Shula, you'll see that's true. I was studying his stuff when he had Larry Csonka and those very successful teams of the early 1970s. They ran the heck out of the ball. That was their deal. And then Shula switched to Marino, and his team's throwing it all over the place. Don Coryell is considered a passing guru. Back when I was playing for him in college, we ran every stinking down. I was the tight end, started my last year and caught three passes. We never threw the football. We ran over the top of everybody. And then he got Don Horn in there and Haven Moses and a few guys, and started throwing and loved it. The next thing you know, he became Air Coryell. Coaches have a tendency after a while: when they get something that is very successful, they then go pick a player that will fit that role for them. You see what I'm saying? They have this thing going, and it seems to work. OK, now they go pick a guy that seems to fit in here and can do the same thing as the guy they have. But in general, I think you've got to take what you have and fit the system to it—if it's a John Riggins, you're going to do certain things; if it's Joe Washington, you're going to do different kinds of things; if it's Terry Metcalf, you're going to do other things. If it's Joe Theismann, who can run out of the pocket and do all these things, you're going to do that. If it's Randall Cunningham, you better be doing the things that Cunningham does. If it's Mark Rypien, you'd better not be trying to get him to do much of these things some of the other guys do. So I think you adjust to your talent, but I think you have a tendency, after a while, to pick the talent that fits some of the things you like to do.

Q: What is the best advice you've ever received in regard to what eventually propelled you to your success as a coach? Not necessarily related to sports even.

JG: I don't think anybody ever gave me something like that, that was one key. I think it was on-the-job training for me. I spent 28 years in coaching and I guess I spent 16 years getting ready, being an assistant. It was all those years, 16 years of working under different people and working with assistant coaches and working with players. It was a gradual accumulation of experience in working with people. I don't think I could point to one thing.

Q: Did you have a mentor, as such, when you look back over the guys that developed you into a final coaching product?

JG: In football? Yes. I think Don Coryell, who I played for, then coached for three different times. I coached for him at San Diego State, coached for him at the Cardinals, turned around and coached for him at San Diego. He probably did the most for my career because he had amazing ability to just gamble on things. He was one of the most gutsy guys ever. He took me when I was coaching and shifted me around. I had always coached offensive line, for 10 years, and Jim Hanifan had always coached backs. But when Coryell got the job with the St. Louis Cardinals, he called me and I said, "Hey, I'm not going to take the job, I'm going to try and coach defense here at Arkansas." He called me back and said, "Hey look, why don't you come up here and you take the backs. Hanifan will take the line." It was a gamble, but he gave me that opportunity. And later on, when I was at San Diego, he made me the offensive coordinator and let me work with the quarterbacks. One time he told me he was going to hire Ernie Zampese, who had coached defense his entire life. We didn't have anybody else on that staff out there that was really a good offensive person. Coryell said, "I'm going to take Ernie, and I'm going to put him with the offense." And I said, "That is the dumbest thing, Don, I've ever heard. We need help here. It's me and Hanifan. We need someone who's got offensive experience." In three weeks, Ernie Zampese was a better offensive coach than I was. I mean, Coryell had guts. I learned a lot from all those other head coaches, but I'd say Don was probably the one who meant the most to my career and gave me the most chances.

Q: Did your coaching philosophy develop over time?

JG: It was definitely things that I learned over time in how to treat people, how to motivate people, how to discipline people. And a lot of it, like I said, it's got to be a feel when you work with people. It can't be something you write in a book, and say "Hey, I'm going to go do this, this, and this." I think you've got to have a feel for working with people and I think nothing quite replaces the experience factor of really working with people and learning it on the job.

Q: Was there a point where your philosophy became completely set?

JG: I think you continue to change. I've said you change 30 percent a year, roughly. So if you're sitting still, in three years, you're out. But I did develop. The first year was kind of hectic, kind of grabbing. But very quickly there, we developed a little system with the Redskins—things we believed in, for instance running the football. I don't care if you can stack this thing up, there's probably one football team that won a Super Bowl that threw it all the time and that was Bill Walsh with the 49ers. And that probably ruined a lot of teams, because they tried to emulate that. In general, I believe you've got to run the football and play defense and special teams. And then we developed a system. You don't want the defense being able to see what you're working on week by week, so we changed a lot from week to week.

Q: And is it important to have a philosophy if you're a coach?

JG: Yes. I think, if you don't have convictions you're in trouble, because, believe me, you're going to be tested. You're going to be tested by the front office. You're going to be tested by losses. And one of the things that happens to coaches sometimes is they don't have anything to believe in. I think a lot of guys have gone to defeat—I've heard that over and over again—because they're changing from week to week. They're coaches who don't know what they believe. That's the first recipe for disaster. And normally, you'll find the good coaches—what they'll say about him at some point is, "This sucker is stubborn. He won't listen to anybody." And normally, I tell them that's a pretty good trait. You'd better look at that guy twice, because chances are that if he's that stubborn, then he's got convictions. He believes in something. So don't misrepresent stubbornness. Now I think he's got to be able to look and analyze when he's made a mistake. But don't misinterpret it.

I tell people, when they ask me about picking coaches, that I would get a guy who's got a little bit of an ego. I wouldn't let ego scare me too much. Of course you can take that too far, obviously, but I'm talking about he's got to believe in himself and he's going to be a little stubborn now, because he's got convictions. Because you're not going to shake him easily. He's going to analyze it and say, "No, I believe in this." There's plenty of times people came to me and said, "That one-back offense is dead." I've had people tell me, "You can't throw the ball in the one-back!" One of the league's great coaches told our front office people, "Hey, that's what's wrong with the Redskins." His team was beating us, and he told our front office people, "Hey, you can't throw the ball in the one-back." They came to me and said you've got to change and all this stuff. I said, "What? Who told you that?"

I remembered that, and the next time we played them, we threw for 410 yards.

Pat Head Summitt

Only UCLA's John Wooden has won more NCAA national basketball championships. Even before reaching her 47th birthday, University of Tennessee women's coach Pat Head Summitt has already coached 24 seasons and won six national championships and nearly 700 games.

Yet she had contemplated a job change when her team lost 10 games on its way to claiming a second straight national title in 1997. "It was pretty bad there for a while, though," she said of the up-and-down season. "I was questioning everything. I wasn't even sure we had the ability to compete, much less win a championship a few months later. I was more than a little surprised by the way we turned it around."

In the wake of that turnaround, Summitt then somehow found the energy to win a titanic recruiting battle for Naismith Award winner Tamika Catchings, the 6-foot daughter of former NBA center Harvey Catchings, and managed to sign three other prep All-Americans.

Despite the coup of those signings, Summitt is aware of the fallacy of expectations. Her highly regarded recruiting class of the early 1990s never won a national title and didn't even reach the Final Four until they were seniors.

Summitt, it seems, has seen every scenario over the past three decades. She was a mere graduate assistant when she was named to replace Margaret Hutson in 1974 as women's basketball coach at the University of Tennessee.

Her pay was a stipend. "It was about 250 or 260 bucks a month," she recalled. "My second year, I went full-time teaching and coaching and my salary was $8,900. I ate a lot of those really cheap hamburgers back then."

A recent pay raise has now boosted her salary package to about $400,000 a year, a sign of the progress in the women's game, progress that can be traced directly to her influence. Her program is the winningest in the history of women's basketball. "I think Tennessee has been a leader in women's basketball," she said. "The support we have had comes from the very top."

Her Lady Vols have won 55 of the 66 NCAA tournament games they've played. Even Wooden and Kentucky's famed Adolph Rupp can't match those numbers.

Summitt played collegiately at nearby University of Tennessee–Martin, where she developed an excellent all-around game, good enough to earn her a spot on the 1973 World University Games team. Her senior season in 1974 was interrupted by a knee injury, but Summitt battled back to make the 1976 Olympic team with which she earned a silver medal.

Eight years later, she coached the first United States women's team to bring home the gold medal. She did all of this, of course, as the very young head coach at Tennessee.

What followed would be national championships for her Vols in 1987, 1989, 1991, 1996, 1997, and 1998. She is just as proud, however, of the 100 percent graduation rate for all players who remained with her program four years. Her programs have also produced 10 Olympians, 14 Kodak All-Americans, 40 international players, and another 20 competing in American professional leagues.

It was thought that Summitt herself might move to the WNBA or its rival American League as women's professional basketball gained momentum in 1997. But she signed a contract extension with the University of Tennessee that will carry her past the millennium.

"I love coaching the collegiate game," she said.

Billy Packer: Is there any such thing as the thrill of victory?
Pat Head Summitt: Certainly. I think the thrill of victory comes when things all fit together and you see a team execute. In some cases, it varies with me as far as thrill of victory because different teams win in different fashions. Some are ugly; some are beautiful, but in the end there's always that thrill, and you accomplish as a team and as a staff a victory that is obviously significant to every person on the team or in that program.

Q: Is it possible to not obtain the championship and yet still feel a thrill of victory?
PHS: Well, that's tough for me. I think we've set a standard here in which it's hard to leave the court or end a season with a defeat and feel that we've really been victorious. However, there was an exception there. Two years ago, when we lost in the championship to Connecticut, I felt like we played a good game. We played well enough to win until the last four minutes, and obviously, they made

big plays and we didn't. So I didn't walk off the court feeling the season was a loss or the game was a total loss or a total disaster because we had had great year, but we did not leave the year with a championship.

Q:How about the agony of defeat, and how long does that weigh on you?

PHS:(Laughing.) Oh, I hate to lose. I do. I just absolutely get physically sick. How long does it weigh on you? I think it all goes back to how you actually lost the game. Was it a matter of effort or execution? Was it a matter of players? You know there are situations, there have been times when we were just outmatched. I think you walk away from that and you handle it. You put things in perspective and you say, "We lost to a better opponent today." When I really struggle is when I feel it comes down to something we can control—we being the players and staff. And if it's effort, then obviously I'm usually upset with the players and everyone else. If it's execution, I'm the first to take blame for that because that's my job, to prepare and to be ready to execute and to hope that a team will go out and respond.

Q:In regard to putting together a championship team, what do you think are the key ingredients?

PHS:Well, I think if you're talking in terms of just putting together a team that can eventually compete for a championship, there's a long list there. You win with players. So you want the positions intact. You want a "go-to" player in the paint. Obviously, if I'm looking at two positions, I'm looking down the middle. I want my go-to player in the paint and I want that point guard that can be the quarterback of our basketball team. I think when you get to the women's game now, versus say maybe five years ago, you really have to have versatile players. You have to have creators and you have to have shooters. I think you have to be able to really spread the floor, and the three-point shot is obviously an important part of the game. However, we won the championship last year and we were 12th out of 12 teams in our league in three-point shooting. But I think that if you get all the pieces to the puzzle, then you're looking at players that are really very versatile, and no weaknesses, basically. You can handle it. You can pass it. You can shoot it off the pass. You can put it on the floor. You can pound it inside. Philosophically, for me—in looking at a championship team—I've always felt that you had to go out and play great defense every night and board with people. And that's been, just philosophically, what we've tried to preach; that offense sells tickets, defense wins games, rebounds win championships. If we get our personnel to buy into our system, and obviously taking care of the ball and shot selection go hand-in-hand with our defense and our boards. So, to me, it's having that personnel and understanding also that not every player is a go-to player. For us, Chamique Holdsclaw is a go-to player. We have Renee Laxton, who is more of a role player. And when you're building a championship team, it's important that everyone understands her role. We preach team concept. We're not a star system, but we certainly know that roles will vary among players.

Q: Aside from the raw talent and personnel, looking back at your championship teams, was there any common thread that they all seemed to have in terms of things other than talent?

PHS: I think chemistry has been really good for us when we've won championships. I think when you have good chemistry, you're looking at an unselfish group; which leads to a team concept which leads to players that will do the little things. They'll do the dirty work and let the better players step up and really rise to the challenge of execution. When I say that, I mean we've got players or we've had players like, say, on our '87 team, for example, that knew they would come in the last two minutes of a game, if we were in a delay, and handle the ball for us. They would come in, obviously, if the player in front of them got in foul trouble. They had to set screens. They had to make passes. They had to be a defensive specialist. So, I think it would be the chemistry and the unselfishness in looking at handling their role for the good of the team and not being disruptive. You can tell an awful lot about a basketball team in watching their bench. When we've had championship teams, our bench has really been as much into the game as our people on the floor.

Q: What is your take on motivation?

PHS: What you see is what you get, is what I think for the most part. There can be short-term motivation, but the purest form of motivation is self-motivation. Now while I think I might be able to come in and motivate individuals, I think that unless they have it inside, unless every day they want to step out and compete—and it's important that you get competitors in your program— but unless they really want to do it themselves, it's not going to be anything that will be consistent or long range. I don't think you can take a 17- or 18-year-old and change her personality. You may alter their behavior for a short period of time, but I just go back to "what you see is what you get." And that's why I really like to understand personalities—not that there is a right or wrong personality—but when we're going to play basketball, there's some that I prefer to be on the floor than others.

Q:How important do you think it is for the leader of a championship team to establish personal relationships with those athletes he or she works with?

PHS:I really think it's the only way. Whether you're winning championships or playing games at a different level, I think a responsibility that I have is more than just being a coach. You know, we're called a coach; what is a coach? Well, a coach wears a lot of different hats. I mean a coach can be a teacher, a mother or a father, a friend, a counselor, a psychologist. Certainly, my philosophy and the system that we have here at Tennessee is that we see three dimensions that we must be prepared to deal with: the person, the player, the student. I think as a coach, I need to understand it's more than X's and O's. It's about caring about individuals. It's helping with time management or helping them with a family crisis or being there to let them know, first and foremost, that we care about them as individuals. And then that carries over right into academics. I mean, we have a 100 percent graduation by our players, but that's by design. That's important. That's why I have a job. That's why they're here. And so they understand, hopefully—if they are in line with our thinking, that "I'm more than a basketball player. That's a small part of my life." Basketball is a way in which we teach life skills. And by teaching these life skills—we can only teach these life skills if we're really trying to prepare young student-athletes for life after basketball—and that's a commitment we've had in place and will always be in place in this program. And it's been key in a championship situation. Chamique Holdsclaw said [in 1997] after we won, one of the first things that came across the air was, "I love Tennessee, it's a great place," but she made reference to the fact that the coaches care about me as a person, and I think you have to have that.

Q: The word "potential." We hear it so often about teams, about individuals. Is it a curse or is it something that you can see and you can bring out in people? Or is it something where a person has potential sometimes and it never happens?

PHS: Well, certainly we talk potential a lot in this game, and if we see a great athlete, we expect her to become a great player. If we see a great player, we think she should perform at a certain level. Obviously, we have a standard set in our mind for what a great athlete should do, or what a great basketball player should be able to do. But players don't reach that potential because of physical abilities alone. They have to have that motivation, and they have to have, really, desire and commitment to the game. I could be the most knowledgeable coach in America, and not work at it, and then I'm below average. I could be the most talented basketball player in the country, but not really work hard, and so therefore I will never really reach my potential. I always tell our coaches in recruiting, I don't want to have to go out and use my imagination. I want to go out and see what a player is willing to commit to do on the floor. And then if we need to work on skills, that's fine. But that heart and that head, is so important when you're talking potential and development.

Q: In regard to satisfactions and disappointments in your life as a coach, what would be your greatest satisfaction?

PHS: The consistency that we have been able to maintain in this program in the area of graduation rate and national contenders. It's not necessarily that we've won NCAA championships but we've been in the hunt every year, and we've been able to handle success, and that's been a real challenge. We've been able to handle success in the classroom, and continue to promote academics. So I would have to say it's been twofold; it's been the consistency in our academic and athletic standards and performance in this program.

Q: In regard to the great successes that you've had, is there ever the fear of failure?

PHS: I've had the fear of failure, sure. But, you know, really it's not something I've really focused on. And when I think about it, recently, I don't think I've thought much about losing. I think that it's really important, as a competitor, as a coach, as a teacher, to focus on what you need to do and what you need to make happen, and not what could happen. And so, our emphasis is on execution, not winning. We're talking about how we need to go out and perform today. And if you execute and you're prepared, then that takes care of it.

I'm not even going to talk about failure. That doesn't enter my mind. That might be something that crosses my mind after a bad practice. I might say, "If we don't do better than this, we're going to get beat." But when it comes to game time, I don't ever think about losing.

Q: And you never think about the fact that you've accomplished so much, and, "Gee, suppose next year we're not very good, or suppose I've reached the peak of my abilities as a coach?"

PHS: No. No, not at all. If I had that fear, I'd probably go out with a championship, and this last one would have been a good one. I've had people say, teasing me, maybe family members, "Don't stay in it. Look what's happened to so-and-so in the profession. He's lost his touch. Or she can't relate to young people anymore."

I think the thing I've tried to do, Billy, is really stay in tune with change. And change is not necessarily bad or negative. A lot of people will say, "Wow, you've really changed, you've mellowed." I view change as positive and right along that line, as long as I'm willing to make those changes and get to know the young people in today's world and continue to study the game, then we're not going to lose here. Not much. We may lose a little, but we're getting players, and as long as you get players, you're going to win a lot.

Q:When you were first getting started, did you think that there were potentially any shortcuts to success? Or do you see any now that you've had so much success?

PHS:No, my staff would tell you I always do things the hard way, anyway. I think that's just within my personality. I don't think there are any shortcuts. I think there's a right way to do things. I am constantly preaching that, even to our players. We don't want to take shortcuts. We want to go that extra mile and do the extra work. I think mentally that gives you an edge because, if you do cut corners, then you know in the back of your mind that you haven't really paid the price, that you're not really as prepared as you need to be. And we want to cover our bases in terms of preparation.

Q:The word "loyalty," we hear so much about it now. Particularly, you're in an environment where a lot of it is required. You've got the academic side of life. You have the sports side of life. Is it, and does it have to be, a two-way street with your ballplayers?

PHS:Definitely. I think it has to be a commitment with both parties. It starts with your staff and goes through with your team. We talk an awful lot about loyalty and, we view our program, our staff, our team as a family. And we're here to protect each other. We may have our differences along the way, and we may have an argument like you have with your family. We may be able to talk about each other face-to-face, but no one else is going to talk about a team member or our program. We spend a lot of time on the subject of loyalty, and family, and what our commitment will be to each other. I think that goes hand-in-hand with respect. You have to have the loyalty and you have to have the respect. And with your players, yes, it needs to be in place. But it's not something you assume will happen. It's something you really work on and build on.

Q: Do you have personal and team goals that are set before the year? Do you sit down before the year and say, "I think we can be X," or do the goals just evolve? What are your goals?

PHS: Well, I think the program has really set a standard, and every player knows it. When I'm recruiting players, invariably, we talk about winning championships. That's a given. And every year we want to do our best to win a national championship and an SEC championship. But, what I do is I leave it up to each team. It's an individual situation for each team in terms of what their goals are. We've not talked about it before the start of our season, we've not discussed their goals. We will get to that, and we will establish if they want to win 20 games, 20-plus games. It depends. I think players can be realistic for the most part. I think they're realistic. I've had some teams in the past that wanted to go undefeated. I didn't want that to be a goal. I really didn't. I let them set that goal, but we didn't reach that goal. We did go undefeated three years in the toughest conference in women's basketball, and that was their goal, which served as a great motivation for us during that time. So I think it's important to allow players to participate in establishing goals. For me personally, it's to win the championship every year or to put a team in that position.

Q: Suppose you've got one spot, two players. What characteristic will be more important in terms of the final
championship? The physical ability or the mental?

PHS: You've got one player to pick for a championship. I would
say the mental. I think when you get to that stage, knowing also what the other four people are going to look like,
I want a player that's going to be able to make the good
decisions, think on her feet. I guess it was Lou Holtz who
said, "I'd rather have a slow person in the right spot than
a quick person in the wrong spot." I think certainly it's
true in the sport of basketball that execution is as much
mental as anything. And I'd take that smart player.

Q: In regard to the word "competitor," is this something
that you see in a person and bring out? Is competitiveness something that players either have or they don't?
And can you make a team more competitive, or is it just
something that's God-given?

PHS: Well, I think you can see it in individuals, first of all. I look
for competitors. I look for competitors when I'm recruiting.
I watch players play to see how they handle success and
failure. I look for players from winning programs because I
know they've been in competitive situations, and they've
won and they understand how to win. Can you bring it out?
I think you can bring some of that out, but I don't think that
you can all of a sudden make someone a great competitor.
They either have it or they don't. Peer pressure, game situations and practice, obviously you can simulate some things
in the practice that I think can stimulate more of a mind-set,
"I want to win, I'm going to compete." But that's nothing in
comparison to having a player that steps out there and says,
"All right, I'm winning; I want to win today." And when
you work on a team, or work with a team, you hope that
your competitors will be able to rub off on the other players,
and I think they do. Michelle Marciniak, her competitive

spirit was contagious. And she brought emotion to the court for other players. And that's something that I think can happen and create some change. But again, if you got it, you got it. If they don't, don't expect them to be at the top of their game as a competitor.

Q: The biggest career mistake that you've made?

PHS: (Laughing.) Oh gosh, I've made so many. The biggest career mistake? Probably when I coached the Pan Am Games in Puerto Rico, and we had a situation with some controversy on our team about shoes and which shoe in particular some players wanted to wear. And we had hoped to move out of the village into the hotel, and then we were told at the last minute by the USOC we could not. And the men were out of the village. We had some adversity come up, and we didn't handle it well. When we went to the court, we weren't ready to play. If I could have that day over again, I think I could get those players better prepared mentally. I just thought I did a poor job. I didn't have them ready to play, and it cost us a gold medal.

Q: In regard to preparation, what is more important—the day-to-day preparation or sitting on that bench making adjustments during the course of the game?

PHS: Day-to-day preparation. Ideally, you want players to go out and play and make a lot of those decisions. And that limits what you'll have to do in a game. The game's important, but all that preparation, day to day, will prepare players, and if players are prepared then you get to sit and watch. Yes, you need to be there and ready to make some adjustments but the adjustments are few if they're ready to play.

Q: In regard to the adage that teams play as they practice, have you found that to be true, or are there times when it's something you really can't forecast?

PHS: For the most part, I would agree with that. I think that basically what we try to do is determine, one, how we want to play, and once we determine style and how they want, as a team, to perform, than that's the way we expect them to perform every day in practice. So it becomes a habit. So that when the game starts, you've already had enough practices in game situations, and when the game starts, it's just a carryover, an extension of practice. I would have to say it all starts right there.

Q: Pat, nobody is more organized than you are, so let's try to quantify this a little bit. The use of time in the preparation and the proper use of time, how important is that to success of a championship team?

PHS: Well, I think it's important. I think time management and organization are obviously critical in terms of how, as a coach, I manage my time to allow me to prepare and organize for players' time. And certainly, time in practice, time in the game, we're constantly working with a clock, time and possession. And I try to look at my job the same way. I have X number of hours in my day, and I need time to watch film, I need time to prepare for practice, I need time for staff meetings. Then when I get to a court, I'm working with a clock constantly. So in this business, it's critical. A time-out, is what, 60 seconds, maybe 90 seconds? I talk to my staff, organization, my players about the need to understand how to position themselves on the bench, how to really listen. The communication there is critical. In this business, if you're not aware of time then you're not very prepared.

Q: In regard to the delegation of authority, you mentioned your staff. And we see again, there are different philosophies on the part of coaches. How important do you think the delegation of authority is in developing a staff that can build a championship?

PHS: I think first of all, it depends on individual philosophy, and I'll certainly give you mine. If you're trying to develop coaches to move on in the profession, then I think you may see them as learning from you. I have a veteran staff. I want a veteran staff. I feel like with 29 players out now as coaches, or former GAs as coaches, I want a staff that's going to help the program and help the basketball team, and be able to help me on a daily basis. So, I delegate a lot. I think it's important to hire people that you think are smarter than you, or better than you in certain areas, whether it's in recruiting or it's specific to X's and O's, or it's personality in dealing with player relationships. And then I delegate an awful lot. We have over 80 years of experience, coaching experience, on our staff. That's been a real key for us. We can go to practice. We've already talked philosophy. We can break down our teaching and be very specific. We can spend a lot of time with individuals. We can spend more time in watching film because there is a trust, that loyalty, and therefore our staff has the freedom. Not only do I want to delegate, I want to give them the freedom then to go operate.

Q: **In regard to your philosophy as a coach, do you continue to build it? Was were your thoughts about how to put together a program the first day you took the job here; how much has it changed over the years? And is it important to have a philosophy?**

PHS: It's important to have a philosophy. When I took over the program, I'm not sure I had one. I was 22 years old. It was my first coaching job. I was really in over my head, and so mine was just day to day—trial and error. And what I realized, and certainly learned very quickly, is that you've got to have a system. And I'm not sure that the first 10 years I had what I would call a consistent system. Defense was always very important in terms of my philosophy and how I wanted our teams to play. The defense, the work ethic was there. Offensively, we're very structured. I think that with my personality, people would probably say, "Pat has to have too much control on the offensive end." But I think as time went along, and I had an opportunity to really study the game, certainly coaching the '84 team, the Olympic team, just the two years prior to that, in scouting the international clubs, I learned more basketball in those two years than I had learned prior to that. And I think that I certainly established a consistent philosophy from that time on because I got to watch every style of offense and defense, and just a variety of philosophies. And it was overwhelming. But I was thinking, "I've got to have a system." So certainly, prior to '84, I felt very committed to a system.

Q: **It's kind of interesting you mention '84—and I'm going to digress here just a little bit—the game of basketball was played by women for almost exactly the same number of years as it was played by men, and yet you really have been involved with the incredible growth of the American game for women, and accepted not only nationally, but internationally. Take me back to when you took over the Olympic program, in effect, when there was no chance to win. As a matter of fact, it was almost ridiculous to think the American women could compete against the Soviet Union at that time. What was that like, that challenge, and how much did you look forward to it, or did you feel it was a challenge that would be impossible to ever handle?**

PHS: Well, I first played against the Soviets, competing against the Soviets as a player. And I was a junior in college. It was in '73. And Billie Moore, who was our '76 Olympic coach, was the assistant there. We went to the World University Games, and they beat us in the opening game by

51 points. It was just incredible. I just can't tell you how we were so overwhelmed. They were so much better, and they executed. For them to shoot 75–80 percent was just the norm. They could execute unlike any women's or men's team that I had seen play. But when I came back and we played in '76 and Billie was our head coach there, and we lost to the Soviets, I even thought in that time frame we're going to close the gap here. I started coaching internationally in '77, and didn't have a chance to compete against the Soviets until—what? '79—and, you know, we went to the wire with them. From '79–'80, we started playing much closer. And then '83 in the World Championships, we should have beaten them. I think I made a defensive mistake as a coach at that particular game. I should have put Anne Donovan on the ball. She's 6'8", and pressured the inbounds. We didn't switch on a down screen. I knew who was going to get the ball, and they won. They won at the buzzer. But we were in a position where I really felt we could get them in '84. Unfortunately, because of the boycott they were not there. It was a great disappointment because I really felt, "We're going to beat these guys this time around."

Q: You give advice so often now to coaches and players and young people coming along. What was the best advice you were ever given that's helped you develop championships?

PHS: Without question some of the best advice that I received came from Billie Moore. She's the most professional person I've ever known. And her advice to me was to always do things the right way and be a professional. And I think that's really helped me. Her advice was that there's a right way and a wrong way to do things, things are black and white. Do not live in the gray. Do not move into the gray for any decision. Keep things as they should be, and do them the right way.

Q: In regard to Billie, obviously, I've seen her teams practice. Without question, if you ever saw one of her teams practice, watched her execute in the game, Billie could have coached men or women on any level, and done it successfully. How difficult was it for you and other coaches of women's basketball to feel the acceptance that you now have? Was there ever a time you felt it was never going to come? Or am I being naive to say that it has come?

PHS: I never concerned myself with that. I just wanted to do the job I was doing, and do it to the best of my ability, and make a difference for young women. I thought that was just a matter of, it'll happen. Another thing bothered me more than the question, when will the coaches be accepted? What bothered me was, when will people out there, when will the public, so to speak, appreciate the work and the execution, and the level of play of the women's game? I wondered if that would ever happen.

Q: Do you feel it's here?

PHS: I do. I think we've arrived. The media, the television exposure is just tremendous. The impact has been phenomenal, and not only in the last five years, but even in the last year. With the ABL and the WNBA, there's obviously some more opportunity for exposure and for us to establish ourselves. But we can't rest on that. We have to continue to promote our game.

Q: You know we have seen, obviously, some male coaches have championship teams on the female side. Do you ever think you'll see the day that we have a female coach such as yourself who certainly would be capable of coaching a men's championship team?

PHS: I don't know, Billy. I don't think I'll live to see it. I think there's still a barrier. If you look at society and you look at the women's game and what's expected, I think women are expected to coach women. I think it's okay for men to coach both. Will that ever change? We have some women now even coaching on the high school level or junior college, maybe a Division II or III school. But Division I? Never say never, but I would not anticipate as a head coach that we would see that in our lifetime.

Q: Well—I'll throw out a crazy one. Will we see a woman president of the United States before we see a woman lead a team to a national men's championship? Which one comes first?
PHS: Yes. Yes.

Q: A woman president?
PHS: Yes.

Q: (Laughing.) Oh, that's kind of tough. Let's talk about discipline, can a team win a championship without it?
PHS: I've seen a couple that I thought were not very disciplined win championships, but I think discipline is a must in any program. If you don't have discipline, then you're a long shot from winning the championship even if you've got great players, and even if you've got an outstanding staff. I think in order to win championships, you have to have some discipline in the program.

Q: You have had so much success on all levels. What keeps you motivated to want to do it again?
PHS: Well, I love the game. I have a tremendous passion for the game and for working with young people. It's something that motivates me to go out and work on a daily basis with individuals, and watch them develop—and to see their game, obviously, to see them get better, to see the results right there. You get instant feedback in this

profession. And I like that, whether it's good or bad. We're constantly being reinforced for what we're doing on a daily basis. I love working with kids. I mean I just love it. If I were not coaching—and I've often wondered this— I'd be in a classroom somewhere. I'd be working with kids on a playground. I'd be, obviously, somewhere spending my time with young people. They give me energy. I just love it. It's in my system so that's why I keep on doing it.

Chuck Noll

Chuck Noll spent his playing days running plays in and out as a guard in Paul Brown's Cleveland Browns offense. In 1969, at age 37, he was named head coach of the Pittsburgh Steelers, a team that had enjoyed just eight winning seasons in its previous 36 years of operation. "We will change history," Noll promised his first day on the job.

He never quite accomplished that, of course, but he did amazing things with the team's present and future, beginning with his very first draft selection, defensive tackle Mean Joe Greene out of North Texas State. Also in that '69 draft was defensive end L. C. Greenwood.

A year later came quarterback Terry Bradshaw and cornerback deluxe Mel Blount. Linebacker Jack Ham was the prize of the '71 draft, along with safety Mike Wagner and defensive linemen Ernie Holmes and Dwight White. From 1972, the Steelers harvested running back Franco Harris. But 1974 was the best of all, bringing receivers Lynn Swann and John Stallworth, linebacker Jack Lambert and center Mike Webster.

"Weapons," was how the young coach described his draft picks. The first sign that Noll was going to be able to turn the Steelers around in a big way came in December 1972 when Harris made the "Immaculate Reception" that defeated the Oakland Raiders and gave the Steelers the first playoff win in their long, miserable history. It was obvious the team's fortunes had changed. The major key was the "Steel Curtain" defense, led by Greene and his cohorts on the line.

By January 1975, Noll and his Steelers claimed their first Super Bowl, a 16–6 thumping of the Minnesota Vikings. Over the next five seasons, they would add three more Super Bowl titles, including two victories over the Dallas Cowboys. The Steelers' fourth title came in 1979, over the Los Angeles Rams. Through it all, Noll maintained a low-key, intense approach. "Winning a fourth Super Bowl should put us in a special category," Blount said in '79. "I think this is the best team ever assembled. They talk about Vince Lombardi, but I think the Chuck Noll era is even greater."

Billy Packer: Chuck, is there such a thing as the thrill of victory?
Chuck Noll: (Laughing.) Well, you know, when you prepare your people properly, and they're grounded in the fundamentals, you expect to win. And victory is not a thrill, as such. It's your stepping-stone to the next thing. The preparation has always been the key, getting ready for it, and getting your people ready to meet all the situations.

Q: So, that thrill of victory is not something that's lingering? You're on to the next challenge when it happens?

CN: Oh, very much. When the game is over, the preparation for next week starts. You have, maybe, a few hours, and you start thinking about the next opponent. But the preparation was always the key, the fun part, getting everything going. And then you play the game and you expect to play it well. If you don't, it's very disappointing, obviously.

Q: Well then, how about the agony of defeat?

CN: When you lose, you know you're not going in the right direction in a sense. You may be asking people to do things they can't do. You may have misjudged your opponent or whatever, but the defeat is a great learning situation because it makes you probe a little bit, makes you go back and think about what you're doing and try to get on the right track. I spoke to a group one time, and the CEO told me, "You know, you're lucky, you've got a scoreboard." I didn't know what he meant at first, but that's right. When you keep score, you don't go off on a tangent, and continue going in a direction because you have something that tells you, "Hey buddy, you'd better get it right. You'd better look at things again."

Q: What do you think is the key ingredient of a championship team?

CN: People. You know you can't do it without the talent. There's a difference. I mean there are a lot of talented players around, but you have to have talented players who are good people. And that's really the difference. Attitude is the thing that separates people, by far. You have to be ready to work together. You have to function; football is the quintessential team sport. You don't do it by yourself. It's something that everybody has to play a part, everybody has to contribute. When I go out, and I talk to a group, I try to throw out the word "teamwork." We used to have a key phrase for it. It was, "whatever it takes." You do what you have to do to make the team successful. And that means the effort, that means carrying the load. You don't sit out there and measure someone else's contribution, and then match that. That's losing.

Q: Chuck, were you in situations where without the best talent you were able to maximize the circumstances?

CN: You know, that's tough to say. It really is. You know we always wanted to win. We wanted to put our best foot forward. We wanted the best foot forward for each player, so you try to not ask somebody to do something he couldn't do. You wanted to make sure that they were able to do it, and you put a game plan together for your season based on everybody showing their best side.

Q: Is motivation something necessary to create a winner, or do winners already have inside them self-motivation?

CN: It begins with self-motivation. I don't question anybody who comes out on the football field. But some are motivated greater than others. It really comes back to if you have to have exterior motivation. I'm talking about if you have to have someone kicking you in the fanny to make you go. That's only going to work while someone's kicking you in the fanny. There are times you're going to be out on the field and you're by yourself, and you have to reach down and pick it up. There may be guys around you that motivate you as well as a coach, for example. We were playing with as many as 50 people sometimes, and you're not going to get into each one. They have to be able to rub off on one another, and we were fortunate to have that kind of situation.

Q: Could you name somebody that in your mind, had that supreme self-motivation. And then maybe somebody

who developed it as he went along with his character building?

CN: Well, probably, I could say that the guys that we had really had the desire to win—which is what it takes. They have to want to do it. I've had fathers come up to me and say, "Hey, I've got this talented kid, all he needs is a coach to motivate him." Well, if the kid doesn't want to do it, there is no motivation that's going to do it. Maybe the father wants him to do it. You know, the father is motivated, but the son may want to play the piano and not play on the football field. And if he doesn't want it deeply, himself, it's not going to work. It doesn't matter who's yelling at him or screaming, which is the normal thought of motivation. Motivation, in my mind, was always there's a "what-to-do" and a "how-to." The what-to is easy, but the how-to, the technique that makes it happen, is where we'd spend a lot of practice time. And when people know how to do it, then they want to go out and do it. So motivation was not yelling at them and screaming. That's not going to cut it, but if you give them an assignment and work on the technique that gets it done, then you're going to have guys who want to do it. And to me, that's motivation.

Q: **So many times we see championship teams and you see sometimes the participants talk about the love for each other. There are other times we see championship teams, and the guys don't even seem to get along. Are personal relationships necessary to have a championship team? Do they have to be positive personal relationships?**

CN: Well, personal relationships, I'm not so sure. What happens, I think, is when you develop the bond or a trust where you say, "I know this guy that's playing next to me is going to do his job because he's demonstrated that he can do it." Now he may be sick or he may have an injury or he may have something that's going to slow him down, but the other members of the team trust him to do his best. And you have that kind of a trust relationship that you build over time. And if you have that, some people call it love. You know, we had our teams get together 10 years after for reunions. And you come back and the spark is still there. You can see it. They respect one another. They trust one another. They know that if I'm trouble, this guy's going to pick it up for me. It's that kind of thing that makes for championship teams. And that's something that builds over a period of time.

Q: As the leader of the championship unit, can you sense and do you have to sense when there is somebody out of synch with the rest of the team, somebody who could become a cancer that would kill the opportunity for a championship?

CN: Very much. You have to be a team member. You have to put the team first. You know you can get a lot of people that are "I Guys." They want to do it for themselves. They say, "I've got this contract where if I carry the ball this many times I'm going to get more money." All those kind of things are wedges that get in the way of "whatever it takes," of the team mentality. One of the impediments to teamwork are people who are concerned about credit. They say "I'm doing that, I should get the credit." Well, if the team's successful, there's enough credit for everybody. If the team isn't, then the same guy's going to point the finger and say, "It's his fault." That's a destructive thing. You're never going to be a champion if you're a finger-pointer. The only finger pointed is at the mirror. You take care of yourself. You're the only one that you can control. And you have to have that kind of attitude. Again it comes back to, as I said earlier, attitude separates people. If I'm an "I Guy," and it's only me, I'm not going to be a good team member and I'm not going to build a trust relationship. And guys are not going to build that bond. You can have people like that, that can be great talents, but they can destroy your team. Ultimately, the best team wins. Not the best individual. Football is not track. This is the quintessential team game.

Q: Is it more difficult to maintain success or is it more difficult to get to that level where you are number one?

CN: That depends on your people. If you can maintain your attitude, then you can maintain this winning thing. Now there are other factors, obviously. Injury. And there's a certain amount of luck that's involved in it. But attitudes change. You can have people who can be successful one year and they play well as a team, and all of the sudden, they want to write books or do endorsements and they forget about what got them there. The hard work and functioning as a team. Suddenly you turn that "I" thing around a little bit and it all falls apart. You know, that's why it takes special people. Attitudes change. You can see guys who come to the end of the road, for example. They know, "This is my last year. Now I'm not concerned about being the best or being the best team. I'm worried about being paid," for example. And that gets in the way. So, it really comes back to attitude. As long as your attitude is that same winning attitude, that "whatever it takes," you're in good shape.

Q: If you think about the great Steeler teams, you think of the "Immaculate Reception" and Franco Harris. Was he there because he was supposed to be there, or were you guys just lucky on that play?

CN: I think it goes back to Franco's beginning in football, something he may have gotten at Penn State or in high school or whatever. You know, when your assignment is over, you don't stop. You want to see what else you can do. And that's exactly what happened. Franco had an assignment. He carried it out, and then he saw the scramble happen, so he started downfield to be a receiver, and the ball was thrown down. And he started reacting to the ball because you want to get down there and see if you can become a blocker, that type of thing. These are all attitudes, habits that are built in practice. You get a lot of people who say, "Aww, you just want to play the games, you don't want to have to worry about practice." Well, practice is where the habits are formed. That's where your trust relationships are built. That's where all the good things in putting a team together happen, and that's why it's so important, and that's why that happened. It was the culmination of good practice.

Q: One of the things we hear in sports and in business is the word "potential." Is potential almost a dangerous word when you start thinking about developing a winning team?

CN: Well, no, you'd like to have potential (laughing). If your potential is limited, you're not going to go very far. But you may have potential, and usually you speak in terms of individual talent when you say potential. Melding it together. Getting them to work together. Getting them to be a team is when you start realizing potential. Some people call it synergism. It's one of those things where the whole is never equal to the sum of its parts when you start talking about performance on a football field. Maybe in mathematics or in science or in machinery you can add up the parts and you're going to have the whole. But when you're talking about a team, it's never the whole is equal to the sum of its parts. It's either greater than or less than depending on how they work together. That's really the quintessential team. If you do work together, well, you're going to be greater than the parts that are thrown together.

Q: What's your greatest satisfaction looking back in terms of what you put together with those championship teams?

CN: It comes back to people, again. Having been associated with people with great attitudes. We talked about before about what happens when you come together, when you have success and when you're working together, there's the bond. If it's not working, then you have a disdain for one another. (Laughing.) It works that way. So it behooves everybody to develop that attitude. It comes back to, where do these kinds of attitudes come from? And in a sense, the primary team is the family, a marriage. And if you get people that haven't experienced that good team-work, you have to make them understand its value. That's where you develop the attitudes that make winning possible. The big thing is where do these attitudes come from? Basically winning attitudes start in the home. You can develop some of it outside, on the football field.

Q: As a coach, how do you face failure?

CN: Well, number one, you don't want to have fear of failure because that kind of locks you in. It doesn't allow you to realize your potential, if you go out there with the idea, "I might fail." You go out and you just let it happen, let it flow, and if you've prepared yourself properly, failure is something that you don't expect. You expect to have success. And I think that's an attitude again, that you have to develop.

Q: When you first got into coaching did you find people to imitate? Did you find shortcuts to take?

CN: Well, number one, you never want to be an imitator. You know, if you're an imitator, you're a poor second. If you want to be a champion, you have to do what you do. You have to stay within your personality. You have to do what you think is right. If you are wishy-washy and flip-flop because someone else is having success with this particular thing, or if you want to go to that offense or you want to make all kinds of changes, all you're going to do is screw yourself up. You have to have basic beliefs. I was fortunate enough to grow up with coaches that had that philosophy—coming probably from Paul Brown. You had to be basically sound. If you're basically sound and fundamentally sound, then it's going to go, it's going to fall into place. But you don't want to go from one end of the spectrum to the other. Somebody's having success with the run-and-shoot or someone may have a fast break offense, and you haven't got fast break people. You can't do what they're doing. You have to meld your people, do what they do best, put their best foot forward and do what you believe in.

Q: Is loyalty a two-way street between coaches and players?
CN: That's part of the trust relationship until the agents come in and try and drive a wedge (laughing). That's what it's all about. There has to be a trust between players, between players on offense and defense. You can't have coaches fighting coaches, offense against defense, that type of thing. I mean there has to be a oneness of thought, a singleness of purpose, and then the attitude that goes with it.

Q: What was your feeling about goals? What was the structure of your goals, if you did set them?
CN: They were always team goals. Individual goals were never something that we stressed. We wanted to do it as a team. In fact, contract structures were set up that way. Team merit. You know, if the team was successful, then everybody should benefit.

Q: So your goals were always oriented that way? You didn't sit down and say, "Well, let's see, this year I think we can be 9–3," or this year, we can do things of that nature?

CN: No, not really. We wanted to win every game. And you set out to win every game. When you didn't, it was a disappointment, obviously. Our goal was to be the best team. We had goals where we wanted to improve our running game or our passing game or defensively, we wanted more turnovers. We wanted to structure things that way, but they're team goals, not individual.

Q: You had players like Terry Bradshaw and Mean Joe Greene, guys that provided tremendous leadership but who had much different personalities. How did you identify leadership potential?

CN: We used to preach that everybody's a leader. You're either a negative leader or you're a positive leader. But everybody contributes, and everybody has to be a part of it. And again, when someone may not be able to carry the load, someone else has to step up. That's the whole idea of whatever it takes. You're not always going to be a hundred percent healthy; you're not always going to meet the same challenge. The burden may be on our offense or on our defensive line, for example, or on our secondary because of the other team's offense or the other team's defense. The burden shifts, and you've got to be able to step up and carry the load when you need to. So that's the kind of leadership we want. Everybody's a leader. Now if you have someone who is a complainer, that guy's not doing it, a finger-pointer, that's negative leadership. Leadership comes from everybody.

Q: Can you turn a negative leader around?

CN: Sometimes. If the guys that carry the load, your best people, have the great attitude and are good team players, then you might be able to carry a few that are a negative influence. If your good people can carry you, it's fine, but you're looking to replace negative leaders. There's no question.

Q: If you're making team cuts and it comes down to a guy with smarts or a guy with more physical talent, which would you opt for?
CN: Well, you really need both.

Q: I'm making you make a choice (laughing).
CN: That's a difficult thing to say because you have to have the real people there. Is the potential there to get smarter, in a sense, or to get more experience? There are some people that come and right from the get-go, they have a super grasp of what you're trying to do, and some, it takes a while. That's why you have taxi squads and all kinds of things. When you have to make a decision, you try to evaluate for the long term as opposed to short term. If you're going to keep somebody and he's going to keep screwing up for you, you don't want him around. Again, it comes back to your perception or what you believe is long-term value to the team, not immediate, but long-term.

Q: Terry Bradshaw was once saddled with the misrepresentation that he wasn't very smart.
CN: Well, let me say this first, that's a bad rap.

Q: Obviously, I know he's a very bright guy.
CN: Terry called his own plays. In an era when the plays were being sent in from the bench, so that's number one. I came up in the Paul Brown system where I was one of the messenger guards, also, carrying the plays.

Q: With Otto Graham, who was considered brilliant, right?

CN: Who was fine. But, you know, that system doesn't lend itself to the quarterback being in control on the field. That's why we spent a lot of time in meetings, in preparation, quarterback preparation meetings, going over what we wanted to do, and Terry Bradshaw did a good job of that. He called his own plays and controlled it, and I think that had a beneficial effect on our football team. Then the media gets ahold of this rap that he was getting about not being very smart. You know we drafted him number one. There were a lot of people that would have liked to have had him because we had a lot of offers for trades.

Q: Can you make somebody more competitive, and what makes a competitor?

CN: I would say that's a gene. I really do believe that. We've had guys that were really great competitors. Terry, as you mentioned, Joe Greene, John Stallworth. You go down through our whole thing, and probably the guys that were the most underrated on our teams was our offensive line, who were very competitive and very skilled. They weren't really big guys, but they were technicians and they wanted to win in a big way.

Q: When you look at the great dynasty teams in pro football, were they dominated by people with great competitive nature?

CN: Oh yes, no question. I think you can't survive in the game over a period of time if you're not a competitor. If you don't have—I'm talking about a real serious competitor, you're not going to survive.

Q: When you look back over your career, were there mistakes that you felt that you made? Would you go back and change anything if you could?

CN: I think the number one thing that you have to do—everybody is going to make mistakes, and you can't wish them away—but, what you have to be able to do is to learn from the mistakes and not let the mistakes drive you. You can't say, "I'm not going to do this because I made a mistake the last time we did that." And the mistake gets in the way of a good decision later on. Which happens. A lot of people function that way. If you make a mistake, you acknowledge it and put it aside, and learn from it. And say, "I don't want to do it again but it's not going to be the driving force in my life."

Q: Do you practice as you play? Did you feel that practice was the key?

CN: Very much so. Yes, I believe that, and we were probably as physical in practice as anybody. And it's a long season, but you try and temper it. You do it early in the week and let your people recover. But you have to keep that tempo. The tempo of the game is what's really important. You have to have running backs that will be willing to run the length of the field because this is building habits. After the ball is thrown, you have to have people retreating to get in the play because the play is not over. You have a lot of guys that'll rush the passer, and when the passer throws the ball and they stand, they turn around, and you might as well get a $50 seat. Charge them is what we used to say. You've got to continue from whistle to whistle. You have to establish that mentality in practice.

Q: Did you ever have a player who was a lousy practice player but came on game day, or did you feel that guys basically showed what they could do in a game based on what they did in practice?

CN: We had a lot of that early, especially with rookies coming in that you don't know. You'll also have guys that are great practice players, that show well and get in the game and are not very good at it. You have other guys that the challenge excites them and it's an adrenaline flow and they perform much better in the game than they did in practice. But the effort still has to be there in practice.

Q: In regard to the management of time, I don't think that I've come across anybody, including executives in business, who is more concerned about time and the use of time than coaches. How do you feel about the importance of the use of time?

CN: No question about it, and efficiency. You know you have to be efficient in your preparation. You can work your coaches to death, too, and they're so tired and they can't get taught on the field what you have to get done there. So we tried to be efficient. And there was a very big stress on becoming more efficient the longer you're in the game. You try and eliminate the preparation mistakes that you're making, and make it more efficient.

Q: We often think about a professional team where the head man gets, obviously, an awful lot of the credit, and in some cases an awful lot of the abuse when things don't go right.

CN: The abuse may be right (laughing).

Q: How about the delegation of authority with your staff?

CN: Extremely important. You evaluate what you're doing, you get together in meetings, you talk over what you want to get done, and there should be a meeting of the minds in your staff meetings. And then you go out and let them do it. There are many times I've had coaches who will tell you, "It was successful for me to do it this way," but they were doing it a little different. I can't force them to do it that way because if I do that, we're going to have a lousy effort. There's such a thing as "pride of authorship." You want your assistants to be proud of their contributions, to get the feeling that they are giving much to the team. If they can go out and they believe in what they're doing, then they'll be able to sell it. They're really the contact with the players, as opposed to the head coach in football because you have so many people. Your assistants have to sell what you're doing, what you believe in. Of course, the head coach has to sell the assistants. It goes on. So that's the delegation and that's important.

Q: Doing that means you have to live with the conflict when the head coach decides to overrule the assistant and change the way things are done?

CN: Oh sure. You let somebody go and he believes this is the way to get it done, and if it's not working that way, it's time you have to have another meeting of the minds. You get in staff meetings, you know how coaches' staff meetings are, there's heated discussion. There's no question about it, but from that heated discussion should come something worthwhile.

Q: In regard to a formula for success, obviously, everybody's looking for it. I mentioned shortcuts before. Is there such a thing as a formula for success?

CN: I don't think anything is cut and dried. Number one, as I said before, you don't want to imitate somebody else. I used to go to coaches' conventions, coaches' clinics, and you get somebody up there and he's selling what he's doing. "Ahhh, This is the way to do it." A lot of these coaches then will go out and they're going to do it that way. And they're changing every year, and really don't have any basic beliefs. That's a sure sign of not how to do it. You're not going to be successful. You have to do what you believe in, and what you can teach, because again, it's not the what-to-do. The how-to is so important. The techniques that go with it.

Q: What is the best advice you were ever given as it relates to your coaching success?

CN: Well, I think as a player, I had coaches that very much stressed technique, the how-to. And it proved successful for me and as a result, I think, I've taken what I learned from them and built on that.

Q: Do you, in order to be successful, have to have a philosophy?

CN: Oh yes, no question. You have to believe in what you're doing, and have to have faith in yourself. If you don't, all these other things are going to change it, and you're not going to be successful.

Q: How many years did it take you to build your coaching philosophy?

CN: I went right from playing with the Browns to coaching. I was hired without any coaching experience at all. I started in 1960, and it was a learning experience for me. I was fortunate to be with Sid Gilman, who was a great football man. I learned a tremendous amount from him. We had an interesting staff, you know. Al Davis was the receiver coach. He and I used to fight a lot at that time. Of course, as a player I thought I knew everything there ever was to know. I'd listen in meetings, and I was able to go out on the field and pretty much execute it. I got a rude awakening right off the bat when I found out you can't just tell them. You've got to go out and show them, and work through it. Teach technique and you may have to do it over and over and over and over. The first time you try it, it's not going to be necessarily grasped. It has to be sold, the technique that I'm talking about. Somebody may have had success in high school or college doing it a particular way, and you come in there, and you're trying to say, "Well, on this level, it's a little different." There's going to be a resistance. You can't just use words. Words may start the process, but, boy, there's a lot of work that goes behind it if you're going to change the mind and get the belief sold.

Tommy Lasorda

Some sportswriters over the years have admired Tommy Lasorda for his inspirational and motivational touch with his players. Others have attempted to depict him as a borderline buffoon, a light version of Casey Stengel or Yogi Berra, a guy with average abilities who survived with the superior talent provided by his organization. But if Lasorda has anything in common with Berra or Stengel, it's a deep understanding of the game and a knack for producing odd, pithy quotes.

"No matter how good you are," Lasorda once said, "you're going to lose one third of your games. No matter how bad you are, you're going to win one third of your games. It's the other third that makes the difference."

At the very least, it's a perspective born of experience. Lasorda labored as a lefty pitcher for most of 14 years in the minor leagues, an effort that netted him only 26 major league appearances for the Brooklyn Dodgers and Kansas City Athletics.

He began his career in coaching as a scout for the Dodger organization and eventually worked his way into a run as a minor league manager. In 1972, he moved into the coveted slot as a Dodger coach, which in turn left him in position to manage the team when Walter Alston stepped aside in 1976.

Lasorda's first two teams, in 1977 and '78, each won pennants only to fall to the New York Yankees in six games in the World Series. He claimed his first World Series championship in the strike-shortened 1981 season when his Dodgers whipped the Yankees in six games. His Dodgers won division titles in '83 and '85 only to lose in the league championship series.

Then came the magical 1988 season when Lasorda's Dodgers upset the highly favored Oakland Athletics in the World Series in five stunning games. In all, his record is perhaps a testament to his understanding of the people playing for him, and to his sense of humor.

"There are," he once explained, "three types of baseball players—those who make it happen, those who watch it happen, and those who wonder what happened."

His secret was his touch, as he often explained. "Managing is like holding a dove in your hand. Squeeze too hard and you kill it; not hard enough, and it flies away."

Billy Packer: Tommy, is there any such thing as the thrill of victory and the agony of defeat?

Tommy Lasorda: Oh yes, there is, Billy. I've said this time and time again, the man who puts more effort, more time, more energy into his job, is the one who will suffer more in defeat. And over the years, I've really enjoyed winning, and I've despaired losing because losing is just a very, very tough situation with me.

Q: When you lose, how long does that feeling last, and can you profit from it?

TL: Well, when we lose, Billy, the most important thing is that when I walk into the clubhouse the next day, no matter how dejected or tired or depressed I might be, I have to put on a new face. I have to put on a winning face. I have to put on an enthusiastic face. I've got to put on a self-confident face, because if I walk into the clubhouse dejected, tired, and depressed, the attitude and the atmosphere of the clubhouse and the club is going to be that way. But if I go in with enthusiasm and self-confidence, all of those things are contagious, and I can help spread them.

Q: What do you think is the key ingredient in a championship team?

TL: A championship team, to me, is when you have a team who will, number one, play for the name on the front of the shirt, and not for the name on the back. Because when they start playing for the name on the back of their shirt, now they become individualists. And to me, individualism will win trophies and plaques and honors, but teamwork will win championships. I try to impress upon my team that if you take 25 players, a manager, a coaching staff, and an organization, and we all get on one end of a rope and pull together, we can pull the rest of the clubs with us. But if half get on one end of the rope and half get on the other end, you can pull all day long and all you're doing is pulling against yourself.

Q: In regard to the talent, did you ever feel that any of your championship teams won with less talent than maybe

some of the other clubs, that you won because guys were just willing to do what you said, pull together?

TL: A good example of that, Billy, is the 1988 Dodger team. We were much, much inferior to the Mets in the playoffs, as far as talent was concerned. And we beat them in a very tough seven-game series. And then the whole world knew that the mighty Oakland Athletics had a power-house. Bob Costas even came out and stated on television that this may be the worst team put on the field in World Series history, the '88 Dodgers. And of course, I took that and ran with it. We beat the Oakland Athletics in a five-game series, and everybody knows that we had a bunch of no-name guys, but how we won was all of them playing to the best of the their ability. All of them playing in an unselfish attitude. All of them proud of the uniform, and all of them believed they could win.

I remember Don Baylor with Oakland saying, "Hey, we want the Mets to win so we can play the best team in the National League." When we beat them in five, I told the writers, "Go over and tell him he just got beat by the best team in the National League."

Q: When and how do you start developing that champion-ship attitude on a ball club?

TL: You start in spring training. That's where it begins. You tell the players, do you want to be world champions? Naturally, they're going to say yes. Say okay, then I'm going to tell you what it's going to take for you to be world champions. You have to think and believe. First, I want you to get in shape physically, mentally, and fundamen-tally. Because when I mean physically, you have to work really hard and get ourselves in the best physical condi-tion we can. When I say fundamentally, we've got to work hard on the fundamentals of baseball and execution, be-cause games are won and lost because of either executing fundamentals or the failure of executing fundamentals. And when I say mentally, I want everybody on this team to believe we will be the world champions of baseball. If you believe it, then you will practice like a number-one team, and if you practice like a number-one team, then you'll play like a number-one team. And if you play like a number one team, that's exactly where you'll finish.

Q: Can a leader, a coach, a manager motivate players to become champions, or is that something that has to come from within the individual athlete?

TL: Motivation is very, very important as far as the leader of the team is concerned. First of all, I classify a leader as someone who walks out in front of his men, but he doesn't get too far out in front to where he cannot hear their footsteps.

A guy asked me one time, what are the number-one qualities that a manager or a leader should have? It was very difficult to put it down into a certain category. But I went to church and I heard the priest give a sermon. He talked about Solomon, who was the paragon of truth, and he was pleasing to the Lord. And the Lord said to Solomon, "I want to give you any gift you want." And Solomon said, "The greatest gift that you can give me, Lord, is an understanding heart." And I think that's what every manager or coach needs, an understanding heart, because when a player doesn't do well, the manager or coach has got to understand how that player feels. That player probably feels worse than anybody, and that manager or coach has to understand that.

I believe that everybody in this country, from the President of the United States on down to the lowest hourly worker, at some time or another needs to be motivated. Because there are times, Billy, when we think we're doing the best we can when in reality, we aren't. Something has to motivate us. Something has to get us to a higher degree of competition and a higher degree of performance. People say to me, "You have to motivate guys making three and five and six million dollars a year?" I say, "Absolutely. Motivation is very, very important on an athletic team."

Q: Is it important for the leader, the coach, the manager, to be liked by the players?

TL: I always felt that maybe they're not all going to like me, but I hope and pray that they all respect me. And the only way you can get respect, Billy, from your players is you've got to earn it. You've got be honest with your players. And you've got to make them understand what it's going to take for them to be successful.

I'd like for my players to like me, because I always tried to build a family attitude. I told my players we spend more time with each other than we do with our families, so you've got to get along, we've got to respect each other, we've got to love each other and we've got to do everything we can to help each other.

Q: So you really think, if possible, it's good to develop a personal relationship with the guys who are playing?

TL: No question about it, as far as I was concerned. I did. I developed a very close relationship with my players. Billy, first of all, I told them I want them to bring their sons in the clubhouse. I want them to because they're away from home a lot, so bring your son to the clubhouse. Make them see what a big league team is like, number one. Number two, I wanted to know all my players' wives' names. I knew all their children's names. I went out to eat with my players. When I first became the manager of the Dodgers, Al Campanis said to me, "You can't go out and eat with your players."

I said, "Why not? Who wrote that rule? I need those players."

And he said, "Managers don't just go out and eat with the players."

I said, "Let me ask you a question. Let's say I have to speak at the Rotary Club tomorrow and three of my players are there, do I sit at the same table and eat with them?" He said yes. I said, "Well, if I can eat with them at a Rotary Club, why can't I eat with them at a restaurant? What's that got to do with me managing them. What's that got to do with me earning their respect. That's got nothing to do with it."

I felt I really needed those players. I told them how much I loved them. I told them how much I needed them. And I told them how much I wanted to be a part of them.

Q: The word "potential," is that a blessing or a curse for either a ball club, or let's say a rookie coming on the scene?

TL: Well, I think potential is a great thing to have. I think it's a great thing to talk about. And I told our players, talent that is used develops. Talent that isn't used will waste away. If you have the potential, then you've got to perform and utilize it. And then you have to utilize every ounce of energy you have. No, I don't think there's anything wrong with potential. Because potential, in my opinion, means that there's ability there.

Q: We hear the term "role model" so much today. Does it apply to the coach in the eyes of the players? Does he have to be a role model?

TL: Without question. I told my players I wanted to be their father away from home. I wanted to be able to help them in every aspect of their life. I believed that, and I said this about a manager—a manager or a coach of a team, he has to be a role model to his players, because they have to respect him, they have to appreciate him, and they have to look up to him. And I said this time and time again.

We need more role models in this country. I told my players that they have to be role models to the youngsters because they have more impact on the youth of this country than anybody. The youngsters don't want to be a fire chief or a governor or a mayor, a police officer. They want to be athletes. They want to be like the big leaguers. I said, "If you major league players, including me, spend more time trying to impress upon the youth of our country how important it is for them to get a good education, that education opens many doors to success."

And if we'd spend more time trying to impress upon them to stay away from illegal drugs, we'd have an impact. Number one, it's against the law. Number two, it's harmful to their body. Number three, all it will do is lead them down the path of destruction. Those youngsters would listen to these players, in many instances, quicker than they would their own parents.

I believe in role models because when I was a youngster growing up, I had my heroes. They were Babe Ruth and Lou Gehrig and Joe DiMaggio and Hank Greenberg and Jimmie Foxx, and Charlie Gehringer and Mickey Cochrane. Those guys were my heroes. And I believe that players today need to be role models.

Q: The greatest satisfaction you ever had as a manager?
TL: That question is pretty wide. I've had a lot of great satisfaction, and for me to put it to one particular situation would be difficult. Being named the manager of the Dodgers, I thought that was a great thing that happened to me. But more important is the players that have played for me. I loved them. I appreciated what they did for me. And the satisfaction that I got was to see those guys becoming

outstanding young men, and playing the game the way it was supposed to be played.

Q: How about the biggest disappointment?

TL: Oh, you always have a lot of disappointments. Losing. Losing was a big disappointment to me. I think one of the worst things that I've ever encountered is when we got beaten by the Cardinals in the 1985 playoffs. That was one of the worst defeats that I've ever suffered, because of the fact that we felt we could beat them, but we didn't. So you have a lot of down times, but the good times far exceed the tough times, Billy.

Q: In today's world, with the press scrutiny, the talk shows, the press articles that are written, is it tougher than in the past to do your job as the leader of a ball club?

TL: It's tougher because of the situation the way it is today. Players have multiyear contracts. They have guaranteed contracts. The have no-trade contracts. You have the press always there to observe what you're doing. And I think it's a lot tougher today. Managing today, I felt, is tougher than like when Walter Alston managed the Dodgers. Because in those days, you didn't have those no-trade contracts. In those days, you didn't have those multiyear contracts. In those days, you didn't have these guys making enormous amounts of money. And the press is always there to observe everything that's going on. It's certainly tougher today than ever before.

Q: How about the feeling of facing failure? Did that ever come up for you?

TL: I think the fear of facing failure has to be there at all times. I think this is what generates your interest. This is what motivates you, is the fear of failing. Abraham Lincoln once said, "Where there is fear, there is a great deal of courage."

Q: Have you ever found, looking back now, that there were any shortcuts that you could have used to success?

TL: Well, you always feel that you could have done better, Billy. And I think that comes with experience. I feel that I learned a great deal as we went along in managing. I think that after my first year, compared to my 20th year, I felt that I was better prepared for the team. I had the team better prepared to play, but I think as you go, with experience, you learn a lot more.

Q: We hear so much about loyalty. Does it have to be a two-way street?

TL: Einstein once said that an ounce of loyalty is worth more than a pound of knowledge. I believe that. Give me loyal people and I'll beat you. I think loyalty is very, very important in our lives. I've been with the Dodgers for 48 years. And I've had opportunities to go elsewhere for more money, but money is not the most important factor with me. It's doing what I really and truly love to do. I work for the greatest organization in baseball. I'm proud of the Dodgers. And I've never failed to tell everybody how proud I am to be working with the Dodgers. I said there are four things in my lifetime that I have never regretted one day of, and that is number one, the love I have for God. I never regretted loving God. Number two, I've never regretted loving the family that God gave me. Number three, I've never regretted living in the greatest country in the world, the land of opportunity, the United States of America. And number four, I've never regretted one day of the 48 years that I've been with the Dodgers.

Q: That's loyalty. Do you ever, when it's January and you're coming out and getting ready to go to spring training in February, do you ever set goals for the season?

TL: Every time I went down to spring training, Billy, I always felt that my teams were going to finish number one. I wanted them to believe that. I wanted them to know what I felt. I wanted them to know that I believed in them. And anything short of first place for me, was not a success.

Q: Is a winning coach or leader born with the leadership qualities or can they be developed?

TL: I think they can be developed. I don't believe you're born with anything. I think you're born with health, and then whatever you want to be, and whatever the effort that you put into what you want to be, that is what determines it. And I wanted to be a manager. And first of all, as a player, I wanted to play in the major leagues. Well, I reached that level but not to the degree that I had hoped for and wished for and prayed for.

Then when I became a manager, my goal was to be the manager of the Dodgers. And that dream became a reality and I managed the Dodgers for 20 years. And believe me, I think that is very, very important in handling a ball club. I think you have to make the players believe. They have to believe in you, number one, and they have to believe in the organization.

Q: Two players are basically the same coming into spring training. One may have an edge in regard to physical talents. The other guy has the edge in regard to execution and let's say the intelligence and attitude. If the fine line comes down, you've got to pick one or the other guy, which one of those attributes are you probably inclined to go with?

TL: I'll take the guy with the lesser talent and the more desire and the execution ability. I'll take that guy over the guy with the talent.

Q: Can you create a competitor or does he have to have it inside?

TL: No. I think you can create that. I think a good example is . . . I can give you two good examples. Wes Parker, for example. When I took Wes Parker under my wing, I was a minor league manager. This guy had never hit over .220, and I made him believe in himself. I made him believe that he could hit, and by golly, he did something that only 10 guys had done in the history of the major leagues. He hit 10 home runs or less and drove in over 100 runs.

I talked with Orel Hershiser when Orel Hershiser came to pitch for me. He was not the best competitor that you wanted to see. He had a reputation of being the kind of guy who did not have that real desire when times were tough. I think through endless hours of being with him, I made him believe in himself. And I created a winner, and he proved that over the years as he became a tremendous competitor and a very, very successful winner.

Q: What's most important in regard to the final outcome, the pregame preparation or the in-game adjustments?

RA: I think if you've got a team prepared to play the game, then you're going to find out that you've got the results. I think preparation, when opportunity meets preparation, then I think you're going to have the successful results. Preparing a team to play, because if they can do it over and over and over again in practice, then they'll be able to react in a game.

Q: In regard to all the clubs that you had, did you find that the champion plays as he practices?

TL: I believe that. I found that out, that whatever effort they put into their work, that's where the results will be. I've had some great teams playing for me. I know the '77 team that I had, my first year as a manager, was a great one. I went around the country telling everybody that we were going to beat the Reds, because the Reds were coming off back-to-back world championships. They had won the world championships in '75 and '76. I took over for the Dodgers in 1977. I knew one thing. The talent was there on the ball club. All I had to do was make them believe in themselves. Four guys did something that had never been done in the history of the big leagues that year. Four guys hit 30 or more home runs on the same team. Steve Garvey hit 33. Reggie Smith hit 32. Ron Cey hit 30 and Dusty Baker hit 30. We won the pennant and we were in the World Series against the Yankees simply because they believed that they could beat the Reds. And this was the most important thing—getting the players to believe. And that was a very, very exciting year.

Then in 1981, we brought the world championship back to Los Angeles where it belonged. We beat the Yankees. Because the Yankees beat us in the '77 World Series, and they beat us in the '78 World Series. And my father taught me growing up, that there was an old saying I had to live by, and that's "because God delays, that does not mean God denies." I used to say my prayers, and I used to say, "Dear God, if you can see it in your heart to put me in another Fall Classic, please let it be against the Yankees." And in 1981, my prayers were answered. We beat the Yankees in six games, and that's told the facts, because God delayed, God didn't deny.

Q: Did you have any mentors that you had coming along as a manager, and are they important?
TL: Oh yes. Without question. My mentor was Al Campanis. Al Campanis taught me more about the game of baseball than anyone. He was a disciple of Branch Rickey, and I was a disciple of Al Campanis. And the Branch Rickey theories carried on through this organization. Peter

O'Malley was a very, very important part of my life. My father was my idol. He taught me more about life than anybody did. Ralph Houk. I played for Ralph Houk. He was a great leader, a man who taught me a great deal about how to conduct myself and how to play the game. I always said if I could be like anybody as a manager, I wanted to be like either Ralph Houk or Al Lopez, because they were my idea of outstanding managers.

Q: The delegation of authority, we see that so much in business and life. Is that important to head up a ball club?

TL: I think it's very, very important to delegate authority because you have to have men, and you have to have a good coaching staff who can carry your philosophy with the team. And you have to have players willing to be coached. I tell my players, "If I holler at you, it's constructive. It's only to make you a better ballplayer. I love you very much but I want you to be the best man you can be, and the best ballplayer you can be. And it's my job to get that out of you. So however I have to do it, I'm going to do it. But I'm going to get the maximum effort out of each and every one of you."

I'm in the Hall of Fame. I didn't get in the Hall of Fame because of my athletic feats. I never got a hit for the Dodgers, I never struck anybody out for the teams. I never hit a home run. Whatever success you achieve as a manager or coach becomes a reality only because of the contributions of your players. My responsibilities are basic. I have to get those 25 guys to all get on one end of a rope and pull together. I have to get those 25 guys to play for the name on the front of their shirt and not for the name on the back of their shirt. I have to get those 25 guys to be proud of that uniform that they're wearing. I have to get them to play the game in

an unselfish attitude, and if I can do that, then I'm going to be a successful manager.

Q: What's the best advice you were ever given in terms of what created the tremendous success you had as a manager?

TL: The best advice that I was ever given, was given by Al Campanis, who taught me to be honest with your play-ers. To understand them, you have to be a father-confessor. You've got to be able to understand how they feel, and I think that is very, very important, because we learn in three ways in life, Billy. We learn by conversation. We learn by observation and we learn by participation. We all have the opportunity to improve ourselves. And I know one thing, Al Campanis and Peter O'Malley really helped me a great deal in my 20 years as manager of the Dodgers. But I must say this, and I believe this as much as I believe that I'm breathing: I thank God for all the wonderful players who have played for me, all the guys who made it possible for me to walk down the streets of San Francisco or Philadelphia or New York or St. Louis or Chicago with a smile on my face, knowing that I have just tasted the fruits of victory. I also thank God for the fact that these players gave me everything that they had. And I appreciated everything that they've done for me. And they made it possible for me to be inducted into baseball's Hall of Fame. Without them, it could never have been accomplished.

Q: Talking about the players and the teams, is it important to establish discipline? Do there have to be rules?

TL: There are rules in life that we have to follow. We have to follow the rules of the Lord. We have to follow the rules of our employers. Every team has to have rules. I don't like to have rules on the ball club. I never had too many rules, because I didn't believe in having too many rules. I told them, "You want me to treat you like a man, I will treat you like a man if you act like one. I don't have to have any rules. If I see you're not putting honest effort into it, then we have problems." But I didn't have too many rules. I never had a curfew in the 20 years I managed the Dodgers. I never had a curfew.

Q: To be successful, do you have to develop a philosophy?

TL: Without a doubt. And the philosophy is that you've got to believe in yourself. That's a motto and a philosophy that I have really stressed. You've got to believe in yourself. Self-confidence is, without a doubt, the first step to success. And I made a lot of players believe in themselves, because there are times when they doubt themselves. There are times when they're not sure of themselves. That's the time they need me to put my arm around them and encourage them, and let them know how much I appreciate them, let them know how much they contribute to the ball club, how much we need them.

Q: Did this ever change for you? As an example, you mentioned your first year managing the Dodgers, a life-long dream come true, now you look back some 20-some years later, is there anything that changed in your thinking over that period of time?

TL: No, I don't think so. I think basically my philosophies were the same. Basically, my attitude was the same. I believe that the only thing that changed was, I learned a lot. No question about it. But my attitude, my philosophy, and my love for the job never changed. I loved my job so much that I wished we could have played 365 games a year. That's how much I enjoyed putting that Dodger uniform on. That's how much I was proud and honored. To me, it's a privilege. It's a privilege to be the manager or a coach of an athletic team. To me, you have an obligation, a commitment and a responsibility to wear that uniform with pride, dignity, and character. And that's what I tried to impress upon my players over the 20 years that I managed the Dodgers.

Mike Krzyzewski

The Mike Krzyzewski story is a classic tale of basketball prosperity. The son of an elevator operator, he was raised in a middle-class household and played Catholic League ball as a high schooler in Chicago. His abilities on the court brought him to the attention of the new young head coach at the United States Military Academy in the mid 1960s, a fellow by the name of Bobby Knight.

Krzyzewski went on to become Knight's point guard at Army, where in three varsity seasons he led the team to a 51–23 record and two appearances in the National Invitational Tournament.

After graduation from West Point in 1969, Krzyzewski spent five years in the army, three as a coach of service teams and two as the head coach of the U.S. Military Academy Prep School.

Having reached the rank of captain and completed his service, Krzyzewski resigned in 1974 and joined Knight's staff at Indiana University as a graduate assistant, just as the Hoosiers were embarking on their 31–1 campaign for the 1974–75 season. He spent one year in Bloomington, then accepted the head coaching job at Army, where in his second season he directed the Cadets to a 20–8 finish. In five seasons at West Point, Krzyzewski compiled a 73–59 record and a reputation for discipline and man-to-man defense that made him Duke's choice for head coach in 1980.

His teams struggled during his early seasons at Duke, but by his fourth season his young club had earned a spot in the NCAA tournament. Two seasons later, his team would make its first appearance in the NCAA tournament Final Four, where the Blue Devils lost to Louisville.

Over the next four seasons, Krzyzewski's teams would reach the Final Four another three times with each opportunity ending in defeat. Without a doubt, however, the most painful of the losses was the 1990 thrashing issued by the University of Las Vegas–Nevada Runnin' Rebels.

The Devils were young, with three freshmen and two sophomores in the top eight players. The offense, in fact, relied on freshman point guard Bobby Hurley.

In the championship game, UNLV made quick work of Duke. Coach Jerry Tarkanian's guards harassed Hurley into numerous turnovers. First the lead was 21–11, then 47–35 at the half. UNLV was up 57–47 with 16 minutes left and settled the issue by scoring 18 unanswered points over the next three minutes. Tarkanian's Runnin' Rebels blasted their way to the title, 103–73, the largest margin of victory in tournament history.

"It was scary just watching them," Duke's Alaa Abdelnaby said."They engulfed us."

The next season, the Runnin' Rebels again dominated the college game. They were a powerful force during the regular season, crushing opponents by an average margin of 29.4 points per game.

Each win brought more declarations that the Rebels were the greatest team of all time. California-Irvine coach Bill Mulligan, who had coached against John Wooden's great teams at UCLA, was a Vegas booster. "I know Wooden says his teams could beat Vegas," Mulligan said."But he had guys starting who couldn't play on this Vegas team. I've been coaching for 35 years, and to me, this is the best college basketball team I've ever seen."

To many observers, the Rebels seemed like a sure bet to power their way to a second national championship, finishing the season with a 36–0 record and a 46-game winning streak. Tarkanian, ever the worrier, didn't agree."We're certainly not unbeatable," he said.

UNLV's dominance did little to lessen Duke's humiliation."It was devastating," Bobby Hurley said of the 1990 title game. Hurley told reporters of his recurring off-season dream: He's in a swimming pool surrounded by sharks. But after dreaming frequently, the young point guard said he grew used to swimming with the sharks. At least in his dreams.

Hurley seemed to gain maturity over his sophomore campaign, and some observers felt the Blue Devils were a stronger team. Forward Grant Hill, the son of Dallas Cowboy great and former Yale star Calvin Hill, was only a freshman, but he was a slashing, driving player and a solid defender. Those skills went a long way toward eliminating Duke's deficiencies.

Also stepping to the fore were center Christian Laettner, guard Thomas Hill (no relation to Grant), Antonio Lang, and small forward Brian Davis. They and Greg Koubek, the team's only senior, gave Kryzyzewski the depth he needed.

But the Devils still played "young." They finished the regular season with only six losses, then played their way to the ACC tournament finals, where they suffered yet another humiliation, a 96–74 loss to North Carolina.

With a 26–7 record, Duke entered the Midwest Regional and quickly recovered. In order, they turned aside Northeast Louisiana, Iowa, Connecticut, and St. John's to reach the Final Four in Indianapolis, giving the 44-year-old Krzyzewski his fourth consecutive appearance and fifth in six years. UCLA had been to 10 straight Final Fours from 1967–76, and Cincinnati had made five straight, from 1959–63.

Although Krzyzewski's team had never won the title, he was the tournament's winningest active coach, with a 25–7 record in NCAA play. "It's because he's got his system down to a science" center Christian Laettner said of his coach. "He knows what he's doing every day and every week, and it's all geared toward playing well in March. You need a certain talent level, but he brought the talent here. And he knows what to do with it."

Krzyzewski had jokingly sworn before the 1990 championship that he would grow a beard and change his name if Duke lost. But afterward he did neither, choosing instead to go back to the system that had served him well. There was no doubt that he hungered for another shot at the Rebels. That came when Vegas won the West Regional. It would be Duke and UNLV in the national semifinals, a dream rematch if there ever was one.

Duke's primary goal was to keep it close and hope that either UNLV point guard Greg Anthony or forward Larry Johnson got into foul trouble. Most important, the Dookies had to get confidence early, which they did, jumping to a 15–6 lead. From there, Laettner kept them going with 20 first-half points. (He would finish with 28 and seven rebounds.) That, in turn, infused the rest of the roster. Freshman Grant Hill played excellent defense and scored 11 points with five rebounds. And Hurley swam with the sharks, scoring 12 points (including critical three-of-four shooting from three-point range) and getting seven assists.

The Rebels, meanwhile, helped the Duke effort by making only 9 of 15 free throw attempts. With 3:51 to go in the game and UNLV leading 74–71, Anthony picked up his fifth foul on a charging call. Instead of using freshman backup point guard H. Waldman, Tarkanian inserted reserve forward Everic Gray, which left the Rebels without a driver at the wheel.

Duke caught, then passed Vegas. In the final seconds, Laettner hit two free throws for a 79–77 lead. Johnson had the ball with time on the clock, but he passed it to Anderson Hunt, who took a three-pointer and missed. Duke had halted the UNLV winning streak at 45 games.

Krzyzewski's players celebrated deliriously. The game had worked just like their coach had told them. "We talked about it all week," Grant Hill said. "We had played a tough schedule; we'd been in a lot of close games. We knew that UNLV had been winning almost every game by 20 or 30 points. Coach told us that would be our advantage. If we could get to the final minute close, they'd fold."

In the championship, Duke cooled red-hot Kansas in the first half. The Blue Devils shot 59 percent from the floor. Then they pulled away with a 13–4 run midway through the second half. They led 61–47 with 8:30 to play, but the Jayhawks closed to within five points. Duke answered with another run, pushing the score to 70–59 with a little over a minute to go. From there, the Blue Devils claimed their first title, 72–65.

"We wanted to give Coach this one. He's earned it," said Hurley, who finished with 12 points and five assists.

Krzyzewski said it was nice that his players said they won the championship for him. But he added, "Kids shouldn't play for coaches. They should play to play together and to have fun."

There was little doubt that it had been fun.

"It's nice," Krzyzewski said, "to say we finally played well in April."

Having done it once, his team promptly surprised the country by doing it again for 1992, giving Krzyzewski back-to-back championships. Today, his teams continue to rank among the best in college basketball, annually reaching 20 wins and earning a berth in the NCAA tournament. His 1997–98 team, in fact, spent much of the season ranked as the nation's top college team.

Billy Packer: Is there any such thing as the thrill of victory or the agony of defeat?

Mike Krzyzewski: Yes, but not necessarily in the context that the fans see it. For a coach, at least for me, the thrill of victory is seeing success, not necessarily the win but seeing success in the eyes of your players. To me that's the ultimate of success.

Q: Is there any way, in a defeat, that you can profit by it?

MK: It's the coach's responsibility to profit from a defeat. We've always tried to take a positive out of a loss. However, you don't want to get in a habit of losing all the time, so that's the only way of taking positives. But we try to turn it into a positive thing.

Q: Looking back on all of your championship squads, is there any key ingredient that, before the season started or as it was developing, you could say that this is why we're going to be a champion?

MK: Overall, there has to be a talent level. But the single most important ingredient after you get the talent level is, for me, internal leadership. It's not the coaches as much as one person or people on the team who set higher standards than that team would normally set for itself. I really believe that that's been ultimately important for us.

Q: How do you start if you feel that it's not there but it's attainable. How do you start to develop a championship attitude on a ball club?

MK: You start developing a championship attitude by, first of all, telling kids that they are really good and that they have the potential to become better. Sometimes that is really overlooked, to assume that kids think they're good, as a group. And secondly, to put them in championship-level thoughts—to put thoughts in their head. Like if you're in a preseason tournament we talk to them about, "Well, this is what we're going to face in the NCAA Tournament. This will be like the Final Four. This will be like a Final Eight type of game." So those thoughts are already there, that may be in the future. Because they've already been in them, they'll be in them for real in March.

Q: Is motivation a factor that a coach can instill, or does it have to come from within those guys who are playing?

MK: Motivation should initially start from the players. I tell my players that they need to get to a level by themselves, and then I can try to help motivate them to a higher level. If I have to spend my time motivating them to get to the level they could have already attained by themselves, then we're just going to be a good team. If we can do the other, then we have the chance to be outstanding.

Q: Is it important for a coach to be liked?

MK: It's important for the coach to be respected. Personally, I wouldn't want to coach if most or, in fact all, of the players didn't like me also. But I would never compensate any type of decision, or be less in my decision making, in trying to pursue the "like" part of it. I would really go after the respect. But I would like to be admired, liked, and respected by my players.

Q: Is it important for you, as a coach, to have, while the
guys are playing for you, a personal relationship with
the kids who are playing?

MK: For me it's absolutely necessary to have a personal relationship with the players while they're playing. I think if
I don't have that, then I'm missing out on maybe the best
part of it. Because we have great kids, and you try to recruit great kids, why wouldn't you want something more
than just the basketball relationship? And I think that if
you have more than just a basketball relationship, it can
positively impact the basketball side of it.

Q: You had some kids who certainly have reached the maximum of their potential on the level that you've coached
them, and maybe some who haven't. Is the word "potential" a blessing or a curse?

MK: Potential is more of a blessing. Certainly, if people just
don't allow the potential to develop, I think the problem occurs when they say a kid has potential and then
they don't give him a chance to make mistakes and have
wins, losses, successes, and failures in a development.
Each kid develops at a different rate. So that "potential"
word sometimes, from the fans' aspect of it, puts a little
bit too much pressure on a kid to do it too soon. As a
coach, I would rather have a kid who has potential, but
then my job is to make sure that he's brought along at a
rate where he likes developing his potential. Some kids
have so much pressure on them, that they never like to
develop the potential because of experiencing failures,
and no one's there to support them. That's where, I think,
a lot of problems occur.

Q: The term "role model" is heard so much and thrown
around so much in our society. Do you think it refers
and applies to a coach in the eyes of his players?

MK: Absolutely, a coach is a role model for his players. The coach on a college campus should be that player's best teacher. I think he should be his mentor, his confidante. Inherently, then, you become a role model. I don't think any coach should shirk that responsibility. To me that's his most important responsibility.

Q: The greatest satisfaction you've had in your years as a coach?

MK: The biggest satisfaction is seeing a kid from day one finish on his last day and know that he's improved tremendously. That's going on all the time—the interaction with the player. As far as a singular event, the biggest satisfaction for me was winning our first national championship. We had gone to a few Final Fours, but Duke had never won it, even before me, and Duke had a really good history. And I thought that when we beat Kansas in '91, it kind of validated what all those other guys had done before us. That was the single best moment in my coaching career.

Q: How about the biggest disappointment?

MK: I tell you what, I haven't had huge disappointments. I mean losses are losses. I think if I had to turn one thing back, if I could do it over again, I would coach my '86 team differently in the championship game. I wish I had been older and more knowledgeable, because I really felt that my '86 team was the closest to being the perfect team for me. It may not have beaten all the other teams, or whatever. But it came closer to reaching its potential, I think, than any other team. And I wish that it had won the national championship instead of losing in the final game.

Q: Today's life, with press scrutiny and then talk radio and all the people with opinions, is it tougher than in the past to do your job properly?

We're under much greater scrutiny from people who are not really authorities, or who don't analyze the game, now than we've ever been. And I think it's tougher for the younger coaches who are trying to get their credibility established. It used to be where people on TV, commentators, really good reporters, beat reporters, national press, would follow your team. But those guys followed the game religiously; they knew the game very well. Now with talk radio, they take little sound bites or they take one play or they want to be cute, and there's not in-depth analysis. That's what hurts, not just coaches, but it hurts the development sometimes of players.

Q: The thought of facing failure, first of all does it ever come up to Mike Krzyzewski and, if so, how do you handle it?

MK: The thought of failure comes up to me all the time. I don't like failure. I'm not afraid to fail, but I don't want to fail. It's a sense of great motivation for me. Although when I do, I try to use it positively. But certainly, I face that all the time. That doesn't mean I'm not positive, but I'm always looking for ways that I might fail and then I try to eliminate those things before going into whatever situation—games, recruiting, things like that. Failure is on my mind, most definitely.

Q: Have you found any shortcuts to success, now looking back, of things that you say,"Hey, that would have been a little easier way to get where I am than what I did?"

MK: I don't know if they're shortcuts, but there are better ways of getting there. I've tried to incorporate them more in my later years at Duke. I think the more I allowed my players to be instinctive, the better we became. To try not to overcoach them. To let them get a feel for the game. That doesn't mean not giving them structure or having discipline. But not to overburden them with"my" stuff, to take a look at what they have to offer and kind of simplify whatever system we're running that year to take into account their talents. As I grew as a coach, that's what I've done better. I think I was a little bit more insecure early on, and it had to be more of me. I didn't know any better. As I got some better players I found out that, hey, I don't have to teach Johnny Dawkins exactly the same way that I taught a kid that I coached at Army. Let Johnny Dawkins be Johnny Dawkins.

Q: How do you create respect for yourself as a coach in the eyes of the players?

MK: The best way—the best way to gain respect—is to tell them the truth. Look them in the eye and tell them,"This is the way it is." That means when they're doing good stuff, too. Not just, "Hey, you're not playing hard," or "You're not giving enough." But, "You're good" and "You can be better." When you look at someone straight in the eyes and you tell him or her the truth over and over, that's the basis of your relationship. You develop the best of relationships because it's founded on trust. To me, if I do that with a player, then I think I'm successful with that player and it's just a matter of how successful we will be.

Q: Do you set goals before a season starts, in terms of wins and losses or things you want to accomplish?

MK: I've never set goals of wins and losses. After we went to a couple of Final Fours, I've always talked to my players about the possibility of winning a national championship. The reason I don't do the wins and losses is we approach every game like we can win. If I set 20 wins and getting to the second round of the NCAAs or something like that, my feeling is that once you attain those goals, you might have a certain sense of satisfaction that would stop you from attaining a higher goal. Then you'd be stopping yourself. On the other hand, you might have injuries that occur or different things that might happen, and a team that could have won 24 games maybe won 17, but that's the best that that team could have gotten. I guess what I'm trying to say is, I would rather define success for my team than to have a goal or other people define it for us.

Q: Does a winning coach have to be born with leadership qualities, or can they be developed?

MK: Probably all of us are born with certain qualities that help us. But leadership can definitely be developed. I personally have been fortunate, in a high school setting, to be around great teachers who allowed me to learn more about leadership. Then in college at West Point, it was a school for leadership. I know I developed a great deal there, through trial and error and the guidance that was given to me from my teachers there.

Q: Have you ever had any player or players in your tenure who you felt developed leadership qualities, when the first time or so you were around them you questioned whether that was possible?

MK: Most definitely. I think one of our really good leaders was a kid named Brian Davis, who came to us like kind of a secondary recruit. As a result of being in our system and being around other people who had leadership ability, like a Christian Laettner, he then developed a confidence in his own style where he asserted himself. I've had a few kids like that. But Brian Davis, because he was on both of our national championship teams, his leadership was instrumental in winning both those championships. I didn't think he had that when he came to Duke.

Q: Two players are basically even. You're trying to decide who's going to get certain playing time. One may have

a little bit more physical ability, the other guy with more of an intelligence factor. Which guy probably gets the minutes?

MK: With intelligence you have a greater chance of making other people better. Without giving names to those two people, I would lean more toward the intelligence because basketball is all about making your teammates better, and I think you can do that if you're smart. Some people are quick or strong, but they use their strength and quickness going in the wrong direction. Someone who's a little bit slower or a little bit weaker, if he's always going in the right direction or making proper decisions, will usually beat the other person if there's not that much disparity between the physical strengths.

Q: **Can you create a competitor or does he have to have it inside?**

MK: It's a team process in building a competitor. Certainly a coach—and I find at Duke one of my primary jobs—is to make our kids tougher. We have a school that is one of the best in the country, but it also can be termed somewhat of an elite school whereas it's so nice. There are certain things I have to do to make sure that our kids get tougher. A kid is not going to become really tough unless he has some competitiveness and some toughness in him already.

Q: **What is more important, pregame preparation or in-game adjustments?**

MK: Pregame preparation is much more important as far as the coach and player relationship, in that I find most players, if they start a game and don't have the proper mind-set, it's very difficult to turn that around. In-game adjustments are definitely important, but I would rather have, of the two, my team ready to play at the level it's supposed to play at the beginning of the game. Sometimes they will make adjustments to go higher as a result of being in the game, but they've started off at a very high spot. I think coaching, sometimes during a game, is overemphasized. I'm not trying to lose my job or whatever, because I think it's important. But I think what you do before the game in creating a mind-set is your main job, and the other stuff flows from it.

Q: Does a champion play as he practices?

MK: I really believe a champion does play as he practices. My best players at Duke were my best practice players. You create a consistency of excellence in all of your habits, and therefore the game becomes much easier for you.

Q: You're already starting to become one yourself in many ways, but is it important for a guy like yourself to have mentors in his past to develop like you have?

MK: In any profession, and I can speak for mine especially, it's unbelievably important to have people to talk to, whether you call them mentors or people to help guide you. It doesn't have to be one person, or it could be a number of people over the years. I've certainly been fortunate to have been able to talk to some of the greatest minds in the history of basketball, many of them as a result of my relationship with Bob Knight. Whether it be Henry Iba, Pete Newell . . . whether it be Jack Gallagher, truly one of the top high school coaches I've ever met. Those were all people, and many others, who have given me guidance throughout the years.

Q: What is the best advice you've ever received, whether it be from somebody in your profession or out, that you can think of?

MK: The best advice, when I first started coaching, and I didn't realize it until much into it, was to get—and this is from

Jack Gallagher and from Pete Newell—get as much information and learn as much about the game as you can, but use your own personality to teach it. It takes a while for somebody to have the confidence to follow his or her own instincts, because you see so many people doing a good job and you have a tendency to follow and do exactly what they do. But that was the best advice, to follow your own instincts. Pete Newell and Jack Gallagher gave me that advice.

Q: Is there a formula for success?

MK: I don't know if there's an exact formula for success. I think people have to determine what their formula is, because everyone's a little bit different. In general, I would say definitely hard work. Hard work needs to be looked upon not as, "Oh, man, I've got all this work," but hard work with passion, an open mind to learn, and the ability to use the resources around you to gain success. In other words, you're not going to do it alone. Being a part of a team and developing those aspects usually will get you a lot of success.

Q: Would you comment on the use of time and its importance to your success, or the lack of proper use of time?

MK: The use of time management is incredibly important to success. If you are successful, or on the road to a chance to get great success, you are going to be inundated with a number of different things—many of them that do not have anything to do with the game or the practice. To be able to use time management wisely so that you always give proper preparation for your team is ultimately important. When I've made mistakes with my team in the past, as I reflect, much of it had to do with decisions made concerning poor time management.

Q: How about the ability to say no to requests, because obviously with a guy in your position they're unending.

MK: It's huge. The ability to say no is huge. Also to have people around you who will say no for you. When you do say no, if you're a responsible person, especially if they're good requests, there's a sense of guilt, a sense of disappointment that you might create for that person. Therefore, whether it be an athletic director, assistant coaches, your wife, different people, where you're not the only one saying no for you, I think you'll never be able to handle that burden if you are a responsible person, if you're a good person. Most of them are good, they're from good people; you just can't do them all and still do your job.

Q: One of the things on any successful team is the matter of discipline. Do there have to be rules to have a good championship team?

MK: There have to be standards. I don't like too many rules because rules then can run your team instead of you running it. I like the flexibility of making decisions. Basically with my team I tell them that my one rule is don't do anything that would embarrass you or our basketball program. Then I'm the judge at what those things might be, and it gives me great flexibility. And hopefully, I've developed a relationship with my players where they're not going to say, "Well, you did this with Grant Hill and you did another thing with Brian Davis." If somebody asked me about that I would explain why I did it in each case. Sometimes rules can get in your way, but standards should never get in your way. That's why I would rather create very high standards on my team.

Q: Is it important for a fellow who becomes successful to develop his own philosophy as to how he runs his life, his team, the championship?

It's very important for you to develop your own philosophy. That philosophy is ongoing because you as a person change. I'm a different person at 50 than I was at 45. My philosophy can change somewhat because of new knowledge and I'm a little bit different person. I think a philosophy is a plan. It's what your standards are; it's how you incorporate all the things you think you are into what you are doing. Certainly, I think that is very important.

Q: Mike, you mentioned 50, you have a philosophy now. You say it's ever changing. At what point in your life do you think your philosophy got to the point where it is now? Was it 15 years ago, 10 years ago? Or do you look upon it as ever changing?

MK: It changed dramatically probably in the mid-'80s for me, in that I had been coaching at that point around 9 or 10 years. I think I had enough history, enough contests, with recruiting, handling things in public, and games, to where I felt confident about who I was and understood from the successes and many failures I had, because I had a number of losing seasons. I had two at Duke, I had a couple at Army, and I had been poor in the coaching profession and then somewhat successful, too. But it happened in the mid-'80s. My philosophy hasn't deviated that much, but I'm just stronger in my convictions concerning many of the things that I do now than I was then. But that was probably the start of it.

Sparky Anderson

George L. "Sparky" Anderson was born February 22, 1934, in Bridgewater, South Dakota. He wasn't all that great of a player, but then again many successful big league managers aren't. He played only one season in the major leagues, with Philadelphia in 1959, and batted just .218.

He labored five seasons as a minor league manager, then took over the Cincinnati Reds in 1970 and soon molded them into the "Big Red Machine," an outfit that won four pennants in seven seasons. His '75 and '76 clubs thrilled Reds fans by winning back-to-back World Series.

Anderson's trademark move was his quick replacement of pitchers when they showed signs of faltering, leading to his nickname "Captain Hook."

His success bred its own sort of troubles, however. When his teams finished second two years in a row, he was fired in 1979, a move that stunned and alienated thousands of Reds fans.

The Detroit Tigers, though, were only glad to give him the controls as skipper, and he promptly pushed them to respectability. He was named American League Manager of the Year in 1984. His Tigers won the Eastern Division with a 104–58 record and won seven of eight postseason games on the way to taking the World Series, Anderson's third as a manager.

His Tigers won another division title in 1987, and he was again manager of the year, but his club lost in the American League championship series.

Anderson always hungered to manage competitors. Pete Rose was known as a "me-me-me" guy during his playing days with the Reds, but Anderson didn't mind. "Some people don't like that," Anderson once said, "but I believe in me-me-me players. Give me 25 players who want to go to the Hall of Fame, and I'll take them."

He loved the way Rose used his toughness to change the course of a game. "Take my advice," Anderson once said. "Don't ever tell Pete Rose he can't do something. You'll lose."

Billy Packer: Sparky, you have had so many great successes in your career. Is there such a thing as the thrill of victory?
Sparky Anderson: Yes. I think there is, especially when you're young. I started out at 35, and when you're young, yes, it really hits you. I think as you get older, the main thing you want to do is do your job right. That, to you, is the satisfaction. Maybe you finished third, but you know that you really did your job right; better, maybe, than the year you won. I think that's the satisfaction down the road. But when you're young, that thrill of winning, it's an ego thing.

Q: How long does it last?

SA: I think it lasts until you grow up. And I think what makes you grow up is you realize that you're no genius. You have no immediate answers to the problems that you sometimes face. You have good players and if you direct it right, you can win. If you have mediocre players, you can direct it right and still finish third. But that's when I felt the proudest, finishing third.

Q: How about the agony of defeat?

SA: Very hard, again, when you're young. You will take it personally. I did. I personally took defeat as if it was my fault. And then as you get older, you wake up and realize, "Hey, wait a minute, did I do a good job?" That's the first thing I want to answer to myself. And if I can answer yes—and I've answered no at times—but when you answer yes, then it doesn't hurt.

Q: Can you profit from that agony of defeat?

SA: Yes. You profit by knowing, as I said, that you're not the genius. The genius is in the personnel you have. Now get that personnel to do what they're capable of doing.

Q: Talking about personnel, what's the key ingredient to a championship team?

SA: The key ingredients, whether it's high school, college, or professional, there's no difference on it. The whole ingredient, and don't let anybody ever tell you different, it's the players. If you have good players, you're going to have good teams. Even if you're not there. Just leave your name there and your team's going to play pretty well. But if you are a good coach at any level, it's what you do with that good personnel and how you keep them focused to play. Not to be a bunch of clowns. Be professional. And if you can get them to be professionals and they have that talent, I'm going to tell you something, you're going to look real smart.

Q: When you say the basic answer is talent, did any of your championship squads, in your mind, win with less talent than maybe what was out there with some other squad in that given year?

SA: Yes. In 1987. That would be my my proudest year. When I left camp, I always used to tell my wife where I thought we'd finish. And I honestly said we will finish between fourth and fifth. And we won 98 games, and we won our division and lost to Minnesota in the playoffs. But I told them the last day, remember this day and remember this year; this will be your proudest moment someday when you look back on your baseball career because you did something that nobody ever thought you could do.

Q: How about developing an attitude? You talk about having talent, but do you develop a championship attitude with a team? Is it possible to have a good group of ballplayers who never get the championship attitude?

SA: Yes. That happens. I see it happen all the time. But that's where I say good coaching comes in. In the sense that you develop for your franchise or your college or your high school, you develop a pride that when you come there, you're going to be the best. That doesn't mean the best players. You're the best. You're representing Monroe High School and Monroe High School has a history of winning, and they have a history of acting like professionals. I always maintained this. If you cannot be a professional on and off the field, then all your talent went to waste.

Q: Is motivation a factor in developing a championship team, or does motivation come from within the guys that are on it?

SA: Well, motivation to me is a word that I don't quite under-stand. I think motivation to me is the leaders—that's right from the top, that's from the front office right on down—that we are going to try to do things right here. We might not win every year, but we are certainly going to do it right. And when people see us play, they're going to see a team that acts and performs as professionals.

Q: Sometimes can you have a situation where you, as the leader, from a coaching standpoint, get that extra moti-vation from certain guys on the ball club that help to deliver motivation to others?

SA: Yes. What I used to do, Billy, for instance in spring train-ing, I always brought in six guys. I brought in one of the guys who was going to be an extra man. I brought in a pitcher, and then I brought in four players. And they were the top players. And I'd sit down with them, and I'd say, "All right, we're going to go over all our rules. I just want to touch them and go over them. If there's anybody here that believes there should be a change in one of these rules, we will discuss it, but I'll make the final decision." And we used to sit and talk in spring training that day. And I had them wait after we had finished all our work, and when they'd showered and everything, and we'd have that meeting. Then I'd take them all to dinner that night, after we'd completed it. I said the next day, then, I would announce to the club this is what it is.

Q: And that's the deal?

SA: That's the deal. And that's the way this deal would go. And your guys have made this rule and this is the way it's going to be.

Q: Is it important for a leader of a ball club to be liked by those guys that he's coaching?

SA: I have two rules, and I give that to them in spring training. Number one, you guys are lucky, you don't have to
like me. Number two, I'll give you one that's even better, you don't have to respect me. Now, let me explain
those two rules to you. The reason you don't have to
like me is that I have to earn that. Number two, the reason you don't have to respect me, if I don't earn respect,
how in the hell can I ask you to give it to me? I'll earn
that, gentlemen.

**Q: Is it important for you to have a personal relationship
with the guys on the ball club?**

SA: Every guy works differently. My thing just happened to
be it was a fault of mine. I had to go one-on-one with
guys. I felt I had to know about them. And I had a rule
with myself: The player doesn't have to understand me; I
have to understand him. That's my job. I don't play. But
it's my job to understand everything I can about him if I
can, as much as I can about his family, his upbringing,
everything I could understand about him. I felt then I
could solve some of his needs.

**Q: You had some of the greatest teams that ever existed with
the great Cincinnati teams. For them, maybe this word
wasn't important. The word "potential," is it a blessing
or a curse?**

SA: Well, I think it works even for them. Because that was
our thing, that we always discussed and talked. If I felt
that we had a player who had more potential than he
was giving us. What I tried to do with my coaches was
I'd split our squad up into their personalities, and I
would try then, to put the coaches with the players that
I felt their personalities matched. Then, if in any way
they felt they couldn't handle that particular guy, they
would come to me. And that's when I would come in.

Q: What about the term "role model" we hear thrown around so much today, does it apply to the coach in terms of the eyes of his players? Does the coach have to serve as their role model as well?

SA: I had another thing that I used to tell the old-timers. Put your cotton in your ears. I had a thing, a sign that I had seen on the L.A. freeway. It wasn't a joke. It said, "Don't tell me, show me." And I believed that. I believe that the great coaches show their players. It's there. I said this many times. And I use Dean Smith all the time as an example. I never met Dean, but I used this. If I was going to interview Dean Smith, I would never go talk to Dean Smith. I would go talk to his players at the time, and I would go talk to his ex-players. Then I'd write a story on Dean Smith, and I would know him exactly, and I'd hit him right in my article. He's a role model.

Q: Your greatest satisfaction as a manager?

SA: This is ego, but my greatest satisfaction is, I never sold myself out. What was right to me, was right, and I never sold that out. And I do like to think my players knew, because they used to say, "The old man won't buy that." I would not sell myself out to try to be your buddy.

Q: The biggest disappointment you ever had?

SA: I think the biggest disappointment I ever had was when baseball went on strike in 1994, and they didn't have a World Series. I thought that was one of the biggest mistakes I'd ever seen in in my baseball career.

Q: Today, we see such incredible press scrutiny of every single move a manager makes or a player makes, or a front office makes. Is it tougher, do you think, today than it was in the past to effectively do your job?

SA: I think it's tough if you can't do your job. I don't believe the press scrutiny is tough at all if you can do your job.

Q: How about the fear of facing failure? Is that, at any time in your career, something that you ever thought about?

SA: I think probably my whole career. I will admit that to you. I think my whole career, the thing that drove me to try to do things right, was the fear that I would fail, not only myself, but fail a player. And that's something I didn't want to see—a player that had left and years down the road was in deep trouble.

Q: One of the interesting things about talking to incredibly successful coaches and managers is that almost every one of you have that fear of failure, and you take it almost as a positive, a motivating factor for yourselves.

SA: It is, because of what it does. You are scared. You know what? I don't believe any human being lacks that. No matter how much you know about the game, I think when you first sit down before it begins, there's a little thing in you. It's a thing where you say, "I want to do right tonight, and I want to do a good job." And that's the thing—that little fear keeps you on track. It's not the money. Let's face it, everyone wants to be paid. And everybody wants to be paid what they feel is right, but that didn't come first. Doing the job came first.

Q: Have you found any shortcuts to success based on all of your experience?

SA: No. I really believe that if you take a shortcut, it'll be the last cut. You must be willing, as they say in the stock market right now, to go the distance. And you must be willing to never give up the principles that you believe. Now, you're not right all the time. I look back now, and I made some decisions that were wrong, but, by gosh, I thought they were right. And I've had many young managers ask me, "Well, how do you do it?" I said, "Let me tell you one of two things. First of all, if you have to read books and ask, don't do it. Stay away from coaching. And secondly, coach the way you are. Don't coach the way someone else coaches. That's him, that's not *you*. Be *you* at all times."

Q: Does loyalty have to be a two-way street between player and coach?

SA: Absolutely. Loyalty, to me, is something you have to earn. You earn that. And when you earn it, then it's embedded so deep that . . . like when I got fired at Cincinnati. In the morning, I had told my guys that had been with me all those years, if anything ever happens to me, don't you ever come out in the newspaper protecting me. Because if we are what I think we are together, don't try to show me in the paper where everybody can read it. We know we are. We don't have to have that in the paper. And Joe Morgan called me that morning crying, and he says, "Skip, I'm going . . . " And I said, "Joseph, what'd I tell you? You've got a new guy coming in there. You give him the same respect you gave me. Don't you say a word."

Q: You mentioned earlier that you used to tell your wife when you left spring training, "Here's what I think I'm going to do." Do you think it's important to pre-set goals for a ball club?

SA: I think it's important to know where you think this ball club is. I thought it was going to be a fourth or fifth place club, so I set in my mind, "God, I'd like to shock this world, and really get up there, and win and put this club in second or third; at least show them that they don't know how to pick." Yes, I think it is. I think we all have to have goals, whether we reach them or not. I don't think that's the important thing. I think it's the run, like the guy said many, many times, the run for the touchdown was much better than the score. It's an important thing to be chasing something.

Q: Does a winning coach have to be born with his ability to coach, or do you think it is a quality that can be developed?

SA: I don't know how in the hell anyone can ever define or tell me who could be a great coach. It's the strangest guys in the world. I guarantee you nobody ever thought I'd be a manager. Well, Al Campanis, years ago, when I was a player, once said that I would be the manager. How he ever saw that or knew it, I don't know. But I don't think we can just look at a guy and say, "He's going to be a good coach." I do know this —if he's fortunate enough to start off with a good club, then he has a chance to get over a lot of hurdles that another guy doesn't get over.

Q: Let's assume you're putting your club together in the spring, or maybe even for the long haul, and you've got two guys that are basically the same in terms of where you think they can help the club. And now you've got to make that split-hair decision. What attribute of a player would swing you, his intelligence as a player, or his physical skills as a player?

SA: Well, when it gets to that, to me, it's the intelligence and the toughness of a young man. I think there's some young men, whether they like it or not, they're just very tough. I don't know if they try to be tough, they just are tough.

And there's a lot of them, they just cannot take it when they get a little setback. And they've got great, great, great ability. But the adversity, they just can't handle. And I'll take the kid that, maybe he's a little shorter, but he's a tough kid and he can just come back. You never have to worry about him going home and crying tonight.

Q: Along those same lines, when you think of toughness, you think of guys who love to compete. Do you think a competitor is something that's born, or can you help develop it?

SA: I think he's born. I think he's born and shaped by his family life, as a child. I think everything like that is born. See, I think the ability that was given him, it comes from God. That's for myself. I think he was just gifted with the ability, but the environment that he comes from, I think that then makes his toughness.

Q: Of all the great guys you've managed, they came from obviously different environments. Give me an example of a tough competitor.

SA: Pete Rose. Pete Rose came with less talent. As far as ability, if you took and graded him, he didn't grade out ability-wise, maybe to three or four of the other guys. But that's the toughest human being I've ever been around in my career. I mean you could not beat him, and I say this kindly, unless the coroner pronounced him dead. Even then, you'd say, "Get another coroner. Make sure. If he gets up, you're in trouble." He's the toughest, mentally and physically, I ever coached.

Q: What's the more important thing in your opinion, the pregame preparation, preparing your ball club, or the in-game adjustments and strategy?

SA: The strategy is an opinion during the game. You might be in the other dugout and you want to bunt. I'm in my dugout, and the same type of situation comes up, but my personnel is different and all that, and my opinion is I don't want to. That's all opinions. I believe everything that happens in spring training, basically, is the most important. If you don't get all the things done in the spring that you have to have done with your club mentally, physically, and everything, then when it comes to your practice sessions prior to games, you're in trouble. You can't go through spring training and not get the things done, and then expect all of the sudden you're going to catch up as you're playing.

Q: Does a champion play as he practices? And if so, could you give any examples where maybe that isn't the case?

SA: Well, the really good players are practice players, too. Every single day when you take the field, you basically are going to do the same exact thing. Those guys, you don't have to tell them, they do it. See, the good players have great work habits. That's what I always called them, work habits. They know what they have to do to maintain the ability they have. And you have to work. I've never seen a guy yet that could stand around and was going to end up getting anything done.

Q: Did you have any mentors who helped you move forward as a manager and coach?

SA: My first was a man named Lefty Phillips, who managed the California Angels for about a year and a half. But he was a brain. He couldn't do that in front of the press, but he was an outright brain. And then I was so lucky, I had George Kissel of the Cardinals. He's been there, the guy in charge of the Cardinal farm system, teaching for 50 years. And a guy named George Scherger, who's from Charlotte, North Carolina, I had as a coach nine years. I always used to tell him, "You're the brains around here, and I'm getting all the attention."

It's so important that any young coach starting out has an elderly or older gentleman there that has seen it all before. You haven't seen it before. You say to him, "Oh my god, here, what do I do now?" He can help you. He's seen it.

Q: What's the best advice you were ever given that helped you in your success?

SA: The best advice I ever got was by Walter Alston, my first winter meeting in Fort Lauderdale, Florida, in 1969. I was coming in and I was standing in the middle of the room there, and I see someone waving. It was Walter waving me back to the back table, and there was Lefty Phillips and Walter Alston and a couple of other guys. He said, "Sit here, this is where you belong, not out in the room where everyone can see you."

And he said, "Just remember one thing, you came here because you could do a job, do the job the same way you always did it." I tell many guys that story about him. I said, "Son, the only thing I can tell you is what Alston told me, and he had a pretty good career. You came here because you could do a job. Do the job the same way you always did it. Don't change now."

Q: The manager is in the spotlight. How about the importance of delegating authority to guys that are working with you?

SA: My theory was this: I told them, each one of them had their job, and I told them what I would like done. If there's anything they need from me, come to me, and I'll try to help them, if I can. But this is your authority and I will never bother you. Never spoke once to my third base coach ever in 26 years. Any decision he made, he made. He used to come back and tell me, "Goddamn it, I did this or I did that." I'd say, "Hey, it's over." I just never, never felt that you had the right. You hired them. You told them what you wanted done, and you didn't have the right now to tell them how to do their job.

Q: The greatest asset of a winning ball club?

SA: The greatest asset, and I'm going to give it to you. And that's the reason the '87 club was so great for me. The '87 club proved one thing. They could tolerate the manager and they could tolerate each other. And I said anytime baseball players can tolerate each other, they can have a successful year. Toleration, you know, when you spend that long season together. In football, it's not as much because they don't have as long. But in basketball and baseball and hockey, when you're together that long, if you can't tolerate each other, you're going to have a bad ball club.

Q: Is there a formula for success? And did you ever develop one?

SA: I tell you what, as I told Eric Davis one time when he came to us, "If I ever lie to you, I want you to come to my door and yell it as loud as you can yell it that, 'You are a goddamn liar.'" I believe this, one thing about a coach, whatever you do, whether it hurts you inside to have to tell the truth, tell it, but don't ever tell a lie.

Q: How long did it take you before you developed your basic philosophy?

SA: I started when I was 35, and I think, by the time I was about 42 years old, seven years into my Cincinnati job, that I had myself totally together as far as getting past the ego trip, knowing that I just wanted to do a good job at what I did. The money thing will come. Fine. I never got into how much more will I get if it do this. I finally whipped it at 42.

Q: And from that point on, did you tinker with it or was it mostly locked in place?

SA: I think you change inside of you as you go because you say, "Hey, wait a minute, now, that wasn't right. They're doing it for me, but I think that's being a little overbearing, here, you know." I think you should never be ashamed that you might have made a mistake. If you made a mistake, just walk in one day and say, "Hey, we're going to do it this way." Don't explain it. But it's going to switch to this.

Q: I regard to the style and the system, do you think it's very important for a guy coming along to develop his own philosophy?

SA: He'd better. It's like anything. If you don't have your beliefs, you're in trouble. George Kissell told me this one time, "If you look at a picture, if there's a tree tilted, you ought to know something's wrong." It's the same way when you walk on a ballfield. You ought to be able to look right out there. If you can't look out there and say, "Hey, wait a minute that ain't right, something's wrong out here," then you're not seeing what this is all about. Coaching, to me, is something where if you have to train yourself, you're in trouble. You should be able to just see this stuff.

Dan Gable

Dan Gable's career has been marked by a dedication (some would say workaholism) that has produced a host of honors, titles, and championships. After an undefeated high school career in Iowa, he entered Iowa State and won NCAA titles (at 130 pounds in 1968, and at 137 pounds in 1969), only to lose his one and only match as a senior, in the NCAA finals at 142 pounds in 1970.

He answered that devastating defeat with three intense years of work, seven days a week, to prepare for the 1972 Olympic Games in the Soviet Union. The Russians had declared their intention to find someone to beat Gable in the lightweight division. But even a knee injury couldn't prevent him from powering through his six Olympic matches without surrendering so much as a point.

He retired as an active wrestler soon after (although he has briefly attempted comebacks) to turn his focus on coaching. He became head coach at the University of Iowa in 1977 and from 1978 to 1986 coached the Hawkeyes to nine straight NCAA titles.

Billy Packer: Dan, is there any such thing as the thrill of victory and the agony of defeat?

Dan Gable: There is in my sport. The longer I coached the more I got to the point where I could be a team champion or coach a team champion, but then have an individual within that team not quite reach his goals, and that would really bother me. And I don't think it happened so much at first. I mean it hurt. But when I first started coaching, it was like when you win a team championship, there could be some kids that had let down on an individual weight class and didn't quite get to where they wanted to get, but the thrill of the total team still outweighed it. But the more and more that I coached, the more I've been successful, the less likely that I would leave the championship setting feeling that good about the total situation. And it's almost like you don't really get spoiled with winning, but you almost take certain things for granted and start looking into other areas that I think keep a person from being really, really satisfied.

Then again, my coaching goals are high. I've always had an extreme high, an ideal situation for winning. Instead of just winning, for me the issue has bordered on wanting total victory. By that I mean, if we have 10 weight classes, my total goal from the beginning was to win all 10 weight classes. That's just not reasonable. People say that's unrealistic. But, ultimately, the more I won, the more I felt like I couldn't have an individual letdown.

I've seen the agony of kids' defeats, after they've really trained hard individually. The agony can always be there. And it probably happened to me the biggest time in 1995, the year at home, when our team dominated the championships, but my one wrestler, Lincoln McIlravy lost the finals. And I saw the agony on his face even though our team won. So that really hit home, and it's probably one of the reasons it's driving me to fairly early retirement, which is not totally set yet. But that situation is coming, just by my not being able to handle a loss.

Q: Do you ever profit from the agony of defeat?

DG: Oh, yes, you do. I don't think you can continue to do so, year in and year out, but you can have some real crucial defeats that can set the tone for your whole career. And mine definitely was. My last match in college was an example. I had gone undefeated in high school and undefeated in college, but in my last collegiate match I lost it as an individual. I didn't know it at the time, but that match made a huge difference in my performance over the next two years as an athlete, in the world championships and the Olympic Games. It made a huge difference. And then in my coaching philosophy, it also made a huge difference. There have been other defeats, too, that have caused me to reevaluate my whole approach and try not to end up in that particular situation again.

Q: What is the key ingredient in your mind of a championship team?

DG: Well, it's very difficult to tear the two words apart. By that, I mean individuals and a team. To me, you have a championship team when everybody is contributing close to what they're capable of contributing. But at the same time, it's hard to just say worry about yourself and not worry about others without becoming disrupting because everyone trains differently with different philosophies.

It's a fine line, and it's one that you as a coach have to work at very, very carefully to make sure that you don't disrupt a team with a group of individuals. But when you have that group of individuals clicking for what they need, and still understanding the total team concept, then you're going to have a championship team.

Q: **In regard to an individual, if talent is not the answer, what is the key ingredient that makes a guy a champion, if he's not the most talented individual?**

DG: Whether you have talent or not, that's a big factor to me. The higher level you get to in sports performances, you need a little bit of everything to be good. However, I would still take the young person or the athlete that had the attitude over the talent. But it's difficult once you get to that extremely high level of competition, where talent and all the hard work factors have to be at their maximum.

For a person who wasn't quite as talented as the other person yet who wanted to be the champion or wanted to have the opportunity to be the champion, I would tell them that sometimes attitude and effort can allow them to overcome superior talent. But at the highest levels of competition you often find people with the whole package, the talent, the motivation, the effort, and the attitude.

Q: **How do you start to develop, for a young guy that comes in with you, the attitude to be a champion?**

DG: Well, that's where you have done your homework. That means the environment that he is in is going to help determine his work ethic. And that really is a crucial factor, from a coaching point of view. Because otherwise, you're probably going to go to the level of your work ethic in that particular room or that particular practice area. And so, as a competitor, you need to make sure that you're being successful, not just through talent, but through a work ethic that is second to none. Sometimes young athletes come in and see people who are already champions, and they'll take on the reflection of what's there, they'll emulate the successful model.

Having that hardworking, talented, successful role model is probably more important than just a group of talented guys. Having that work ethic in the training room will also bring on consistency year after year. If you're lucky enough to get a talented kid who can lift up the team work ethic, then you are on a roll.

Q: Is motivation a factor on behalf of the coach, or does it have to come from within the individuals?

DG: It's nice to have both. But, no, I really feel changes can be made even though young people come in with a certain attitude or come in with a certain level of motivation. I think it's difficult. I think it's hard, but I think it can be done. And again, it's probably going to depend a lot on the majority and the minority in the wrestling room. If the majority of your team is work-oriented, that will help the marginally motivated to develop.

On the other hand, if your team has a large number of athletes not ready to commit to the work level, then that marginally motivated athlete will make little progress, or he'll even fall back.

But I would say, yes, motivation can be changed. But it's important to have the influence of teammates to make that change. That's where recruiting can be a really big factor, no matter what the level of competition. You want to get the kids who are motivated to work, who want to listen, who have already had some pretty good learning before they got there as far as attitudes, as far as motivation. You can put all those motivating factors together and things can work. But otherwise, running a team of marginally motivated athletes can be a day-to-day struggle.

Q: Is it important for a coach to be liked by those that he is coaching?

DG: My athletes have to love me. And I'm not saying it in a bad manner. I'm not saying it in a light manner. I'm saying it in a manner where they have to understand me to the point that what I put them through, that there's a reason, a good reason. If they don't see that reason, then they're going to have a difficult time being pushed and reaching that level. And there's a couple of things that I'll point out here. At times, that team of yours will look at you with daggers. But they only look at you with daggers, and they don't go beyond that, because of the respect, because their competitive nature keeps them focused on the fact that you're pushing them for a reason. There's also an understanding, that at times that they're going to look at you with admiration and respect. And even at the time they're shooting daggers, it's only a momentary reaction where that respect still comes back before something bad happens.

Q: Is it important for you to have a personal relationship with those athletes?

DG: I think that's really crucial. I just don't know how you can actually make good decisions, ones that are going to help that young person, without knowing him, without communicating, without having a relationship. And I think vice versa, as well. It's very important.

Q: The word "potential," is it a blessing or a curse?

DG: If you see improvement, if you see athletes striving to realize their potential and they go beyond the level they started at, then it's a blessing. If they go in the other direction, it could be a curse.

Q: Is it important for a coach to perform as a role model for those guys who are playing for him?

DG: It's the only way you're going to develop that relationship we talked about earlier. Because if somebody looks up to somebody and there's not much to look up to, in his heart, it's not going to affect that person. There's a fine line being a coach, and you don't want to cross that line, whatever that line is, where you lose their respect and you lose the ability to influence them.

Q: In wrestling, you actually work with your athletes on the mat, unlike some of the other great coaches that I've talked to, in other sports where competing against the athletes is not a factor. How does that change the coaching relationship?

DG: I think it's very helpful, but it's almost like you're wrestling that particular individual and you're still being aware of what's going on. You're combining the concept of being an athlete with the concept of being a coach, much like the player-coach in pro basketball. You have to merge the perspective of athlete and coach. The benefit of that is pretty big.

Q: What's the greatest satisfaction you've had as a coach?

DG: Bringing people to new levels of excellence. Seeing young people excited to be a part of something even though they may not necessarily be the champion. But it just so happens, that if you're doing things right, a lot of them develop into that winning championship record or form. Seeing young people stick in the program even though they weren't some of the very best wrestlers, and leave with the excitement that the very best wrestlers have left with, then you know you're doing something right.

Q: How about the biggest disappointment?

DG: The biggest disappointment, probably, is when you have an athlete leave your squad for negative reasons. Those are probably worse than even somebody becoming academically ineligible or whatever. Somebody who actually left with kind of spite in his heart or mind, if that happens. I'm trying to think of one right now, and I can't think of any. I hate to have somebody within our system leave, and be very anti-our system or the program for some particular reason.

Q: Dan, this is a question unique to you. In regard to you being one of, if not the greatest wrestler in the history of our country, and also the greatest wrestling coach in the history of our country, were your personal satisfactions greater as a participant or as a coach?

DG: Coach. That's not even close. Coach, by far. Something within your control, that's being an athlete. You can almost get to the point as an athlete where you pretty much know what's going to happen. But you can't do that as a coach, even though I sometimes felt I pretty much knew what was going to happen in competition. For a coach, you don't have the same control over the events as when you're an athlete. The absence of that control factor for a coach means that the challenge is greater, that the satisfaction can also be greater. Because you have less control over the circumstances as a coach, when great things happen, it's exciting.

Q: Do you ever have a fear of failure as a coach?

DG: I think everyone sometimes crosses that path, but a well-prepared person, a well-prepared team, doesn't have to get into that situation very often, if ever. But there's been a few times that it's crossed my mind. But we have rarely, if ever, faced total failure, just because of great preparation.

Even though I loss that last match in college, and even though a lot of the headlines said "Gable Fails," and that's maybe the way I felt for a while, the bottom line was I really didn't fail. I was second in the United States, but at the same time, there may have been some factors there that kept me from performing at my best level, and so I may have failed some part of my training, some part of my training process, but there was more good than bad and that's the real key.

As a coach you could get to the point where you could have a lot of fears that you were going to fail, but the only way that you feel like a failure was if you were totally unprepared.

Q: Have you ever found any shortcuts to your successes?
DG: That word is not really one that I even like in my vocabulary, but there are shortcuts. I'd probably use a different word. For example, I'd talk of "the quickest way to get to be successful," rather than call it a shortcut.

To me, it's mostly a matter of common sense, understanding your sport, understanding the people that you deal with, understanding the skills and techniques and tactics instead of spending a lot of time here and there. Here is what you need. Now to me, that's more like an understanding instead of a shortcut. And it's the by-product of experience. But that word could actually cause mental shortcomings as far as toughness, and I wouldn't put it in my vocabulary.

Q: How do you create respect for yourself as a coach in the eyes of your players?
DG: It takes time. I think you can walk in with respect, based on what you've done in the past, if you've been successful. But you have to build it even though you've been to the top. It takes a relationship and it takes a day-to-day

sincerity. It takes a work ethic that's even greater than the one you're trying to teach to that athlete. Maybe a long time ago, a guy could get away with "do as I say, not as I do." But today is different than yesterday. And it's almost like, "Do as I say, and I'll do that same thing." It takes a lot of being genuine, and it takes a lot of time and effort. And not too many mistakes, and when you make a mistake, you own up to it.

Q: Do you ever set goals for your teams in terms of what it is they are about to accomplish?

DG: All the time. I'm a little exaggerated, but I work with young people who have already been fairly successful, not at the beginning. And I always have been that way, so I'm probably a little high on the goals for a lot of people. I call them idealistic situations, maybe a little bit unrealistic, but possible. But I just don't want anything that's going to shortchange somebody, that's why I'm probably at that higher end of goals. But, yes, goals are in front of me. We write them down. We look at them. We see them daily. We talk about them all the time, and if it looks like they're very difficult to reach, we still won't alter them. But we'll alter our training process to help make that goal still possible, or we'll alter our mind-set right up to the time of the last competition.

Q: Does a winning coach have to be born with leadership qualities, or is that something that can be developed?

DG: It's kind of a similar question to what you talked about earlier about athletes. I think there's a lot of science that we don't totally understand, but we're learning more and more about it. And there's a lot of things that come out and say we have all these things we were born with, and we can't help this, and we can't help that. But I think we can. Even though you're born with a certain mind-set, I think that environment and who you're rubbing shoulders with, the more you do research and the more you try to help yourself beyond others helping you, will put you in that leadership role. And some of it's a little bit luck, by that I mean born into a good situation or born with that good situation. So some of us have easier times than others.

Q: Along those same lines, can you create a competitor, or is that something the guy has to have inside himself?

DG: I have young people right now that are reserved inside themselves, but there's a way to bring out that fire. It's different with each athlete, but as a coach, you've got to find that way. And sometimes, we as coaches never find that way on that particular person. But you don't give up trying. You keep looking for that little button that's going to bring that out of that particular person. When something doesn't work, you go to the next. I'm talking about within rules and regulations. Within ethics. I'm talking about things that are good, not just bringing them from one level to another at all costs. You don't coach with an at-all-costs attitude. You coach with a real attitude, with one that's going to make a difference, that you don't have to depend on luck. You just kind of make your own luck.

Q: In the sport of wrestling, what is more important, the pre-match preparation or the in-match adjustment on behalf of a wrestling coach and a wrestler?

DG: Pre-match preparation. I think the other one's important, too, but there's no way you'll have it and there's no way you'll be able to make the in-match adjustments without the pre-match preparation.

Q: Does a champion play or wrestle as he practices? Have you ever had a lousy wrestling practicer, and yet he could still perform when the match comes?

DG: Many of my great wrestlers have not been that great of practice wrestler in terms of winning and losing practices or just being successful. But I'm not going to say that they've skipped practice. All of them have been very hardworking, or most of them have been very hardworking persons in the practice room, with great attitudes in the practice room. But a lot of them have not been that great in the practice room but something just turned on and clicked when the competitions began, and that's what it's all about. And that's where it's important to do it. Even though it's nice to be able to have both, the most important one of the two is to have it in the competition. And I think that is something a lot of coaches misunderstand, especially in a sport that has a lot of people on the team. And so some people never get to express their opportunity, and the coach misses the boat by not really knowing that your best athlete is on the bench in terms of competition.

Q: **Could you give me an example in the worldwide competition of an American champion, even an Olympic champion, who was not necessarily a great practice wrestler, but could just turn it on when he got on to the mat?**

DG: I can give you several examples, but I can just give you two sets of twins right now that I would have to say that have meant a lot to me and the Iowa program, and the wrestling world because they're Olympic and world champions, and they were national champions. The Badig brothers and Terry and Tom Brantz. Ed and Lou Badig won gold medals at the 1984 Olympics, and at the 1996 Olympics, Tom Brantz won a gold medal and Terry was a two-time world champion going into that event in '96.

   Those four guys, they got more accomplished in practice than just about anybody else. A lot of things happened each day in practice, with that experience of going over and over their preparation and competing in practice. It was just there on a daily basis, but something turned on, something turned on, a different frame of mind, a different gear, whatever it was. Their game face. And they were match people.

Q: Do you feel that a person, to become a successful coach, has to have a mentor or mentors whom they have received input from?

DG: I think it's good. I think it's nice. I think it's probably going to make it easier, but, no, I don't think they have to have a mentor that they're looking up to specifically as to what they're trying to accomplish. I think they will have someone someplace, whether it's a higher form, or whether it's a parent, whether it's a loved one somewhere. I think there's something there that probably will drive the best out of them, but it doesn't have to be in their particular sport. It doesn't have to be exactly in their line of duty. And then you might even say that somebody might have something within his own system that might even drive him, but I don't know if I can really say that's the easy way.

But I couldn't say that's the correct way or that's the way I would like it. Because I think we have to be bigger than ourselves, and I just don't think one self can really bring the best out of us without some external factors.

Q: What's the best advice you were ever given, in looking back over the many successes that you've had?

DG: I think being a very good listener. That doesn't mean believing everything you hear. It means hearing everything and sorting out what's important.

From the beginning, I've been almost a little gullible, in the sense of believing everything my coaches told me. As the years went on, I probably did more checking on what was being said to make sure that was correct. And I think being gullible probably hurt me a little bit except maybe in real commonsense situations.

Sometimes the most important listening you do is the listening that comes after you've reached the top, after you've gotten very good and could be susceptible to the idea that you know everything. Even though you're having a lot of success, you still have to be open. That's how you keep growing, keep competing, even after you've reached that high level, because there are a lot of comments, and a lot of people out there who can affect you and help you and teach you.

Q: The use of time, and your ability to say no, how important is that in being successful?

DG: The use of time is really critical. And I always say it this way: When you get up in the morning, you can write down 10 things that are important to you to do that day. Some people would say the list should be 20, because there are a lot of things you've got to accomplish. Fitting the requests around your priorities is a challenge. Sometimes you have to say no to worthy people with worthwhile requests, and that's difficult.

Q: In regard to establishing discipline on a team, do there have to be rules?

DG: I don't like rules. I don't like being backed into a corner, and not having a way out. Because you always forget something. You always have something that comes up that you can never think about. Or there's something new that comes up. And so you're in a corner, what do you do then? Well, you hope to make a judgment, but then now you're breaking a rule, and I don't like breaking rules. Still, there are circumstances that require rules and even individuals who need rules. I still haven't solved it.

Q: In regard to your career, have you developed a Dan Gable philosophy for success?

DG: Oh, not one I that could just put out in black and white and say, this is it. Because as soon as I put it out, as soon as I write it down, there's some changes being made or there's something being discovered or I'm learning something else, that throws a little chink in that formula, and now I've got to go back and rearrange it. But that's what's good about the learning process. My life philosophy is that I'll change for the better. I'll take the good, leave the bad, and whenever necessary, I'll upgrade myself.

Q: You would say it is basically an ongoing process. It's not like 10 years ago you basically became who you are today and it stayed there.

DG: Exactly. You hit it right on the nose. You know, from that point of view, it's an ongoing process requiring changes. And then when you find out you made one that wasn't better, you change it back to what you think is best. So you'll make some mistakes along the way. You know, a loss every once in a while will straighten you up. You know, that's okay, so long as you don't get used to losing. It'll get you back going in the right direction.

Bill Walsh

Bill Walsh aspired to be an outstanding head coach, but it took him years as an NFL assistant to prepare for his ascension. Even that effort didn't produce the desired result at first. Walsh spent eight years as an assistant with the stern but brilliant Paul Brown of the Cincinnati Bengals. When Brown stepped down in 1975, it was assumed that Walsh would take over, but Brown named Bill "Tiger" Johnson as his successor. A deflated Walsh moved to the San Diego Chargers for a single season as offensive coordinator before taking the job as head coach of Stanford.

In 1979, having acquired the reputation as an "offensive genius," Walsh was named the head coach of the San Francisco 49ers. His first two seasons resulted in 8 wins and 24 losses, but in the process of that agony he witnessed the rise of quarterback Joe Montana.

Walsh's third season resulted in a 16–3 record and a exhilarating Super Bowl victory over the same Cincinnati Bengals team that had passed on hiring him six seasons earlier.

Yet when Walsh's team plummeted to a 3–6 finish during the strike-shortened 1982 season the next year, he felt a disappointment so deep that he actually contemplated retirement.

Instead, he pressed on, and that perseverance was rewarded with the 1984 season in which his 49ers ran up an 18–1 record topped off by a 38–16 victory over Miami in Super Bowl XIX.

Walsh again achieved championship status in 1988 when his 49ers returned to the Super Bowl and once again defeated the Bengals. He stepped down after that third Super Bowl title, only to return a few years later as the head coach at Stanford.

Today he serves as a consultant to the 49ers.

Walsh's trademark, of course, was the famed "West Coast Offense," which featured short ball-control passes and required both the quarterback and his receivers to read the defense and make adjustments during a play.

Strangely, observers questioned whether Walsh was tough enough to be an NFL head coach when he first began, but just the opposite proved true, mainly because he had the ability to eviscerate a player or assistant coach who might challenge him.

"Players were afraid of Bill," recalled former 49ers backup quarterback Guy Benjamin. "They knew better than to talk back to Bill. They'd be gone the next day if they did."

He was known for never allowing his relationship with his players to grow too comfortable. "Bill was always challenging you," said former 49er receiver Dwight Clark, now an executive with the team. "You never felt you had it made."

As a result, even the most lauded veterans knew from the start that Walsh would trade or release them if he had an option to make his team better. "Bill would never have hesitated if he thought that was the best for the team," Benjamin said.

Billy Packer: Is there such a thing as the thrill of victory?

Bill Walsh: Well, there's the relief of victory. I think in football, in particular, with fewer games than basketball, you're actually relieved with victory because you've just completed one step in a long series of steps toward what you hope will be a championship. To me, the only real thrill occurred in championship games at the end of a season, in which I could look back and say we've actually accomplished this. We've gotten to this point. Now there's exhilaration following any win, but for the head coach it's most difficult because by 10 o'clock that night, you're already looking at the next opponent, saying, "Oh my god, they're really going to be ready for us, and this will be the toughest game of our season."

Q: How about the agony of defeat? Because certainly with all the great championships you were able to accomplish, there were those days, whether they were individual games or life experiences, where the agony of defeat also presented itself.

BW: There's no question about that. I can still vividly recall virtually every loss that occurred while I was coaching the San Francisco 49ers or Stanford. Those losses are vivid in your mind because you can always look back and critique yourself and remind yourself you could have made different decisions. And often the evidence was there. Everything was there for you to make the right decision, and occasionally you made the wrong one and lost games. So, I typically relive every game that I've coached soon after it occurred, and I typically find those mistakes I made, even in the greatest victories. I've never coached a perfect game.

Q: In regard to the score, itself, is victory defined by the score or sometimes, is there satisfaction in regard to a job well done?

BW: I don't like to think the score is the factor. We had some big victories over Dallas during my tenure with the 49ers where the score got pretty high. It didn't bother me that much although we never poured it on. But typically, you don't look at it that way. To me, you look at the execution and the performance of your football team, and the score is another factor. So if our team performed well, occasionally even in a loss, where I could look back and say we played up to our full potential, then I'd get the gratification from that. But the score, itself, can be unfair to the opposition if you're looking at big scores, unfair to your own athletes and misleading to everybody.

Q: The key ingredient to putting together a championship team?

BW: Oh, boy. There really isn't one other than hard work, not profoundly stating goals that are really unreachable, not getting yourself distracted by what you will someday do. To me, it's day-to-day hard work, and making sure everyone is working for the same single purpose—and for us, that's winning on Sundays. In my initial start with the San Francisco 49ers, we were the worst team in professional sports, and the first thing I had to do, and you can't do it in one memo or one presentation to the staff or squad, one thing I really did—I wanted us to do was reach our full performance. Not look at any grandiose goals but get very competent at what we do, and become very competitive, and everything else will take care of itself.

Q: Surprisingly, you did not say to me to get the best talent. Is it possible that you can have the best talent and not develop a championship team?

BW: There's no question about it. Handling talent is critical. But I think as a basis, I think it's becoming very well-coordinated in molding a group of people to think in the same direction and being willing to sacrifice and give of themselves, and develop an enthusiasm and energy for what they're doing. And then pay close, close attention to all details that are established. Now, talent's another story. You're always looking to attain the best talent, but by using the formula I spoke of, you're going to do the best job of attaining that talent. And that's being thorough, objective, planning for the near future and the long-range future, being able to see what a given athlete can do for your team. So often in sports, professional sports in particular, people say this guy is only good enough to get you beat. This guy, you'll always want to replace. Well, my position was, don't worry about that kind of language. What can this person do—what single thing can this person do to help us win a football game? Can he cover a kickoff? Can he catch a punt? Whatever he can do. I want redeeming qualities out of my athletes to be able to make judgments on them.

Q: Is it possible to take the best players and not have the best team?

BW: No question about it. We've seen that time and time again. People really never know if they were the best players. The only way you find out is when they go somewhere else and become great players, and then you say, "Wow, we had all those athletes on the floor at one time and we couldn't win." The chemistry's there. The direction's there. And it's just vital that people be conditioned or molded to think in the same direction, and to have the same focus as everyone else. And that's the job of a head coach to develop that. That's the job of a CEO in a corporate environment to develop that. And that's become a science.

Managing people, motivating people, in a sense, inspiring people, but developing an atmosphere in which everyone is fully mobilized. And that's become an art form. And those coaches that best do that are typically those who win.

Q: You used the term "motivation." Is it possible to motivate someone who does not want to be motivated? Is there a science to that?

BW: There is. I think the science is peer pressure. You're never going to be at your best unless the athletes are reinforced by each other. My feeling, as I matured, and I was best able to relate it to others, was that each player is an extension of the other. And the players have to understand that. They're all connected, and they demand of each other. When you develop an atmosphere, when the players demand of each other and expect of each other and will take nothing less, than you've done a good job as a coach.

Q: Personal relationships. I've seen in my time around sports, and around business, that you have CEOs or head coaches who are sometimes very close to their players. You have others who are somewhat removed. What do you feel about the personal relation between the head master and those guys who make up the championship team?

BW: Well, the great coaches, the Pete Newells of the world, were men who had excellent rapport with their players. Humor became a major factor in the unity of the team, but they didn't become too familiar. They didn't find reason to look at a player as anything more than on the court a player. So as I used to watch Pete Newell's California teams practice, there would be hilarity at times when everyone was bent over laughing, and at other times, he was a total taskmaster. So I think the coach should dem-onstrate an interest and a sensitivity to his athletes or her athletes. And at the same time, familiarity is going to be a problem because now you add more factors into the judg-ment of your athlete. And the athlete, in a sense, shouldn't feel totally comfortable around the head coach. They should enjoy his company or her company, but there should be just an uneasiness. And Pete, I'm probably a disciple of his more than anyone else. With Pete Newell, everyone was just a little uncomfortable and really wanted to satisfy him. And at the same time, he showed enough interest in them, that they knew he was really, sincerely a person that was looking after them.

Q: **As a close friend of Pete's, myself, and obviously a dis-ciple in a way, because he and I have discussed the game and the way people coach many, many times. As times change, could a Pete Newell still be successful? Could a Bill Walsh? I mean, we see every year it seems like the athlete changes, does leadership have to change, as well?**

BW: I think it modifies, certainly, and evolves. I don't think there's any question that Vince Lombardi's style as we knew it would be more difficult to convey to the athletes now than then. But Vince would have adapted, and Pete would have adapted. And I guess, you and I would have adapted. You adapt to the circumstances, and the coach that has good general intelligence and is alert and sensi-tive to other people and their feelings, and who thoroughly enjoys being with other people, will adapt to the surroundings. It's more difficult now; there isn't any question. And some of the moves that you would use, some of the format that would be used would have to be altered. But it's being done here with the San Francisco 49ers right now. And it's been done with the Chicago Bulls, and I can name any number of college programs where it's effectively being done. But, as you point out, it's much more difficult because the players have been conditioned by network television, primarily, to consider themselves unique to everyone else and try to prove it whenever they can.

Q: The word "potential," we hear it so much in life and business and in sports. Is it a negative or a positive word, and how do you equate potential to eventual performance?

BW: I would recite to the team any number of times, any number of ways, that it's my job that they reach their full athletic potential. And I think the parameters for that are really . . . people are thinking more physical than anything else. They look at a person as an athlete, and they're looking at his or her physical aspects of it. But potential can be limited by intelligence. It can be limited by the past, by an athlete's ability to relate and connect with others. There are a lot of things, I suppose, that limit the person who has a real gift athletically. But, it's always the job of the coach that the athlete reach full potential. I see many perennial—and I know you see them all the time—perennial losing programs in which there's an excellent coach, and he's effective. But he just doesn't have the talent pool that other people have, and we have to measure that person by whether the athletes are reaching their full athletic potential.

Q: What would you say has been your biggest satisfaction as a coach working with players?

BW: Well, as an assistant coach, it was always producing . . . being part of the package that developed a Kenny Anderson or a Dan Fouts or a great football player. To think that you tutored that person to that level. As a head coach, it's really hard to pin down. I suppose the obvious would be the greatest satisfaction you receive is in winning the championship or winning the Super Bowl. But now, as I reflect, I cherish my relations with my former players, even the guys who were sort of disgusted with me at times, especially when I asked them to retire. But I take great pride in the fact that there were any number of players that became Hall of Fame athletes that may very well may have become that because they worked with me. Not so much that I'm unique, but they could have gotten with the wrong team, and never reached their potential. So, to be a vehicle for an athlete to become truly great is really the highlight of a coach's value system.

Q: **Of course, I've read articles—there have been many articles written about a Joe Montana, who we all know is a Hall of Famer, superstar—but I've also read an article recently about a young man who fell on great adversity; who thanked you for staying part of his life. Did you get just as much satisfaction out of a Montana becoming rated as maybe the greatest quarterback of all time or a young man who kind of faltered by the way and has been able to redeem himself and his life?**

BW: It's the job of the coach to take a responsibility, a professional ethic I guess you would call it, where he has a sensitivity and a feeling for each athlete with whom he comes in contact. And I take great pride in the fact that guys who are now in their 50s, who played for me with the Stanford freshman team, have a great regard for me. And when I meet with them, they'll tell me stories of things I've said. And a lot of it was connected to humor, but I think that it's critical that the coach have the same empathy and feeling with everyone. So as a head coach, I was very distressed if any of my coaches treated the top player differently than the man on the bottom of the roster. The minute I felt it or even had a hint of it, we'd have to get that straightened out.

Q: One of the things that we often see is that quest for the ultimate Super Bowl championship in the sport of football, and then a guy wins or a team wins. How about the thought of facing failure after the big season? Is there a real problem facing failure?

BW: There really is, because I think failure is the key, critical word that haunts everybody. And it's perceived differently by many people. I've coached high school teams where we've lost the league championship, 28–14, and felt that we'd done a marvelous job because our team didn't stack up against theirs. But in the eyes of a young reporter for the local newspaper, we failed miserably; they blew us out. And that's where I would find it most difficult to deal with the media. So failure is a key factor. I think the bottom line for the coach and his squad is how they deal with frustration, disappointment, and failure—how they deal with it. Because I would remind our football teams, they're going to lose a game. I certainly don't prophesy it, in a sense; I don't want it. But I know it will occur. If we have an evenly matched schedule, somebody's going to beat us, because they're going to be at their best when we play them. But it's how we recover from a loss, and how we deal with failure. And I think that's really the best way to judge and to analyze a coach and a program—it's how they rebound from frustration and failure.

Q: One of the things that I think everyone goes through in life, regardless of what the vocation may be, is that you're looking for a secret to success. I wonder if that ever happened to you going along. I know when I first went into the coaching business, coach Wooden was the best; I was going to find out what his secret was and then follow him, and obviously, I'm going to win. Are there such things as secrets?

BW: For the coach, the secret is, number one, your inventory of the knowledge of the game itself, your technical knowledge. Nobody can take that away from you, and you'll always have it. So you must be a student of the game, and a lifelong student of the game. Even toward the end of your career, you're looking for the newest innovations and creations in your sport, and the newest message of teaching and programming your athletes. So technical knowledge, to me, is critical if you're looking for longevity in the coaching career.

And next, of course, is an absolute and total sincere interest in other people. A compassion when necessary. And the willingness to drive a person, even allow him to feel uncomfortable a little bit as you coach him, but with the purpose of making him a better athlete and learning as much as he can socially from the job he's doing.

So technical knowledge, to me, is absolutely critical. If you don't have it, you're depending on someone else, and at some point, this person is deciding whether you're going to win or lose. You need that as a head coach. Second is your compassion, feeling, interest, and loyalty to your athletes. Now, third, you can go on and on, but third is being able to organize and orchestrate a program—all facets of it. And these are the kind of things you hopefully learn before you become a head coach, not after. If you've been fortunate enough to play for Pete Newell or someone, you've learned probably the most effective way and efficient way to teach and coach, and you then become a disciple, and you have the best chance of success.

Q: Your heralded attack, the well-known "West Coast Offense," basically came out of great principles that you established. Is there tremendous satisfaction to know that now Bill Walsh has so many disciples on all levels? We're not only talking about the NFL, but the college

game, the high school game. That has to create some great satisfaction for you, doesn't it?

BW: It really does. I hate to think I'm at the stage of life where this is supposed to happen, but it's here. Who would ever believe I'd be at this stage of life? All of us are stunned when we finally realize we're in our 60s. But sure I take great pride in the fact that any number of my former coaches and players now have careers in coaching, and have done very, very well. And it's not so much a so-called West Coast Offense, as it is coaching principles and relationships, and style of dealing with athletes and the competition. I think more than anything else, I take great pride in that. The fact that Dennis Green at Minnesota does not necessarily run the West Coast offense, but in a recent interview, he was speaking of coaching philosophy, coaching style, organizational structure, and dealing with the individual skills of an athlete, those were the things, I guess, he learned from me. And I, in turn, learned from other people.

Q: You used the term "loyalty." We see so often today cases of loyalty being a one-way street. How important is loyalty in building the championship team?

BW: It's a commitment, you know. There are all kinds of personalities, and some people, inherently, are going to be critical of what's going on around them. I don't consider that disloyal. But now I think if a person personally plots to disrupt or disturb or destroy things, that's when loyalty becomes a factor. But there are varying ranges of personality. Some people are just sort of negative and semi-critical of everything that goes on in their lives, and that never really bothered me. But when an overt act of disloyalty occurred, well then it was in contrast with everything you're attempting to accomplish and it has to certainly be dealt with. But the thing I didn't want or expect was absolute conformity and absolute loyalty to me. I'd much rather deal with people who have a loyalty to themselves and to their professional career, and to their values and ethics. If they'll live those kinds of things, if their personal makeup is along those lines, I'd much more appreciate them than somebody saluting me every morning when I come into the office.

Q: Suppose you've got to make a cut on your ball club or you've got to make a decision as to whom to draft; you have to make a decision as to whom to start at quarterback. Would you say intelligence or physical presence would be the most important characteristic?

BW: There's a formula out there, and I think at any extreme, it could be an incredibly gifted athlete who is rather dull. You can deal with that person, but not in large numbers on your team. Or an extremely intelligent, capable person, who gives you everything he has, but with lesser athletic ability. You can deal with that extreme, too. And hopefully, you'll have those two extremes as part of the makeup of your squad. But the bulk of your squad must consist of people with functional intelligence for the sport itself, and who have the athletic ability to play their particular position very competitively with the opposition. So it could come to pass that you have a very, very gifted athlete who is somewhat limited mentally. It's up to the coach to find, to offer that man a vehicle to use his abilities on the field, that's the coach's job. The coach also needs balance on his club and functional intelligence. It's not high IQ. It's the ability to deal with the circumstances themselves in each particular sport, whether it be water polo or women's soccer or whatever. Their ability to deal with that particular activity and play with an open mind, and play naturally and not be manufactured as an athlete. By the way, there's natural instinct and intuition by degree in all of us. In some athletes, it's there almost in excess, and those are the kind of athletes like Joe Montana or Ronnie Lott, and when you come in contact with them you're just in awe of them right from the first time you see them.

Q: So it's an instinctive feel they have? A Deion Sanders has an instinctive feel?

BW: Right. I think so. There is just a natural intuitive gift they have.

Q: Can you spot that? You walk on a field, and the first day you see a Ronnie Lott, you say this fellow is special?

BW: You'd better. You hope you do. Some coaches don't see that. They don't even account for that. They think anyone that plays for them has to be manufactured by them. So there isn't any latitude given for a natural creative, competitive performance that can be offered if the athlete is given some latitude. In my case, it was with Joe Montana or Steve Young. You personally have seen it many, many times in basketball, and when you spoke of people having teams with great firepower, great talent, and not doing well, typically, it's the coach who doesn't understand to offer those latitudes. And again, that's the proficiency of the coach, his ability to weigh and measure how much latitude an athlete should have, that has a gift. And again, when you look at coaching in that sense, it's a science.

Q: The word "competitor," we see some fellows that just walk out on the field—like a Dick Butkus, who walks out on the football field and goes full blast all the time. Is that inborn? Is that something you can help create? Are there guys who don't have competitive instincts that a coach can help develop or does he just bring that to the field with his genes?

BW: I think you bring a lot of that to the field with your genes. But again, it's the coach's job to nurture and enhance and develop whatever capacity a man has for that to its fullest. With Dick Butkus, it's finding a way to let him explode on that field and still play in an organized sport. For others, it could be a rather hesitant athlete who doesn't have whatever confidence in himself that it takes to bring him along as far as you can. So it's the coach's job to bring a man or a woman as far as you can in the sport, to allow that competitive zeal to demonstrate itself. And it includes reaching back and pulling people up with you, not discarding them. And often, through exchanges and through getting close to the athlete, you can find a way to give them the opportunity to break through any fear or trepidation they might have. And it happens all the time in sports. So you're not always establishing that "only the Dick Butkuses can play for me." Unfortunately, you don't have that many of that type, so you're always trying to pull those hesitant athletes along so that they can have an opportunity to find themselves and compete.

Q: Do you practice as you play? Is that true—that you practice as you play? Or have you had situations where teams didn't necessarily relate to that? Even championship teams?

BW: Well, I'd hate to see a lackadaisical team just frit around the practice team, then go win a championship. That basically means they didn't have any competition in the championship. If you have competition, and whenever you take the field, you feel the other person is one point better than you—that's the psyche I always worked toward, no matter who they were. If you feel they're one point better than you, then every minute you have with your team has to be of value. So our practices are related directly to playing the game itself. There are no drills that

are just drills to take up time. Everything we do is concentration on some aspect of the game, and very close
concentration. So when our players take the practice field,
there's a lot expected of them. And number one is absolute and total concentration on what they're doing. And
we give them reason to have that state of mind because
we're always doing something very practical and succinct
to the game itself, related to it. Not just going through a
series of plays or drills to get them over with. So if you
see a team or a group of players who are bored with practice, the coach isn't doing a good job. It's that simple. If
you see players who hate practice, their coach isn't doing
a very good job.

Q: **You mentioned a word that leads right to my next question. The utilization of time, how important is that to
the success of a championship team and coach?**

BW: If the players feel that you are using every minute on the
field to prepare them to win or to compete, then they're
going to be willing to give you every minute of their time.
But if there's wasted, loose, lackadaisical moments out
there, the players lose their concentration and lose their
appreciation for practice. So with the San Francisco 49ers,
every play that is run has a practical application, and the
players know what it is. Every situation and every drill
that is run, players connect it directly to the game itself.
One of the misnomers or the misleading conclusions that
young coaches reach is they have toughness drills, or they
have drills that we decide who has more courage than
anyone else. Or they have drills that were really space-
fillers because they don't know what else to do. So the
absolute bottom line in coaching is organization and preparing for practice. And that doesn't occur the day before
the practice, or the night before. Or the day of. That occurs in the off-season when a major calendar is established

and every detail is organized weeks before it ever takes place. In my particular case, I would take my vacation. Part of it would be establishing the first four-and-a-half weeks of training camp. Every practice. Every drill. For every coach. And with that in mind, I knew exactly how many minutes my defensive backfield coach had for tackling. On what days he would do it, and what the drills would be. And this covered the entire spectrum of the game of football. Every situation was covered. From having the ball on your own 1-yard line, to having the ball on the opponent's 1-yard line. Playing with 10 seconds remaining and trying to score, and as is the obvious example of taking the ball the length of the field in the final drive, which we did on many occasions. All those things were practiced. So contingency planning has become the most critical factor in coaching once you get to the organizational level. So that every consideration that is reasonable is accounted for and there is a way of teaching it or explaining it to the squad. So they're never surprised. Now there was a day in Bear Bryant's time, if you said to a team, "Now men, if we're ever behind 28–0, here's what we'll do," the players would have laughed. The whole room would have gone up in the air, and he would never have said that. But now we, in this dynamic, explosive form of football we play, you can be behind 28–0, and you should know what to do. Or you can be ahead 28–0, and knowing your opponent is still dangerous, and know what to do. So, all of these contingencies that can occur in sports are now the critical aspect of coaching the game. And that takes study and concentration, learning, investigating on the part of the coach. And those coaches that have this broad-based, comprehensive of knowledge and understanding are the ones that we'll see in the future that will be succeeding.

Q: You brought me right into my next question. You mentioned the assistant coach, how important to building a
   championship team is the delegation of authority to
   those people that are working with you?

BW: Well it's absolutely critical that the assistant coaches can feel
    comfortable, in a sense at ease, but in control of their drills
    and their time and their athletes. They have to be able to feel
    that. There has to be a relationship that's worked out where
    the presence of the head coach will not affect the assistant
    coach or distract from him teaching his athletes. Today's head
    coach could very well, like in corporate America, become a
    facilitator, where you actually go to a drill and help the as-
    sistant coach with a drill, giving the controls to the assistant
    coach. Where he is in control, and you're assisting him. And
    your ego isn't affected in one way. You're both doing your
    jobs, and the players can see and understand that. An ex-
    ample would be in critical games, I would be the man
    handling the scout squad for our defensive unit. I person-
    ally would be. And in some programs, the graduate assistant,
    the fourth graduate assistant, would be up there doing it,
    and everybody would be yelling at him, and everybody
    would be confused. Well, in my case, I would be the one
    that would be directing that because I wanted our team to
    get preparation in my presence in doing that. So I had sub-
    jugated myself to the defensive coordinator and his staff.
    But that's just part of the ongoing relationships that develop
    on a coaching staff. But coaches should have autonomy, and
    they should be able to drill as they see fit, provided that fits
    into the master plan, and that's been discussed in detail be-
    fore they ever do it.

Q: By the time they walk on the field, the coaches as well
   as the team had better be a unit?

BW: That's right. And the head coach has to know what the
    assistant's doing, and has to have, I guess, approved it, if

you want to say that. And it would be understood prior to game time.

Q: With this great preparation, you're planning for success. Did you ever sit down and decide what is success? How are we going to define success for this given team? You've come off some years where you didn't win the Super Bowl. You came off years that you did. What was the formula for success, or was there one?

BW: There had to have been a meeting of the minds, in our case between ownership and management and coaching, as to where the squad was and what could be expected. And I can remember one particular year in which we expected our team to win more than they lost, because we had a very young team, and we were building. Well, it turned out we won 13 and lost 2 that year. And we exceeded any expected goals or anticipation of anything, and that's a plus. But I think the realistic objective exchanges must be held between all parties. In professional sports, it's ownership, management, coaching, but in the intercollegiate scenario, the athletic director, those key people involved in the program, all of them, sit down and objectively discuss what to expect that year.

Q: What do you view as the athlete's obligation to a team?

BW: I think really conforming and participating and being involved in the organization or in the team is absolutely critical. And living with standards that are established, and living within the parameters of the expectations of everyone else, whether it be being punctual; whether it be concentrating on whatever plans are unfolding for a game; whether it be how you handle yourself during the game in the most severe of situations, how you handle defeat. All those kinds of things build for a sort of a persona that an athlete has to develop to really be part of a winning team.

Q: **The development of your philosophy—is it important, first of all, to have a philosophy, and secondly, how do you develop it?**

BW: I think it's really important to develop a philosophy as you can identify it. A lot of people would like to have the philosophy before anything else. But often it will take some fundamental knowledge of the dynamics of the game itself, and of the options related to rules, and actually of the parameters of how the game is played. With some knowledge of that, then a person, in general, will have a certain slant on what he sees. He'll see things somewhat differently maybe than someone else, and that's when the philosophy begins. But it's so important to have a mentor. At the time, you never think of this person as a mentor, but as you look back, he or she was. In my case, it was my college coach, Bob Bronson, who was years ahead of his time and who really thrived on the technical and strategic parts of the game. But also I worked for Paul Brown, one of the great coaches of our game, and other people like John Ralston and Tommy Prothro. And my experience with Al Davis with the Raiders also added to an inventory of knowledge and appreciation that I have. But then as time passes, you, your own philosophy becomes semi-evident, and you begin to work toward it. And at some point many years later, you say "Well, this was your philosophy," and you look back and say, "Yes, I guess it was" (laughing).

Q: **What is the best advice ever given to you, not necessarily football advice about a specific play or something, but the best advice that you've had that helped you develop championships from any individual?**

BW: It may have been Sid Gilman, whom I had a number of conversations with as we were developing the San Francisco 49ers. And he just said pay attention to every detail, and expect everyone else to have the same commitment, and for everyone else to have an investment in what they're doing, that works with you.

Lenny Wilkens

It has never been about the numbers for Lenny Wilkens. All the same, his career has produced a most impressive set of statistics. Heading into the 1997–98 season, his 25th as an NBA head coach, Wilkens owned 1,070 victories, the most in league history. In fact, if you add up the 1,150 games he played during his 15-year career as an All-Star caliber point guard, Wilkens has participated in more than 3,300 NBA games, more than anyone in league history.

For much of his early career, he was a player-coach, first with the Seattle SuperSonics, then with the Portland Trail Blazers. He returned to Seattle as a full-time coach midway through the 1977–78 season and took a team with a 5–17 record and directed it to the NBA championship series, one of the most amazing in-season turnarounds in pro hoops annals. His club lost to the Washington Bullets, but Wilkens reversed the circumstances in 1979 and coached the Sonics to the championship, a 4–1 decision over the Bullets.

For 1986–87, he took over a dismal Cleveland Cavaliers team that had won just 29 games the year before and promptly directed the club to a string of 50-win seasons and playoff appearances.

He worked the same transformation for the Atlanta Hawks after taking over there before the 1993–94 season, again pushing that club to the upper realm of the NBA. The reward for his consistent success was his naming as head coach of the United States Men's Basketball Team, the so-called Dream Team III, that claimed the Gold Medal in the 1996 Olympic Games in Atlanta, the ultimate honor in a career that has garnered many.

In 1994, he was named NBA Coach of the Year. In 1997, he was the only person named to both the NBA's 50th anniversary list of 10 best coaches and 50 greatest players.

An All-American point guard at Providence College (where he earned a degree in economics) and a first-round draft pick in 1960, Wilkens quickly developed into a seasoned, veteran floor leader, one so capable that he even finished second to Wilt Chamberlain in the league MVP voting one season.

One of five children, Wilkens learned the game on the playgrounds of Brooklyn. He only played one year of high school basketball, but that was enough to launch his career. "Everyone said I was like a coach on the floor," he said of his transition from playing to coaching. "So I decided to find out."

"No matter what I do, people will always say I'm laid-back, but I used to lose my temper much more quickly when I first started coaching. But soon I realized I was never like that when I played the game. I was always in control of what I wanted to do when I played, and I decided I wanted to coach the same way."

Billy Packer: Lenny, is there any such thing as the thrill of victory or the agony of defeat?

Lenny Wilkens: There's no question there is. The thrill of victory, when you're playing as many games as we do, is not just one game, but to me, it's a matter of getting to a championship round and then winning it. There's no question in my mind it's a thrill. Winning an All-Star game, there's a thrill to that, too, because it's the best of the best. And certainly, losing in situations like that is painful. When you're in sports, it's sort of a roller-coaster ride because you're so up and down. But when you lose, when you're a real competitor, there are no good losses.

Q: How long does that agony of defeat or that thrill of victory last for you?

LW: I guess until the next game (laughing). Especially in losing. The beauty of the NBA is that you don't have a whole lot time to feel sorry for yourself, because there's another game coming up and you have to prepare, so your mind has to jump to preparation for the next game. You get over it quicker. And the thrill of victory doesn't last as long as you'd like it to, because even in just winning a regular game, tomorrow night you might be playing someone else, and everything changes.

Q: How about the difference between the thrills or the agony for a player as opposed to a coach. Which one was either more satisfying or more difficult to overcome?

LW: I think the losses, for a coach, are more difficult to overcome. As a player, I knew that I could do better the next game, or I could help the team do better. I could physically be out there. As a coach, you prepare your team,

---

275

and the only way you help sometimes is through a time-out or something like that. But it's the players who are on the floor doing the rebounding, doing the defending, doing the scoring. So all yours is preparation, so I think it's harder for a coach to get over losses than a player.

Q: What do you feel is the key ingredient of the championship team?

LW: I think one of the key ingredients in a championship team is being tough-minded, and really believing that you can overcome any circumstance.

Q: Where does talent fit into the championship equation? Do you think you can ever win a championship, when in your mind, maybe you have less talent to work with than maybe somebody you're going to have to face?

LW: I think that happens rarely. You've got to have talent, first of all. That's a premise we all take for granted. If you're there, you've got some talent. But yes, on sheer hustle, a team can go pretty far. But I think that if the talent is well-prepared and well-coached, you're not going to overcome it.

Q: In regard to developing a championship attitude on a team, is it something that you can feel developing as the season goes on? Or is it something that you can sense from the first day of practice?

LW: The attitude gets stronger. But you can sense that people are about business when they come into camp, and how they've prepared themselves over the summer. If that is there, you accomplish things quicker, because you don't have to spend as much time on fundamentals. But I think that the attitude has to get stronger as you go. What happens along the way if you win tight games, close games, then in your mind, you always believe you're in every game no matter what the score is.

Q: Is motivation something that you as a coach can put into the team, or do you think it has to be something within the team and the players themselves?

LW: I think it has to be within, but I think the coach can help bring it out, if it's there. Most people who are highly competitive, whether it's business or sports, they have something within them. And then, yes, you can bring it out, and I believe that I can do that, if you have it. If you don't have it, I think it's very difficult to instill.

Q: For a coach to be successful, is it important that he be liked by those people playing for him?

LW: No, I don't think so. What I push for is respect. And respect has be a two-way street. And if we have that respect, if we respect one another, we can work together. We don't have to like each other, because when I go home, I may not want to see you again until the next day, and vice versa. But I think that we've got to respect one another. We don't have to love one another.

Q: You mentioned a coach gaining respect. How do you gain respect in the eyes of those guys playing for you?

LW: I think, one, you're consistent. And like I said, two, I let them know that respect is a two-way street. And if you want it, you have to give it. I don't take anything personally. I let them know I'll be there all day to work with them if they want to improve on something. And I'll put the time in. And I let them know that everybody is accountable for their actions—everybody. And I don't treat one guy more special than another. If the bus leaves at 10, everybody's got to be on the bus. And I'm consistent in that. And my players know that. And I'll go to bat for them. I'll work hard for them, but then, as I said, they've got to respond, too.

Q: Is it important for the coach to have a personal relationship with the team leader and those guys who are
playing for him?

LW: I think he has to. They've got to be able to communicate.
They've got to be on the same wavelength. And usually,
your leader is sort of an extension of the coach, to a degree, on the floor. On the floor, the players, someone
amongst their peer group, has to be a leader, and if he
understands what a coach wants, and can implement
some of it, then that makes him even that much more effective and it makes the team more effective.

Q: You've been an excellent player and then a hugely successful coach, the winningest in the history of the league.
Over the course of your career, the game has changed a
great deal. Do you think the player/coach relationship
has changed with the game?

LW: The athlete, no question, is a little different today, but so
is society. And I think that those of us or anyone who has
continuous growth in the world today is aware of how
things have changed. Communication remains one of the
keys in coaching.

The young athlete coming in requires more teaching
today than before, because they're not as solid with fundamentals. A lot of them come out of college after one
year, and what you're seeing also is some of them are coming in from high school. So not only do you have to help
teach them basic fundamentals, then you have to teach
them maturity, help them with maturity, rather. Then teach
them the pro game. So there's a lot more required today,
and you've got to build a trust. And if you build that trust,
then they're receptive to what you're talking about.

Q: The word "potential," is it a blessing or a curse for the
athlete? Or for the team?

LW: Probably a curse (laughing). It's unfortunate, but in the NBA, too often people, they look at a guy's potential and they label him, and sometimes he can't shake that. And I think that's wrong. I think that we should recognize that a guy has potential, but we shouldn't categorize him until he has the chance to be successful. And I think sometimes we categorize a guy too soon.

Q: The term that's thrown around so much in the media today is the term "role model." Do you think it applies to a coach in the eyes of his players?

LW: I think that in a sense, that he sets a standard, and he should be consistent. The players should know where he's at all the time, and know what to expect from him. So in that sense, yes, I think that applies to everybody, though. Consistency is a key ingredient in many relationships.
I recognize that role models begin with parents, but those of us who are looked up to, I think we need to be consistent. We have to do our part.

Q: How about the greatest satisfaction you've had as a coach? Not as a player, but as a coach.

LW: I would say the greatest satisfaction is certainly winning a championship in the NBA, but also coaching the Olympic team to the gold medal. Here, you represent your country on a world stage. I don't think it gets any better than that. I mean everybody in the world is watching the Olympics. And here I have a chance to help them win a gold medal. I think that's the greatest.

Q: How about the greatest disappointment?

LW: Oh, I don't know what the greatest is. There's been a lot of disappointments (laughing). Especially when you don't win and you think you should. I guess when we had a chance to repeat. We won the championship in 1979 when

I was coaching the Seattle SuperSonics, and we went back the following year, and we lost in the conference finals because we had to play at the University of Washington, and not on our regular home court. We had to play on a neutral court. And that hurt us because we split. And we were playing the Lakers, and they wound up beating us. So that was truly a disappointment because I felt if we had been playing at the Coliseum in Seattle, we would have won.

Q: With today's press scrutiny, is it tougher to be a successful coach than it was when you first started?

LW: Well, yes, it is, Billy, because so much is perception. I'm not someone who's going to promote myself. I'm from an old school background. I think if I'm doing something well, you should be able to see and read and understand that. I mean you should be able to see it. I shouldn't have to go out and sell you on what I'm doing. And so yes, I think it's tougher. I think that's because the questions are put to players, especially when the media know a player's not playing much, they go to him and get him to say things that probably he shouldn't say or didn't want to say and expand on it. Everything gets taken out of proportion.

Q: The idea of facing failure. Is that something that ever haunts you?

LW: No. No, because I was taught at a young age that that's just an opportunity to start over again.

Q: Have you ever found any shortcuts in this great success you've had as a coach?

LW: None at all (laughing). It's work. It's putting time in, and understanding and learning and working with people. No, there are no shortcuts.

Q: Lenny, do you ever set any goals for your team in terms of wins and losses, or where you anticipate being at the end of the year?

LW: Yes, I set goals. I set intermediate goals. I give players individual goals, and then I give the team a goal, which is probably my goal, too, of where we should be by All-Star break, how we should be playing by then, and where we should be going after that.

Q: Does a winning coach have to have leadership qualities that he's born with, or is it something that you feel can be developed?

LW: That's a hard one. I don't know. I think it can be developed, but, you know, ever since I grew up, I wanted to take the lead in everything I did. I mean I wanted to be involved because I felt like I could affect the situation. And so when I was a player, it was really easy. I wanted that ball at the end of a game, because I knew if I couldn't do it, I knew who could, and that I could get it to him. And so, I think you need that. Yes, I think some guys do evolve into leaders that maybe didn't realize they could be early. But a lot of it comes early.

Q: You have two guys who are basically the same in terms of their productivity. Now comes a time you have to make a decision in playing time. Are you going to take the guy with the superior physical skills, or the guy with the mental skills?

LW: The mental (laughing). Definitely. I can overcome a lot of physical disadvantages. I could use your strength against you. I can do a lot of that, if I know how. And so, it's not always how strong you are. The guy who has mental superiority will find a way.

Q: We talked about leadership, and I want to also bring up the point of the competitor. Is that something that's also built-in, or can you help build the competitive spirit?

LW: I think you can enhance a competitive spirit, but I think you've got to have that basic drive to win. I think that comes from within.

Q: Have you ever seen a guy who on your first go-round, maybe didn't have it, but through some means or another, was able to become a better competitor?

LW: Well, yes, because usually what happens when you see someone who doesn't have it, sometimes it's only because of a lack of confidence. And if you can build his confidence and show people how to be successful, then they get to liking that, and all of the sudden they step up and become real competitive. But his basic competitiveness was something that was there already. It was just dormant.

Q: What's more important? Pregame preparation or in-game adjustments?

LW: I don't know. I feel they're both necessary. I try and prepare my team, but I feel I'm mentally ready to make any adjustment I have to. And I think they go hand in hand.

Q: With the tremendous rigors of an NBA season, does a champion always play as he practices?

LW: No. You know, I think what happens is . . . we always say how you practice is how you play. I think it's up to the coach to recognize when you have a long season like that, every practice doesn't have to be three hours or two hours. What has to happen in practice is you have to accomplish what you're setting out to do. And if it's to prepare your team and get them ready, and when you see they're ready, then go ahead and stop it. Don't let it drag on or become ragged or whatever. Because then you're going to take away from your sharpness.

Q: Over the years, you've had an opportunity to observe so many coaches and other players—do you think it's important to have a mentor? And did you feel that you had mentors getting you to the point of where you are today?

LW: I think so. You learn from people. I only played a half of a year of high school ball. But that coach at Boys' High, a guy named Mickey Fisher, was the smartest coach I've ever met. And just a half a year I spent with him, talking the game, and him working, making me do things, whatnot, I never met anyone as smart as him. And then when I got into the pro game, I always marveled at how Red Auerbach utilized all his players. He'd take a guy that everybody thought wasn't going to be any good and get something out of him. The other guy was Marv Harshman, who coached the University of Washington. I used to sit and watch his practices, and talk with him. We did a TV show together, and I learned quite a bit from him. So, those were the three guys.

Q: What is the best advice you were ever given, either in or out of basketball?

LW: Well, the best advice was given to me by Marv Harshman. It was when I was a player-coach. I wasn't as calm then as I am now, as people think I am, I should say. I was yelling and screaming at practice one day because a guy didn't see the man on the low post, or didn't get him the ball at the right time.

Marv was waiting for me and watching our practice. And so afterward, when Marv and I were together, he told me, "You know, it was easy for you because you see the floor all the times. You always saw it and it was easy, but they don't see it like you see it. So what you have to do as a coach, is learn how to help them see it."

And I thought, "Yes, that makes a lot of sense." That really helped me in teaching the game.

Q: With all the requirements that you have, the travel, the multiplicity of the games, is the use of time something critical to your success?

LW: It really is, because there are so many demands on you. Whether it's doing promotional stuff for the team or for yourself, or family. All these things compete for your time. And so, I try to use my time judiciously, because it is important.

Q: Do you as a coach feel the establishment of discipline is necessary? Do you have set rules?

LW: It is necessary. I think anyone who is successful understands discipline. We have discipline, I mean when we are going to leave to go somewhere, or the bus leaves at a certain time. Or we have a set time to be in the locker room before a home game. All the things that are important to a team have to be driven by discipline. And I want my players to understand that.

Q: Do you set up a series of rules that are to be followed, and how do you enforce them?

LW: We have team rules. And if someone violates them, they get fined. And, as I tell players, if I've got to keep fining you, then I don't want you.

Q: To be successful as you have been over these many years, do you have to develop a philosophy?

LW: I think we all develop a philosophy. And mine is to always . . . not to worry about things I can't affect or control. I've got to move on, and worry about things I can change. So, I don't let anything get me down. I'm an up person. And I try to stay upbeat all the time, and I find that I can do that.

Q: Looking back now from the day you coached your first team to where you are today, when do you feel that you

established the mental framework of your philosophy? Was it right at the very beginning? Or did it develop over a period of time?

LW: No, it didn't. It developed my third year as a player-coach. The first couple of years were a novelty, and I wasn't really sure what the heck I was doing or why I was doing it. And in the third year, I got real serious about it, and I'd been paying attention and so forth. And I started to try to affect the game in some kind of way by doing things. When I started having success, I started liking this and then, you know, ideas start to form and you start to get opinions about what you can do and what you can't do.

Q: How long has the Lenny Wilkens philosophy, as we know it today, been solid?

LW: I think it's been present for a long time. You embellish everything that you do as the seasons go by, but that philosophy came early, and it was based on a lot of what I saw. And I saw how successful Red Auerbach was with the use of his personnel, and how he did things. So I think it's been there for a while.

Joe Paterno

He loves the opera and still reads voraciously. Not long ago, he went through Joseph Conrad's *Lord Jim* and was stunned at what it revealed about leadership. Needless to say, he's a special teacher. Penn State fans can only be happy that five decades ago Joe Paterno simply didn't have the money to go to law school. He had an English degree from Brown University, where he played football and basketball. He needed direction in his life and figured that becoming a lawyer was a good start. "But my dad and I owed $2,000 when I got out of Brown, and it was going to be a real financial problem for us to handle law school," Paterno recalled.

Instead, he became a football coach.

It was in 1950 that he became an assistant to new Penn State coach Rip Engle.

It was a paycheck, but not something he planned to do for life.

Nearly a half century later, Paterno was still chugging on at age 70, after 32 seasons as a head coach. His successes include seven undefeated teams and 20 Academic All-Americans. He has won two national championships, a hair under 300 games, and an unequaled 18 bowl games.

To find something representative of his style, look no further than his team's uniforms and his own thick glasses and white socks.

"I don't think our uniforms look that bad," he once said. "I think they say something to kids about team-oriented play and an austere approach to life."

His players wear high-top black shoes, white helmets with no logos, and jerseys with no players' names on the back.

It's a style he has carried out of the past and into a future that seemingly has no limits, a rare thing for an septuagenarian. He still runs sprints with his players, walks 20–25 miles a day, and has no thoughts of retiring. In 1996, one of his players, Brandon Noble, told reporters, "I really think he's stopped aging or something."

His mother supposedly died in her 90s with black hair.

Thus, Paterno turns all the energy that his gift of youth has brought to coaching the Nittany Lions. "There's nothing else I'd rather do," he says.

He did have a losing season once. Penn State fell to 5–6 in 1988. And in 1992, his team started 5–0 only to finish 7–5. But he has charged back each time from those setbacks. And now he's well within striking distance of Bear Bryant's record of 323 wins for a Division I head coach.

One of his lessons late in life has been not to press too much. "I have a lot more patience with kids," he said as the 1997 season got underway. "When I was young and aggressive—I was 39 years old when I first started head coaching—I had very little patience and a very difficult job realizing how different kids could be."

He even drew some rare criticism during the 1997 season when he pulled his starters with a 34–3 lead over the University of Pittsburgh. Paterno, though, said he was more interested in reserves getting playing time than pumping up the score to impress the pollsters.

"What I owe to my team is to make sure everybody plays and works hard, and I have an opportunity to play them," Paterno told reporters who questioned his move. "I think that for me to take some kids who look forward to playing on a Saturday and not play them when I think the game is in control because I want to make sure that we win by X number of points so we can preserve a place (in the polls) would be irresponsible."

In the closing minutes, Pitt scored two touchdowns over Paterno's reserves.

"The game is played by kids, college students, a lot of whom do not get a lot of ink, but get the satisfaction of working hard all week, and if things go well, get an opportunity to play," Paterno said. "I think that's more of my responsibility than to try to satisfy the appetite of a lot of people . . . I don't have much respect for their judgment in the sense that because you win by 25 points that makes you better than if you win by 15 points. That's so unreasonable to me that I just don't want to get down to that level."

Billy Packer: Coach, is there such a thing as the thrill of victory or the agony of defeat?

Joe Paterno: I think there is a thrill of victory. I don't think there's any question about that. Agony may be too strong a word. But there's certainly a feeling as if something left your stomach if you lose. I don't think you ever quite get over it. You never get used to it. I remember we played John Robinson in the Fiesta Bowl. And John and I were getting to be friends, and we beat them. As we were going to the after-the-game on-the-field ceremony, he leaned over and said, "You know, this losing is for the birds!" And I think that's the way I always walked away from a loss. And yet keep your perspective. You don't want to go overboard about it. There's always, hopefully, another chance.

Q: Do you profit from losing?

JP: I think you profit more from getting a licking because it makes you zero in on the things you didn't do well. There's a tendency when you win to overlook some of the things you didn't do well. I've always said to my squad, you're never as good as you think you are when you win, and you're never as bad as you think you are when you lose. And you learn from both ends of it, but I do think you learn more from losing.

Q: Is there a key ingredient of a championship team?

JP: I think the expectancy. I think the key ingredient to me, in a championship team, is to plan for it. I think there are a lot of people who want to be national champs. Some of them don't have the slightest idea what it's going to take in any area. I think you've got to literally plan to be champs. You start out understanding there are going to be different things that are going to come up during your season. There's going to be a time when you have a bad day. You're going to kick the ball around, and yet you've got to have the poise and the confidence and the expectations that you're going to overcome that. There's going to be a time when you're going to have to make a drive in the last quarter. In my sport, you're going to have to win a couple of games with specialty teams. You've got to plan for it. And the kids have got to have that kind of expectation, and they get in a tough football mind-set. They'll run a kickoff back the second half. They'll do something. I think you've got to plan or talk about it all the time. I think the individuals involved in it have to think about it all the time.

Q: What about talent as a key ingredient? Have you ever won with what you thought was less talent than maybe somebody might have had to win a championship?

JP: Yes. I think talent is obviously very important. But with 11 people on the field at one time both in the kicking game and on offense and on defense, there's a certain amount of discipline and trust in each other and the ability to do little things that are just a small part of the operation, one eleventh of the operation, over and over and over on a consistent level. And sometimes people with talent don't want to do that. But if you get the combination of the talent and the understanding of what it takes to be able do the things you've got to do in the clutch, and have the poise to do it, then obviously the talent helps. I think you can have talent and not do it, and I think you can win without talent. You've got to have a certain level of talent. I'm not saying you can go out there and win with a bunch of guys who can't run, you know, can't jump and do some things. You can have a better team than the other guy may have if you've got those little ingredients.

Q: Each year, of course, you have a whole different scenario. The changing environment of the college game doesn't allow you to build, in effect, a dynasty. That means that you have to develop a championship attitude on a team on a yearly basis. At what point each year do you begin the championship process?

JP: We've tried to be selective in the people we recruit based on the fact that we're looking for character, people who are going to be with us four, five years. We're looking for kids that we think have a chance to graduate, and will respond to what we feel Penn State expects of them, and vice versa. So, every once in a while you look at your squad and you know, "Hey, we're not going to get it done this year. It's probably two, three years down the road." But you start to plan and start to put people in places, so that if you have some luck, then it works together. And usually that's worked for us. Every three or four years, we usually have a team that I think is a national championship type team. We've either had an undefeated team or we've played for a national championship or we won the national championship. That's pretty consistent over the last 30 years here at Penn State, except once, and that's when I had a very unusual group of kids that I didn't quite handle properly. So, that's about the cycle we've gone through. But I do think you can't just all the sudden say this is our championship year. I think you've got to look down the road, and start to work to it.

Q: Can you motivate players to win a championship, or does it have to be something that the kids have from within that you merely pull out?

JP: Leadership might be a better word than motivation, because when I get a group of people, they don't understand what it's going to take to win a national championship. And our coaching staff, and I've been fortunate because I've been able to keep all our coaches for such a long period of time and so many of them have been through this thing with me, that you start out talking to them about what it's going to take. It's going to take a certain lifestyle, it's going to take a certain discipline, certain commitment. Try to explain the level. And then day in and day out, try to make them understand that it's worth the effort. Now that's probably the motivation part of it. The scene in a locker room after somebody wins a championship is one that nobody ever forgets. You never forget that feeling. And every time you see somebody, whether it's the Bulls win the national championship, or last year it's Arizona won it when they weren't supposed to win it, you talk about it. It takes a little luck, obviously, but it's just something that nobody else does. You're going to have it all your life.

Q: So "winning one for the Gipper" isn't necessarily what you would consider the ingredient of the motivation to be a champion?

JP: No. No, I think they win it for themselves. I think they want to have an experience, a once-in-a-lifetime experience. And I think that's the thing. And as far as the coach or the manager of the operation, he's got to show them how to do it, and he's got to make sure that they're not silly, that they can do it an easier way. There are no short cuts. It's a tough job. You want to be number one. You want to be the best. There's a hundred football teams that get together every preseason, and every one of them might have a possibility of being the best. Which one's going to be it? These are the things that have worked for us. These are the things that if you're willing to do, you'll have a chance to be on a national championship team before you get out of Penn State.

Q: Is it important for a coach to be liked by those players and assistants working for him?

JP: No. Absolutely no. Respected. Fair. As fair as you can be when you're dealing with 120 people. It's impossible being fair to every one of them. And we start off telling them that. One of the things I tell them when we first start in preseason practice—which is where we try to set the tone of how tough we're going to have to work—I say, you know, you may come back here 25 years from now at a reunion, and you may all sit around and you may say, "Boy, you remember what an SOB that Paterno was? You remember what Sandusky made us do? And you remember that day we practiced out there until we thought we were going to drop? The shouting, and the urging and the cajoling and the nit-picking about all the little things." You may come back and gripe about that, but you're never going to come back here and say, "You know, I just wish Joe knew how good we wanted to be; that if he'd just pushed us a little more, we could have gone all the way." We're never going to sell you short. We're going to make you be as good as you can be, and if you're willing to go along with us, we're going to have some fun.

Q: Is it important to have personal relationships with players while they're playing for you?

JP: Yes. I don't think it has to be a deep personal relationship, but I think it's got to be a relationship where they feel free to come and gripe to you about something. They feel free to come and say, "Hey, how come we're doing this?" Or a group of them can come to you. For that reason, I try to meet weekly with 11 or 12 kids at a breakfast group, and just sit around and say, "Hey, we got any problems?" Try and get the kids to come in and talk to their position coach, or the person that recruited them, or come in and talk to me, and feel free to be critical of us. I think that's important, more so today than it was years ago. Right now, the players are much more mature, and they expect more from a coach than just the arbitrary, than just going out there and saying, "We're going to do this," not giving reasons, and if they don't like it, not being able to go in and ask you why. I think you've got to give them the freedom to ask you why.

Q: The word "potential," is it a blessing or a curse?

JP: Well, the old saying, you know, you lose with potential, you win with performance. I think potential, that's just what it is, it's a vague word out there that I really don't know what it means. I think potential is what could be, what might be, but it doesn't do anything. It doesn't pay bills. It doesn't win games. It doesn't make you a good athlete. It's performance. Performance is the key word, not potential.

Q: Today with all of the attention that is received, and all the press scrutiny, is it tougher than in the past to effectively do your job?

JP: I don't think tougher is the word. I think it takes being more alert and more understanding, particularly when you get older, to the environment they live in. It's different than the environment kids lived in 30 years ago, than the environment I performed under. You know, with the media, the agents, the big money, there's tremendous pressure on these kids, the families, and other people to be good enough to be professionals so they can make a lot of money in a hurry. All that is out there. You can handle it. Maybe it's a little tougher, but it's not unmanageable. I think they still want to have success, they still want to be part of a winning team, hopefully a championship team. It's just a question of making sure that they know that you understand the pressures they're under, and try to explain to them why we have certain NCAA rules, why you can't horse around with an agent, why gambling is such a danger to a football team. That's an ongoing kind of dialogue, and in that sense, it's probably tougher, but it's certainly doable.

Q: With all the success that you have had, looking back now, are there any shortcuts, any way to guarantee success?

JP: No. I don't think there are any shortcuts. If somebody's got one, I wish he'd let me know. It's an awful lot of hard work.

Q: How about failures? You've had so much success. How do you face failures for yourself personally, and do you learn from them?

JP: I would define failure in these terms. I don't think you fail when you get licked, I think you fail when you don't do a good job preparing your team, and you don't do a good job the day of a game. We've played some games and lost, and a lot of fans are around here thought we were failures, but we really felt we had done one hell of a job in getting a team ready, and we played well, and the other guy was just better. Just a better football team. So, when you define failure in that light—that you didn't do as well as you should've in getting a team ready, and the kids didn't practice as well as they should've, and we didn't give it our best effort—then that's prayer meeting time. That's prayer meeting time as a staff. You know, that's enough. You realize, "We can't win . . . we're not doing our jobs with our kids." And it's prayer meeting time with your squad. You say, "Hey, you guys, enough's enough. Let's stop screwing around here. You didn't give it your best effort. Let's learn from that. You guys under-stand now that you can't beat anybody unless you prepare well and you're ready mentally from the time we start to play." Those things come into it when you you lose some-times. Other times when we lose, I get the squad together and say, "Hey, look, that's really a heck of an effort."

Q: How do you create respect for yourself and your staff in the eyes of the players?

JP: In the way you handle your life. Whether you're honest with them. Whether you're not a phony. Whether they appreciate the fact that they know you're working your butt off. That you get into the middle of a football game, and you can say to an offensive lineman, "Now look, we went over that stunt there. This is the way we're going to handle it, and don't forget it." They know you're knowledgeable. They know if you've done your homework, you've looked at tapes. You don't consider you're a coach just because they put that title in front of you. You understand what your duties and responsibilities are and you work as hard as you possibly can in order to help them do as well as they can do. I think those are the things kids respect. They don't respect a lot of baloney-throwing and that stuff, patting them on the back every time they do something that's halfway decent. The good ones, if you tell them they did something well when it's not, they laugh at you. They know when they did it well.

Q: Is it important, Joe, to set the goals that you're going to accomplish in a given day, a given year, a given season, or maybe even for a career, or can you do it without pre-set goals?

JP: I don't set goals. We talk national championships every year, but we don't say we want to be at this level by this week, or that level. The only thing I say to our squad all the time is that our worst enemy is time. We're going to run out of time, so we can't waste it. Everything we do, we've got to do it full speed and we've got to work every minute to get better. If we get a little bit better every day, we'll get to be as good as we possibly can be within the time we have. But if we waste time, we can't recover it. And if we go out there and we don't go full speed in practice, we're going to start to create bad habits. Because I always tell them, you either get better or you get worse. There's no way to stay the same. I don't care in your own life. If you write a letter and you're sloppy with it, you've gone backward. If you have some respect for the people you're writing to, when you write a letter, you put some effort into it. That's all we ever preach. We just say, "Hey, let's just get better today. Let's get better. Let's try to play a better game this Saturday than we did last week." And when that one's over, let's get better on Monday and Tuesday and so forth. But always with the idea that down the line, that's going to lead us to a national championship.

Q: So nobody ever sits around and puts in an envelope that you think you're going to be 7–4 or 11–0?
JP: No. Never done that.

Q: Is a coach or player born with leadership qualities, or is it something that is developed?
JP: I think in a lot of cases, most of the cases, I think the kid is born with a certain confidence in himself and a need to be in front of the pack. I think that's most of the time. But every once in a while, you get a kid who's really not sure of himself, and all of sudden, he has some success, and you know, you can feed on that. And he has a little success, and you can almost see him growing in self-esteem, and wanting to be in a leadership role, and that has happened to me with certain kids. But in most cases, I think, they come to you as leaders.

Q: If two guys are basically the same, and you're sitting around with your staff trying to decide which guy is going to get the playing time, and you have two qualities that you have to choose from—one, intelligence, and the other just physical ability—which way would you have a tendency to lean?
JP: It would depend on the level of how much better is one physically and how much smarter is the other one. But if they were close, let's say one guy is six in physical ability

and three in intelligence, and the other guy is seven in intelligence and three in physical ability, I'd go with the intelligence. In football, everything revolves around 11 people. When we put our game plan in and start to get things ready, I say, "Now look, when we go out on the field I want to make sure everybody knows where to line up. I don't want anybody in any doubts about how we're going to line up against those formations or this or that. And I don't want anybody to have any doubts about what they're going to do in a certain situation on offense and so forth." And as good and as elaborate and as diverse as football is today, with so many formations and so many different things you do in the college game, I think if you can't get them lined up properly, then you can't just line up in one thing all day because they'll kill you. You've got to change. In your game, you've got to go from zone to man-to-man in the middle of it, and you've got 2–3 zones and that kind of thing. I think you've got to have intelligence. I asked John Wooden what quality he thought was most important on his basketball team. He said, well, my basketball teams were always intelligent teams. And when I look at that, I think that's the way I teach.

Q: What's more important, to prepare for a game or to make adjustments during a game?

JP: The in-game adjustments won't happen unless you've done the pregame preparation. The pregame preparation gives you the ability to make some adjustments in the game. I think your preparation has to be intelligent enough, broad enough that you can go into a halftime and say, "Okay now, this is what they've been doing to us in there, so we're going to go back and do this. We didn't put a lot of emphasis on this during the week but we went over it. You guys are familiar with it." I think that all has to be built into your preparation. If you're not prepared, you can't succeed. Bud Wilkinson said to me a long time ago, if you haven't practiced something, don't try to put it in during a game.

Q: Can you create a competitor or do those guys and teams that really have the great competitive spirit, is it something that's already there? Can you bring it out, or can you really get a bunch of guys to want to compete?

JP: Well, when you say a bunch of guys, I think there has to be a couple of competitors in the group who literally show the way. Somebody will get in the huddle and say, "Damn it, they're knocking the crap out of you . . . " Something to that effect. But I think you can create a competitor from a kid who's not sure he wants to compete. In a lot of cases, it's because he doesn't *think* he can compete. I think if you can create situations where he can have some success, and he feels that he can compete, I think slowly you can bring him along. I had a kid on my team, I won't mention his name, a year ago, if you said he was starting for me, I would have said, "You're crazy. He can't, he's got no belly for it." But he had a couple of things that happened to him, and he started to come along. He had a couple of good practice sessions. And pretty soon he had another good one. He stayed healthy. All of the sudden now, we were saying this morning, looking at some practice tape from yesterday, "Son of a gun, that kid's really become a good football player. Who'd have ever thought he'd be that kind of competitor?" But that's not easy. And a lot of things have to fall into place for a kid who has not been a competitor to become a competitor, but it can happen.

Q: Do you have a mentor or guys that set the tone for you? To be successful, do you have to have mentors?

JP: Yes, I think it's important to be around people who have won. I used to go to every clinic I could go to and listen, but the best advice anyone ever gave me was "Don't do it the way I did it. You've got to be yourself." So I think you can learn, learn about the profession itself, the organizational parts of it, the techniques that are involved in it. But you really have to be a guy that can take all that stuff, and say, "This is the way we're going to do it. This isn't the way Bobby Knight did it. This isn't the way Bear Bryant did it. This is the way we're going to do it."

Q: Do you feel it's important then to develop a formula for how you're going to do it, and how long does it take you to get the "Joe Paterno formula"?

JP: Well, I don't know how long it would take. Gee, I think it's absolutely vital. I think you sit down before you do anything, before you talk to your staff, before you talk to your squad, before you talk to anybody, you sit down and say, "Now these are the things I believe in. I think this is the way I want to do it." And then you start selling. You sell your coaches. You sell your players. You sell your fans. Coaches and salesmen, it's nothing different. You've got to sell all the time. You can't sell something you don't believe in because you can't fool people.

Q: When did you know what Joe Paterno wanted to do? When did you settle on the formula?

JP: When I was an assistant coach.

Q: Is that right?

JP: Absolutely. I was just angry that I didn't get to be a head coach sooner. I had a couple of opportunities, but I was really waiting for Rich to retire, you know, without pushing. I finally got to the point where I wanted to take the Yale job, and Rich said, "No, you stick around, I'm going to get out of here soon." I was just waiting to get to put it into play.

Q: Do you change it ever? Is it something that constantly changes, or you feel pretty rock solid that that's the basic formula?

JP: Well, the basic foundation of it, I don't change any. We make adjustments. Right now we have a great quarterback and a couple of wideouts, we may throw the ball a little bit more, but as far as the attitude toward practice, the attitude toward planning to win national championships, what I expect of the staff, what I expect of a kid who wants to play, we're not changing that. I'm a no-earring, no-beards, no-hats-in-the-house kind of guy, which you constantly have to sell a kid because they think, "What's the difference if I've got an earring or I've got a beard?" I have to frankly tell them it doesn't mean a lot as an individual, but it means a lot to the team. We've got to find out whether you really want to make some kind of personal sacrifice to show what kind of commitment you want to make to this group. Now, those things, I wouldn't know how to coach otherwise. I don't want hotdogs. I don't want guys that I have to keep telling people we're sorry because they shot their mouths off. Those kinds of things. Hotdogs can be a problem for their teammates. Character, being able to trust kids, being able to get some kids to do some things in the clutch for you, all those things I've never changed. Because I wouldn't know how to coach them otherwise.

Q: When you look back, what's the greatest asset of your championship teams?

JP: The ones, the great ones I've had, some of which just had great people, great players, were based on a camaraderie that went beyond just being friends. And I think we had kids that literally would, you'd think, go to war and die for each other, and trusted each other. I mean there was tremendous trust. They didn't get into tough situations with some guy getting in there and saying, "Well, I'd better be ready to cover up for so-and-so, and I've got to be able to not only do my job, but someone else's." I think that that trust they had in each other was literally built because of how hard they worked together. They worked so hard together, and they trusted each other so much, that when they got into that position to be a champion, they had it. They had it. And I've had other teams that were close to it, but just missed it, and that was the kind of season they would have, 9–2, something like that—when you really knew that just a little more, one or two more kids in there that really worked, they could have won it all.

Dean Smith

He's a cigarette smoker.

He's an overweight liberal democrat.

He's been married twice and fathered five children.

He's been hanged in effigy, yet he's also had a building named after him—the $33.8 million Dean E. Smith Center in Chapel Hill.

He's won 879 college basketball games, more than any other coach in the history of the sport.

He's also a great innovator, having played a hand in the development of the run-and-jump defense and the Four Corners stall game.

One other thing about Dean Smith: He's been loved.

By fans. By assistant coaches. Most of all, by his players.

When Michael Jordan had to travel home after his father James was murdered in the summer of 1993, it was Smith who met him at the Wilmington Airport. Jordan had been able to keep his composure until he saw his college coach.

When they embraced, Jordan broke down and cried.

"The two most important men in my life have been my father and Dean Smith," Jordan said in honoring Smith in the foreword to Art Chansky's retrospective on the University of North Carolina program and its coach, *The Dean's List*.

That is just the kind of closeness Smith has maintained with all of his players, the least and most talented, from the team captains to the student managers. That closeness meant that when Smith eclipsed Adolph Rupp's record for coaching wins in the spring of 1997 it was a time of special celebration for all of the people affiliated with the Carolina program over the past four decades.

And when Smith abruptly retired just months after claiming the all-time wins record, that Carolina family closeness again responded by hugging him in a warm embrace.

"He's been like a father to all of us," Jordan said after hearing the news.

The surprise, of course, would be if Smith's players weren't full of emotion. Perhaps there are coaches who can match his skill at X's and O's or who can equal his knack for attracting supremely talented recruits. But the 66-year-old Smith had no equal when it came to the human side of the equation, to the challenge of keeping a family atmosphere in the largely cynical climate of college athletics.

Time and again his former players have produced stories of Smith's legendary capacity to keep track of the trials and tribulations of their personal lives. He does this not because he is a good politician. He does it because he cares.

The incredible thing about Smith is that over the years he was able to shunt aside all the high-profile plums, the marketing and endorsement deals that have corrupted so many other coaches, to make sure he kept his basketball family first. (Smith was the first coach, or among the first, to share his shoe endorsement contract money with the university he served.) He would give more attention to the lowliest manager from 10 years ago than he would some wealthy North Carolina businessman who wanted to play golf with him.

Even more amazing, Smith never wavered in his philosophy of treating the lowliest and the superstars the same. To some degree Smith inherited this "family" approach from his predecessor, Frank McGuire. But with McGuire, you were either in his family, or you were the enemy. Smith removed the hard edge from the philosophy and lived family to the fullest.

"His program was very much a different style than most college basketball programs," agreed former Tar Heel and Milwaukee Bucks coach George Karl. "He built his program around team and family and togetherness and camaraderie and helping each other. There's so much not even on the basketball court. With your classes. With your assignments. There was always a family kind of unity that I don't think existed anywhere else."

At the same time, Smith showed a striking capacity for what many consider the uglier side of the game, the recruiting process.

Perhaps better than any coach in the history of the game, Smith knew how to capitalize on his own success. In turn, he showed his players how to do the same.

A good number of them moved to the pro level as early entrance candidates, leaving Chapel Hill before their eligibility was used up. It was Smith's policy to study the issues and help inform his players when the financial circumstances for turning pro were in their favor, thus encouraging and supporting their decision.

"I love him for that," says Jordan, an early entry candidate in 1984.

Smith was about the only person in favor of his leaving school, Jordan said.

And once his players got to the NBA, Smith never let them slip out of his thoughts, even players like Sam Perkins who describe themselves as "never part of the elite."

"He calls, he writes, he wishes you luck at the beginning of each NBA season," says Perkins, a three-time All-American for Smith who now plays for the Sonics. "He does that with everybody. You just feel special that someone like him is thinking about you, even though sometimes you may overlook calling him. He's always got an eye open for each of his players.

"You can't pinpoint any one thing about him, except that all his players have this deep respect for him. We all have this feeling for him, even the players that only played a few years for him. We all have it. There's just something about coach Smith that overwhelms you. His persona, the way he treats his players. Yes, he coaches and he yells at you and tells you what to do. It's just him, his warmth."

Pete Chilcutt of the Vancouver Grizzlies says that he frequently runs into NBA players who harbor a bitterness about their college coaches or who speak disparagingly of their college programs. Not Tar Heels, said Chilcutt, who played in Chapel Hill from 1987 to 1991. "One thing all Tar Heels have in common is pride."

The builder of this proud community was born on February 28, 1931 in Emporia, Kansas, and was raised in Topeka, where he played guard in basketball, catcher in baseball, and quarterback in football.

"I've always wanted to call signals," Smith once quipped.

He was nine when he heard his first NCAA title game, the 1940 showdown between Indiana and Kansas, on a Kansas City radio station. The event wasn't known as the Final Four then. Regardless, it was *big*. The basketball bug had bitten him.

Some have implied that Smith, the son of two schoolteachers, wasn't much of an athlete, but longtime Chicago Bulls assistant Tex Winter was the featured speaker at Smith's high school athletic banquet and says the young Smith was multitalented. Winter, the coach at Kansas State at the time, said he tried to recruit Smith to become a Wildcat but lost out to the University of Kansas, where the coaches were able to attract Smith with offers of an academic scholarship.

At the Lawrence campus, he played baseball and basketball and even made the freshman football team. As an upperclassman, he served as a deep sub on legendary coach Phog Allen's stellar teams of the early 1950s. The Jayhawks won the 1952 NCAA title and just missed a second championship with a narrow loss to Indiana in the 1953 title game, during which Smith scored a single point. He spent enough time on the bench there to know that if he ever got a head coaching job he would be sure to substitute early and often.

He got his first basketball coaching job at the Air Force Academy as an assistant, but he also served as head coach of the school's golf and baseball teams.

It was Air Force basketball coach Bob Spear who recommended him in 1957 as an assistant to Carolina's Frank McGuire.

"That's when Frank asked me, after the 1957 championship game, if I wanted to be his assistant," Smith recalled. "At the time, I didn't know that Spear had been bragging on me. But I told Frank, 'No, I don't think I'd enjoy it.'"

By 1958, however, Smith had changed his mind. He agreed to help McGuire at Carolina.

He had been in Chapel Hill just a year when he got involved in the effort to integrate the local lunch counters, not a popular move in the segregation-ridden South of 1959. Asked his motivation for taking a stand, Smith said, "You don't do it to get credit. You do things because you think they're right."

In 1961, the gambling scandal that rocked college basketball prompted McGuire to move to the National Basketball Association, and Smith took over the program.

A local newspaper pointed out that the 30-year-old from Kansas was "not overpowering in personality."

It would take Smith more than four years to convince the Tar Heel faithful otherwise. His teams stumbled along to a 35–27 record in his first three seasons.

In early January of 1965, Smith's fourth team took a 22-point beating at Wake Forest, their fourth straight loss, and pulled into Chapel Hill late that night only to find Smith hanging in effigy from a tree. Team captain Billy Cunningham stormed off the team bus and pulled down the display.

"It made me think," Smith recalled later, "'Gosh, who needs this?'"

The incident, however, propelled the team to a 15–9 record and a tie for second place in the ACC. What would follow was an unprecedented run of winning seasons and tournament appearances, including 17 ACC regular season titles, 13 ACC tournament titles, an Olympic gold medal (1976), an NIT championship, 11 Final Four appearances, and two NCAA titles.

Basketball fans are well aware that Smith's team won its first title in 1982 against Georgetown University. The difficulty amidst all the sweetness, of course, was that Smith had to face Georgetown's John Thompson, his friend and assistant coach from the 1976 Olympics. The situation "carried a special set of feelings," Thompson recalled. "I had mixed emotions about playing against Dean because I have a great deal of respect and affection for him. Dean was instrumental in helping me understand what the college game is about and helping me to structure my thoughts about what I had to do and how I could carry out the things I wanted to accomplish. And here, at the biggest moment of my career, I was playing against the guy who had as much to do with my thinking as anybody. So I had to generate a little bit of competitiveness and stubbornness in order not to think of him as my friend. Because it was Dean, it caused me to be even more fired up."

It was fitting that John Thompson came to Chapel Hill for Smith's retirement press conference in 1997. Smith was never one to go hot and cold with his friends. With Smith, relationships are long-term.

Billy Packer: Coach, is there any such thing as the thrill of victory and the agony of defeat?

Dean Smith: I would imagine any coach would think that. I remember all the losses. In basketball, it's hard not to finish with a loss when you play in the NCAA tournament. So those are the ones that hurt, the season-ending defeats. I'm sure we all put too much pressure on ourselves and our players because of that. Because of that, for so long, I've tried to focus on, "How did we play?" If we played well and lost, I should be happier than if we played poorly and won. So that way I wouldn't be influenced by what other people think. And I was doing pretty well with that until my last year when we were getting ready to play N.C. State. We had just lost three in a row, and the players were tight. We played horribly and still managed to win in the last two minutes. I said, "Forget the stuff about how we played, just get a win."

Q: How long does the feeling, either way—the thrill of victory or the agony of defeat—how long does it last for you?

DS: The thrill of the victory often depended on what the expectations were going in. Our teams in the late 80s, we expected to win. Also, a road win was always a thrill for me. To walk out of a place with the crowd quiet. We'd tell the team, no celebration. Let's wait till we get down to the dressing room, then we can celebrate. I'd say it's okay to jump up and down in the dressing room.

Q: You had so many championship teams throughout your career, and obviously, you played against so many

championship teams. What do you think is the key in-gredient in a championship ball club?

DS: One ingredient that makes a team is obviously players. I think a very underrated part is the chemistry of a team. And their confidence in one another. And unselfishness in our game is huge. And, of course, they have to play hard. We've always said, "Play hard, play smart, play to-gether." And playing smart means you've got to work really hard in practice to repeat things so you'll react even when the circumstances are disorienting, when fans are yelling at you, yet you still know what to do. In the end, there's always a part of luck involved. In the NCAA Tour-nament, maybe one of the tough teams in your bracket will get beaten, opening your path.

What makes athletics and sports contests so special is that there is a winner and a loser. That is determined. There is no gray area.

Q: Have there been times when you felt that the players were not the key ingredient? Have there been times that you lost a championship where you felt you had the best players? And have you won where you felt maybe your guys weren't the best talented, but for some reason as a team they were able to overcome those odds?

DS: Well, in basketball, what is talent? In fact, our worst team to make it all the way to the Final Four, I always said, would have been in '68 when I thought UCLA had the best team I had seen, ever. They wouldn't have been as good if Elvin Hayes, who played at the University of Houston, had been on that team. Because there's only one ball. And that's what I'm saying: Chemistry is so impor-tant. I just can't think of a time when, like you say, talent was the most important ingredient.

A player named Pierce Landry really was crucial to our '95 team. And he's a walk-on. So, I think talent, you must have talent to rebound, certainly, but you can have a situation where the players don't get along and then that's not a championship team. On our '93 team, George Lynch's leadership was crucial, I thought. And Derrick Phelps was another big factor in our character. So I think there's more intangibles that come into play for a championship team. Sometimes teams, by being less talented, have fewer expectations, therefore they do better.

Q: Can you sense, or were you able to sense when there was that something about a group of kids that would enable them to be champions?

DS: To be good, yes. To win that one-point game, you never know that. And that's what we have in our sport of basketball. I suppose in baseball if (Roger) Clemens is pitching, you've got a heck of a chance of winning that game. In football, if you're stronger, faster in the line, your odds jump dramatically. Which reminds me of a quick story. Barry Switzer, when he was coaching at the University of Oklahoma, came in here, and the president of the university asked me to come have dinner with them the night before they played us in football. It's Mack Brown's first year (as the UNC football coach), and I said, "Barry, you know, we've got a new coach, we've got enthusiasm. Aren't you a little worried?" He said, "There's no way they can beat us. Absolutely no way." And I say, "How can you say that?" And he said, "We have too much speed for them."

To me, that means in football, there aren't as many upsets. In college basketball, the underdog has a better chance. Look at Princeton. I love the way Princeton plays. And nobody wants to play them. We don't want to play them. We've played them over the years. But yet you get that underdog role, and they come in. Bucknell beat them last year. They only lost three games the whole year: Indiana, North Carolina, and Bucknell. So they were the favorite at home against Bucknell, and they got upset.

There's strange things going on mentally in championship teams, and that's what makes building one such a challenge.

Q: Can a coach provide the motivation for players to become champions, or does the motivation have to come from within on championship ball clubs?

DS: I think some coaches really believe in the old-fashioned pep talks. The best example would be from years ago, Ray Elliott at the University of Illinois. Most fans wouldn't even remember him. But he was a great coach. His teams would always have two upsets. Beating someone they had no business beating. But they'd also be upset themselves by some little team. I think you can be more consistent down the line by not trying to get too high or too low. The championship teams in NCAA basketball, you really have to be consistent. In the tournament format, it's one lost game and you're out. Indiana upset us in 1984. I thought we were better than they were. And then they were so excited to beat us that in the next game, Virginia, the sixth-place team in the Atlantic Coast Conference, beat them 25 or something two days later. But that's why, perhaps, you're writing the book, because it's so much fun in athletics.

Q: Is it important for a coach to be liked by his ball club?

DS: I don't think that's necessary. I think respect is the word. I think it's extremely important to have the respect of the players. From that standpoint, when you tell them something, they'll listen, and go from there. And sometimes out of fear. I don't think fear is a very good motivation, but at some point in practices, we make that a motivation. Don't let your teammate down. That's why we punish by team, not by individuals. From day one, we have an emphasis for that day in practice. If somebody fails to catch the ball with two hands—say that's the offensive emphasis today—well, if somebody catches it one-handed, well, the whole team runs. To me, that always puts more pressure on a player to respond. Because everybody wants to be liked, and you don't want to let your teammates down. In a clinic, I had a coach come up and tell me that he had a player that he had tried to use that peer pressure with and it didn't faze him in the least. The whole team was running, and he didn't care. And I said, "Well, set him down." And the coach said, "I set him down and gave him a drink of water and made the team run, and it didn't bother him the least, and he's our best player."

I said, "Honestly, I think you'd be better off without him, I honestly do."

Q: If I think back in your whole philosophy and the great run that you've had, it seems to me you never allowed an individual to take precedence over the team situation. That always seems to be a constant factor.

DS: You love basketball, and basketball is a team sport. Jack Nicklaus once told me, "I can't believe these guys get paid in team sports, and they get no-cut contracts. In golf, we have to go out and win to get paid." And it made me think, "Wouldn't the NBA be great if they were paid on wins? If they lost, nobody would get paid. If they won, the best player would get so many hundred-thousand dollars." You're talking about what a beautiful game we would have then.

Q: Yes, athletes in team sports are often paid on potential. What about potential? It's a word tossed around a lot in sports and business. Is it a blessing or a curse to be labeled as a team or a player with potential?

DS: I think the best example may be going to the admissions departments at the universities. What do they go by? The admissions tests, the SATs, are used to project their potential for doing well in college. Would colleges be better off going by a student's record, how he or she has actually performed in school?

As far as athletics, I would tend to go with somebody who has already performed at a successful level in high school. Sometimes that's a danger in our sport. A highly recruited kid sometimes thinks he's already there.

For example, you have the so-called McDonald All-Americans. They can become almost disadvantaged. It's like a really wealthy person sometimes is disadvantaged in that they don't realize they have to continue to work. We've recruited two kids from South Carolina, McDonald All-Americans, really worked hard on both of them, Ricky Jones and Clark Bynum. They're McDonald All-Americans. As it turned out, they didn't even start for Clemson. What I'm saying is, here we were trying to get them. Which suggests you can't necessarily go by potential. We have a young man now at North Carolina, Brendan Haywood, who has tremendous potential. But he also has a lot of work to do, and he has achieved some. To realize potential, athletes also have to do a tremendous amount of work. Sometimes their potential tricks them into thinking they don't have to work so hard. I don't know how to answer your question. But I think we're both on the same wavelength. Potential can be a curse.

Q: Coach, so many of us, over the years, have admired the relationships that you've had with players from the past, regardless of whether they were great athletes or not. You have extended that relationship even to the student managers and other young people who have worked with your programs. At what point do you feel that it's important for the coach to have a personal relationship with a player?

DS: I think that's up to each individual coach. I'm not sure that has a unique part of being a championship team. I just think as a coach, I've seen some coaches who have never seen their players except when they come to practice. And those coaches often do very well, and they care very much about their players. But I chose long ago to take a personal approach, based on watching my dad as a high school coach. After World War II, when they were home furloughed, all his players would come by and see dad, and that's something special. And I feel like a coach is really secondary. The best thing I can say is the Olympics, when the players stand up and get their gold medal, the coach doesn't. I think that says a bunch for basketball. I mean, you're dependent on the players. I always said I owe them. But then I was going to be tough on them in practice. They look back and appreciate the discipline more than anything when they leave. But after they leave, I try and say, "Now, we're friends." I'm not buddy-buddy with them while they're here. But when they leave, "Now, we're friends."

Q: Is it important for the coach to serve as a role model for those guys that he is working with?

DS: I think any professor, any teacher maybe can help by example. But I don't know whether that's essential. You can look at Charley Eckman when he had the Fort Wayne Pistons. He was a former referee, and he liked to joke that coaching wasn't important. In many ways he was everything he wasn't supposed to be. Because of that maybe his teams played loose, I guess.

It's pretty hard to pinpoint an answer on this one.

Q: What would be your greatest satisfaction looking back as a coach?

DS: I don't know. That's a hard one because I've been in it so long, and I felt very satisfied with each team. They're still special. I always felt like I'd made a mistake if we lost. Some coaches think the kid didn't catch the ball or something. He didn't make the shot. And that's something that each time, I tried not to do. I'd tell them, "If you do what I say, and we lose, then I lost the game. You guys win them." Maybe I tend to exaggerate the importance of a coach.

In 1995, we were playing Virginia. We'd gone to an overtime. There were four seconds left, and I drew up a play. I thought they knew it. But because we hadn't practiced it, one guy didn't go where he should have, and we had to take a time-out. We had to get the ball inbounded, and we couldn't. I had to go to Washington after the game to recruit, and my team had the next day off. All the way in to Washington, I was just sick with myself. Why didn't I go with the same play we had worked on?

Q: With all your successes, is there anything that you would change, that was a disappointment to you that you didn't accomplish?

DS: I never set out to accomplish anything in particular. That's the difference. They didn't weigh me on number of wins. I set out to coach, teach, and I thought I would be high school math teacher and coach, but it turned out I never got a chance to coach in high school. At the Air Force Academy and here, each season you just try and get the best you can out of each team, and some teams maybe we could have done better. In retrospect I'd think, "Gosh, if I'd played so-so more or done this." Or I'd think maybe how lucky we were. That's no fun to go back over things. I don't think anybody learns a lot from that. I know you learn from history, but don't live in the past.

Q: In regard to the game today in terms of a coach's life, compared to when you started, there's incredible press

scrutiny, television scrutiny, talk radio scrutiny. Has that made it more difficult to do the job?

DS: I don't think so. In many ways, the media technology has made the job easier. In the old days, on the days the team had off, we, the coaches, would be on the road recruiting. You'd go see a recruit 10, 12 times, which took lots of your time.

I think coaching is easier now, really, from that standpoint. In terms of your time scouting the opposition. With television, now, you have so many tapes on a team. There's 19 tapes. I don't watch all 19 going into a game.

But as far as the presence of the media itself, sure it's much larger. But even back in the sixties, in the ACC, we were on television. So it isn't just like we're all of a sudden discovering it. I will say in 1977, when we went to the Final Four in Atlanta, it just seemed to explode. Something happened between '72 and '77, when it became the national media. College basketball and the Final Four became like the Super Bowl, didn't it?

And today, we have the growth and presence of talk radio. Talk radio, I'd be a sociologist to figure that one out. First, you try to stay away from that. But it's even a big part of coaches' shows. Even on my talk show, I try to hopefully keep things positive. But sometimes you have to have a bad question just to get something going.

Q: What about the possibility of failure? Is that something that crossed your mind often? And how does a coach cope with it?

DS: Well, that is always a part of it. One team is going to lose because that's the reality of competition in a team sport. You're going to go out there and you're going to lose. Now what do you define as failure? I really worked hard to try to evaluate every possession on its own merit—did we get the shot we wanted? Did the other team get a shot we wanted them to take? We even kept score in scrimmages with that in mind. A guy would make a bad shot from three, I'd give him a zero, even if he made it. You miss a layup, you get a plus-three, even though you missed because it was a high percentage shot. We were just trying to emphasize that it's not the outcome, but it's the process for each possession.

On the other hand, failure is not so terrible. I don't think there's been anyone who hasn't learned from failure.

Q: Is it motivating for a coach to have a fear of failure?

DS: I think so. I think that motivation is greater if you've failed before. When it fails, or loses, I think you'll see a team respond—the good, the championship teams will really respond the next night out. And our teams, I think, have always done that except in the NCAA. In the tournament, when you lose, it's over till the next season.

Q: Are there any such things as shortcuts to success?

DS: Well, sure. What are you calling success? If it's just to win games, sure. Take for example, the guy at the University of California, Todd Bozeman. Poor Lou Campanelli's gone, and he comes in. His team is "successful." They beat Duke in the NCAA first round or second round. And he was a success. Yet, the next thing you know, there were allegations of improprieties, and he was released.

Q: Let's say that winning was not the definition of success. I'm talking about feeling that you've really accomplished your goals. Are there shortcuts to that?

DS: I don't think so. That kind of success is generally just hard work. The fact that you're motivated to succeed, the kids have a feel for this. I think we all have a common goal to play well, and that is success in itself. And sometimes we don't play well. Accept that. Learn from it, and bounce back.

Q: You mentioned earlier that a key ingredient for a quality leader of a championship club is the respect. Is that a two-way street between player and coach? Does a coach have to give respect before he gains it? How do you gain respect?

DS: I don't know. In our discipline here (at the University of North Carolina), we're very fair. You have to write the rules down. I mean it's the little things that make a difference. Let's say that one player only had to run the steps 15 minutes for being 15 minutes late. Then, one of his buddies, who is late, he has to run for 20 minutes for some reason. The second player would be upset at the apparent unfairness. So you have to take great care to be very fair. Any time you discipline, you have to treat them with respect as players, and I think it's a mutual understanding that we're here with the same goal. The only difference in goals may be they "want to be a pro." The only difference in goals may be we don't want them to shoot every time they get the ball.

Finally, I think they eventually understand that it doesn't necessarily make you a great player just because you score a lot of points. I remember Tony Laquintano of Virginia, he probably led the league in scoring but they finished last. One of the all-time great basketball jokes concerns Michael Jordan's scoring (Who was the only person to hold Michael Jordan under 20 points a game? Dean Smith.), but I told Michael to get the ball inside to Sam Perkins. Sam's shooting 60 percent, and you're shooting 48 or something.

Q: We've only had one national scoring champ that was on the championship team.

DS: Who was that?

Q: Clyde Lovellette at Kansas.

DS: My gosh, Clyde was, that's true. I know Larry Bird was second. Not Michael, but one of his buddies pointed out that Grant Hill, he only averaged about 14 points a game at Duke. So, you have other good players who sacrificed for their teams. On any true championship team, they don't care who gets the points.

Q: **Did you ever set preset goals in terms of wins for a season? As an example, in October before the season began did you say, "I think we can win 28 games," or "I think we can be in second place"?**

DS: I wouldn't have even looked at that. I know coaches who put down possible wins and losses. No way for me. In the old days, before the expanded NCAA Tournament, our goal was to win the ACC Tournament because that meant you go to the NCAA Tournament. That was our goal. And then, when they expanded the tournament to include teams that hadn't won their conference, our goal was just to be invited to the NCAA Tournament. One major goal. We talked about it in October, November, December, and tried to play well each game. That's the long-range goal that was there.

Then starting I believe in 1993, we put up a picture of the arena in which you're going to play the final game, the NCAA championship, and put North Carolina there. Something so that our players could picture it. Jerry Bell, over at the North Carolina business school, is a good friend, and he gave me a tape once where a guy wanted to lose weight and he put a picture of this thin guy, with his picture on it, a thin body. And he looked at it every morning, and it helped him. And so that's when we started that.

Q: **Looking back at all the great coaches you've competed against, and studied, and played for, do you think that** a coach is born with leadership talent, or can it be developed?

DS: I don't know. There's so many different personalities in any profession. I don't think you can prototype one type of coach, and of course, one that's special to you and me, is Bones (McKinney) and there's only one like him. You couldn't possibly duplicate him. You could do the whole book on Bones. What time is practice? That depends on whether it's sunshine or not, he once told me.

Q: And Al McGuire, he's the eccentric type, too.

DS: And Al. There's so many, I don't think you can zoom in on a prototype.

Q: But is coaching a given talent, or can you develop it? You've had so many now in your family tree of coaches. Let's take your former assistant Roy Williams, who at the University of Kansas is obviously now heralded as one of the brightest of the young guys. Or another of your former assistants, Eddie Fogler, now at South Carolina. I can go down the line with so many of these guys, but did you sense from day one that they had this leadership ability to be a top-notch guy in the profession, or did you see it grow?

DS: Obviously, it grows for anyone. But, yet there is something special about a young man that you can see. I had Larry Brown. I knew he wanted to coach. He used to run the shuffle for all his guys, his little campers up in Pennsylvania. He still loves just teaching, coaching. And Roy Williams. Eddie Fogler. Bill Guthridge. Randy Wiel. All my assistants. John Lotz. That's all I've had.

Q: John Thompson wasn't a bad assistant.

DS: John, he's a great assistant. He's just tremendous. His leadership is exceptional. In basketball, we're all dictators in a way. There has to be one guy who says, "This is the way we're going to do it." So I think we, the coaches, take the blame for the losses, and let the players have the victories. I know John is a dictator. I was, when I was coaching. There's no other way to run a basketball program in college.

Q: You say dictators, but I've also seen you distribute responsibilities to people on your staff.

DS: I didn't delegate enough. I didn't have a staff meeting. I'd come in and say "Here's the practice plan." Then I'd say, "Now you're going to do this." I'd say, "What do you think?" I'd definitely ask the opinion of my assistants. To our players, we let them vote on off-the-court rules, but never let them vote on anything to do with on-court things, such as who gets the ball. I guess I am saying dictator, because you direct each staff member, "You coach the JVs," etc. But you always ask for input. I think the best dictators do that, from the staff, and from the players sometimes.

Q: Can a player become more competitive, or do you think that's something he's born with?

DS: I don't know what creates that. I don't know whether you're born with it as much as it's something that happened in the environment in which you were raised. That's a hard one to figure, because you and I know that there are those that it just kills them to lose a drill in practice. And usually, they're pretty good players.

We talk about talent. What is talent? Part of it is somebody who can make the putt at 18. That's a talent. When you say competitive, I mainly think of somebody's determination. To have Jordan's speed and quickness, but now you add the unbelievable competitiveness, the intelligence in which he plays, that's what makes him so special. And still every year, he gets better. And then the work ethic to go with that, then you might have something.

Q: What's the most important ingredient for success, pre-game preparation or in-game adjustments?

DS: I think the whole program begins the first day of practice. I think it's important. You set the tone. The tone. Certainly to adjust during the course of a game is a part of it. But sometimes an announcer will holler, "Smith better get a time-out." Well, maybe we've missed four easy shots I was happy with, and the other team made four tough shots. I should be happy. There's nothing more to talk about.

I really do believe the first day sets the tone of all our little things, attention to detail, running, hard work, and then, starting to learn how to play as a team, play together. Sure, you have to be flexible. Gosh, if something comes up. Anything could come up. We lose three guys in foul trouble, so adjusting during a game, that's important, yes. But sometimes it works, if I made a good adjustment, and sometimes it doesn't. See, we have a final line that you don't have in other businesses: Did you win or did you lose?

Q: Does a champion play as he practices, or have you had situations where maybe they weren't practicing well, but for some reason, they could get out at game time and execute successfully?

DS: That varies, but generally on my teams, if you don't practice hard, then you don't play. So you never know if you're going to be a champion. Most of our great players have been gym-rats, in the nicest sense. I remember, I won't say the names, three players whom I don't know if they really liked basketball, but, gosh, were they good. Maybe they snuck off and worked in the summer harder than I knew. They would work, but not much. They'd be names you'd recognize, but usually the great ones are gym-rats that just want to keep getting better every day.

Q: Did you ever have a game where you went into it saying two days prior to that the practices were not up to
what you wanted, and then all of the sudden the guys
perform extremely well, or vice versa?

DS: You can never depend on that. We had so many times,
where we practiced well and played poorly. Or we practiced well and played well. Or we practiced poorly and
played poorly.

Q: No formula, huh?

DS: I've been in it long enough, and I've seen no formula.

Q: Do you feel that for a man to be successful that he has
to have mentors, people who he has not necessarily copied, but learned from and been taught by?

DS: I don't know. Certainly, the people whom I've worked
for have been extremely helpful. Doc (Phog) Allen used
the tired signal before I did, but he'd forget about you
if you said you were tired. Sometimes you'd learn I
don't want to do it *that* way. Certainly Bob Spear at the
United States Air Force Academy was a great teacher.
Frank McGuire, who was the head coach at North Carolina when I got there, had an unusual approach. He'd
have been a great football coach. I mean he would delegate it to us to handle practice, but he was still in
charge, very much so. It's strange. I don't know how
you could pinpoint that.

Q: What's the best advice you were ever given? In or out of
basketball?

DS: I don't know. There's so many things. Without going into
theology or philosophy, let's say in coaching. Well, partly,
there's the prayer to accept the things you can't change.
Change the things you can. Have the wisdom to know
the difference. And don't live in the past. And that's a

prayer that's widely known. I think a coach should listen to that prayer very carefully.

Q: Is it important to develop your own coaching philosophy?
DS: I think so. I think it's extremely important to set your standards. I think this is the way the game should be played. Yet you should also be very flexible.

Q: Is it important to have a philosophy?
DS: We have a philosophy of how to play. Now, there's different ways to go about it, but to play together, to play hard. I mean you always insist on effort. And then, to be a smart team. To be prepared for situations. With five minutes to go, be prepared for that. What to do when you're down and in the catch-up game, or when you're ahead, what to do to keep the lead. And all that is a philosophy, but yet we've changed philosophy from year to year based on our personnel. I mean, we never had the same team.

I once asked Bill Fitch, "Bill, why'd you leave the Celtics?" He said, "They've heard that same talk at half for eight years." In the pros, if you keep your stars, you have that problem. In college, we never really have the same team, it's always something new.

Q: Did it take you one year to build your philosophy and approach? Ten years? Or do you feel it's always a learning and catch-up process?
DS: I think it's always about learning and catching up. I recently looked back to an old game because we're getting our old films onto videotapes for Christmas. We were pretty good defensively, looking back through the '60s. We did some of the same things then that we're doing now. The secondary break, we first tried that about '65, and we're still running it. But, yet every year, I think I'm a better coach.

I'd be surprised if everybody didn't feel that they got better with experience. Now, sure there's a time when you might go home with a headache, and forget who the guys' names are. But still I think that's true in any profession, and particularly coaching. You get better.

Q: **Yes, it is interesting because some of the other coaches we've talked to have said that by their second year in the business they had their philosophies in place. Your answer doesn't surprise me because your system at North Carolina has been a multiple system. Over the years one team doesn't necessarily have any relationship to teams that played other times.**

DS: They all have UNC across the front. They love that. I think some things have been constants with us, but not many because you have to adjust to your personnel.

Q: **Let's take that question one step beyond basketball, and talk about you as a person. When did you think Dean Smith, the person, became what he is about today?**

DS: The pastor of a Beckley church here in Chapel Hill gave a sermon once. He had just gotten back from his Yale Divinity School reunion, and some guy had come up to him and said, "You haven't changed a bit." And of course, that to him, was the worst compliment you could ever have. You hope you change each year, and grow.